Gender and Empire

Gender and History

Series editors: Amanda Capern and Louella McCarthy

Gender and Empire

ANGELA WOOLLACOTT

First published in 2006 by
PALGRAVE MACMILLAN
Houndmills, Basingstoke, Hampshire RG21 6XS and
175 Fifth Avenue, New York, N.Y. 10010
Companies and representatives throughout the world.

PALGRAVE MACMILLAN is the global academic imprint of the Palgrave Macmillan division of St. Martin's Press, LLC and of Palgrave Macmillan Ltd. Macmillan® is a registered trademark in the United States, United Kingdom and other countries. Palgrave is a registered trademark in the European Union and other countries.

ISBN-13: 978–0–3339–2644–4 hardback
ISBN-10: 0–3339–2644–7   hardback
ISBN-13: 978–0–3339–2645–1 paperback
ISBN-10: 0–3339–2645–5   paperback

This book is printed on paper suitable for recycling and made from fully managed and sustained forest sources.

A catalogue record for this book is available from the British Library.

A catalog record for this book is available from the Library of Congress.

10 9 8 7 6 5 4 3 2 1
15 14 13 12 11 10 09 08 07 06

Transferred to digital printing in 2009.

To Kiri, Lakshmi, Rochana, Sammy and Toby

Contents

Acknowledgements

It is such a pleasure to look back and recall the professional support and acts of generosity that have enabled this book. I thank the Department of Social Inquiry at the University of Adelaide for hosting me as a Visiting Scholar in late 2001, especially Margaret Allen for her kindness in making that visit possible. I am grateful to the Humanities Research Centre at the Australian National University for my Visiting Fellowship there in 2002; it provided beautiful surroundings, congenial support and precious reading and writing time. I would like to thank the 'Modernistas' at the Australian National University for their collegiality during that southern winter, and for their astute comments and suggestions for the parameters of this book. Thanks go to Georgine Clarsen, Ann Curthoys, Desley Deacon, Jill Matthews and especially to Fiona Paisley for organizing the symposium on feminist history.

I am grateful to the College of Arts and Sciences at Case Western Reserve University for the Senior Faculty Fellowship that facilitated my work on this project in 2002–03. This book, and much else of my working life in 2002 and 2003, benefitted enormously from the cheerful energy, quick-witted intelligence and creative hard work of Juilee Decker, who was the most efficient and delightful research assistant any historian could ever hope for. Terka Acton has been a marvellously supportive editor, good-naturedly tolerating delays with the manuscript caused by family loss and a transoceanic move. I thank my colleague Gillian Weiss for sharing with me her bibliographical expertise on European captivity narratives set in both the Barbary Coast and North America. Trevor Burnard kindly shared with me some of his work in progress on Thomas Thistlewood and helpfully looked over a draft of Chapter One. I am grateful too to the anonymous readers for the press for their helpful readings and suggestions.

As ever, I cannot imagine how this book could have happened without Carroll Pursell. Yet again, his help with bibliographic research, his patience with my endless work schedule, his daily generosity in shouldering more than half of the domestic labour, have all supported my writing. I thank him deeply for his support, companionship, cooking, readiness with a glass of wine, intellectual partnership—and not least his being willing to retire and migrate on the same day, even with the sunshine and parrots as incentives. I wish also to thank all of my new colleagues at Macquarie University for the generosity of their welcome, and their support of my work. This book is dedicated to Kiri, Lakshmi, Rochana, Sammy and Toby, with my love and hopes for their bright futures.

Gender and Empire: Introduction

Until recently, scholars of the British Empire rarely tried to bring the whole empire into a single frame of analysis; rather, for the most part, they have studied it in geographical, chronological, or topical fragments, or as a combination of these. In response to a recent scholarly impulse, and in defiance of what were perhaps the more reasonable self-imposed limitations of older traditions, *Gender and Empire* looks at the modern British Empire as an integrated entity. At the same time, crucially, this book recognizes that the British Empire was always shifting and never a stable unit, its boundaries continually contested, its territorial control changing, and the colonial regimes that constituted it constantly responding to new challenges. My temporal framework is from the latter eighteenth to the latter twentieth centuries, while my geographical reach necessarily and insistently includes both the white-settler colonies and the more studied (at least in postcolonial frames) colonies of exploitation, conquest and rule. Mrinalini Sinha has proposed that to grasp the dynamic and interconstitutive nature of the empire we must think in terms of an imperial social formation, of the simultaneous and interlinked development of metropole and colony. As Sinha suggests, central to making visible the necessarily uneven but combined development of different regions of the world is the analysis of racial, class and gendered hierarchies.[1] This book is grounded in a synthesis and interpretation of a large body of scholarly work produced over the last fifteen to twenty years. In integrating this scholarship, I hope to outline imperial interconnections not previously visible, and to make plain the central role of gender in the British imperial enterprise, both as one of the forces driving and shaping the empire, and as a set of ideologies produced at once in the colonies and the metropole that constituted shifting and pervasive imperial culture.

My aim in this book is to use gender as the primary framework of analysis, and to ask how recent bodies of scholarship applying feminist theory to component parts of the British Empire have changed our historical understanding of it. Using gender as the central category of analysis compels us to examine changing cultural and ideological definitions of masculinities and femininities, and at once allows us to explore such definitions as sites of cultural encounter, and sites of the political contests that have always been integral to colonialism. As Catherine Hall has argued, one of the key insights of feminist theory has been 'the recognition of the centrality of the gender order to the social, economic and political order'.[2] Putting gender at the heart of analysis makes it necessary to look at how class hierarchies and socioeconomic subordination have intersected with cultural practices and discursive formations of the feminine and the

1

masculine. Similarly, hierarchies of gender cannot be understood without examining their inextricable interconstitution with hierarchies of 'race' and ethnicity, hierarchies fundamental to both colonial rule and metropolitan culture in the modern period. Femininities and masculinities have, moreover, been directly linked to representations and practices of sexuality, as I hope this book demonstrates.

In the last ten to twenty years, what had been the moribund field of British Empire history has been completely recast and reinvigorated by the application of postcolonial and feminist perspectives. There is now a whole body of monographs, dealing especially with South Asia, the West Indies and British colonies in Africa, that examine social and cultural aspects of the imperial order and colonial rule. Journal articles on British imperial history have appeared in the pages of the most prestigious historical journals in various countries, including the United States. Most recently, we have seen the emergence of edited collections on imperial history, and we are starting to have collections of documents available too. A number of these anthologies foreground the operation of gender. Notable here is the recent companion volume in *The Oxford History of the British Empire* series: titled *Gender and Empire* and edited by Philippa Levine, it contains both chronological and thematic essays by leading scholars in the field.[3] However, there is, as yet, no single-authored book that seeks to bring together the most influential studies on gender in what is called 'the new imperial history'.[4] The advantage of a book such as this is that it can offer an integrated overview of an already huge and constantly expanding field, necessarily selective as such an overview must be, within a unified structure.

My methodology has been to synthesize the growing body of recent scholarship on gender and the British Empire, to interpret this scholarship, to provide my own analysis of key themes and issues, and to enrich the book with fresh primary-source evidence and narrative. Some primary sources I have relied upon will be very familiar to many, such as the slave narrative *The History of Mary Prince*[5] which has been so widely cited, because it is such a searing tale. Other primary sources may be, I hope, less familiar, perhaps including some of the fiction which I draw upon to illustrate particular points. As historians are now mostly very conscious of, there is no such thing as a transparent historical text, whether it is a scholarly analysis, a newspaper column, a work of fiction, or a postcard. We need to interrogate the context in which any text or representation is produced, and read against the grain for its possible meanings. In large part I have depended upon secondary works, and read them against each other to gain a sense of variance of interpretations, and debates within any specialized area. Not surprisingly, at least some of the debates have revolved around the acceptance or rejection of feminist interpretations. Primary sources – autobiographies, fiction and reports of government commissions, for example – must, of course, be read with care and with questions about their production. Yet they are indispensable as detailed accounts, and as representations of subjective experience, observation or viewpoint. Used selectively here, I hope that they alleviate what otherwise could have been overly historiographical topical syntheses.

Feminist scholars who have critiqued homogenizing and liberal versions of western feminism have helped us to grasp the ways in which imperialism operated by constructing discursive positions for its subjects, and worked to suppress the voices of colonized people. In order to identify the historical workings of colonialism, we need to find the voices of colonized subjects as best as we are able to through the sources available to us. Much of the scholarship on gender and empire has privileged European women as subjects and slighted indigenous or colonized women, some even claiming that European women, subordinated by patriarchy to the rule of European men, have been less racist and more sympathetic than their men to colonized peoples. The complicity-versus-resistance dichotomous assessment of European women and colonialism has real limitations, as Malia B. Formes contends.[6] Rather than being locked into such a binary analysis, we need to recognize the agency of indigenous and colonized people within the structures of colonial societies, within their interstices, and in challenges to colonial hierarchies. And as Jane Haggis warns, it is crucial to avoid colonizing 'gender for white women and men rather than introducing gender as a relational dimension of colonialism'.[7] This book, then, discusses women and men of many different cultures, who inhabited variously racially marked social positions, focusing on different groups within particular topics and chapters. It strives to highlight the workings of gender as ideology *and* as material and cultural practice.

Several premises underlie this project. One is that the field of women's and gender history, still so tied to the American and European history of its origins, must continue to expand its geographical reach and embrace the histories of colonialism that have been fundamental to and constitutive of the modern period. Another premise is that historians of Britain and the British Empire need to relinquish lingering assumptions that only women have gender. As recently as 2003 a historian of the British Empire dismissed women's history with the comment: 'The problem which arises is that in trying to write in a role for women, there is a risk of exaggerating their importance.'[8] If one goal, then, is to render misogynist historical blindness impossible by demonstrating women's centrality, a more fundamental goal is to establish the systemic operation of gender. British historians must recognize gender as a foundational dynamic that shaped all aspects of the empire from the conduct of war, to the drafting of statutes and regulations, to social and medical codes governing sexuality, to stories that appeared variously in *The Times* and in juvenile fiction. Ideas of gender, always linked to 'race' and class, were forged in the colonies as well as in the metropole and circulated constantly throughout the empire. Moreover, I contend that 'British' history in the modern period cannot be apprehended unless we locate Britain as one of the sites of the British Empire and study it in that context. Indeed, the very question of how the empire has constituted the nation, and thus belied the historical fiction of a preexisting or transcendent nation-state, has become a rich area of critical inquiry.[9]

The episodes and topics central to the mainstream history of the British Empire, in which gender can be seen as a shaping force, compel us to see the empire as more than just a scattering of far-flung possessions, more than a grab bag of territories acquired by the British 'in a fit of absence of mind', to quote an oft-used phrase. They reveal political, economic and cultural dynamics that cut across the diversity of colonies, and that can also be seen as structural connections among the modern European empires. They require us to recognize the pervasive ties that existed for centuries between the European metropole and the colonies, the constant traffic that shaped Europe at the same time that it shaped colonial regimes and creole societies around the world. There is no originary moment for the British Empire. The British Isles have been home to peoples of multiple ethnicities for thousands of years. Mercantile links between England and distant parts of the globe accelerated from the sixteenth century, and mercantilism along with other imperatives (including religion) became the basis for an early modern British Empire – a mercantilism to which the slave trade was increasingly important. As Kathleen Wilson and others have shown, the multiple wars and imperial engagements of the eighteenth century were understood and represented in forms mediated by conceptions of gender as well as race. The articulation of Britishness in the period of the Enlightenment linked nation to empire building, 'exploration' and colonial wars in ways that were highly gendered.[10] Yet such connections and articulations were to continue through the modern period, within a matrix of categories of race, sexuality, gender, religion and, of course, class. That interlinkage was especially apparent in the late nineteenth and early twentieth centuries when European imperial control covered a huge proportion of the world, and for European powers definitions of nation and empire were interdependent. As Frederick Cooper and Ann Laura Stoler argue in the introduction to their anthology *Tensions of Empire: Colonial Cultures in a Bourgeois World*

> [I]t is clear that the resonance and reverberation between European class politics and colonial racial policies was far more complicated than we have imagined. ... If there were places where the European language of class provided a template for how the colonized racial 'residuum' was conceived, sometimes the template worked the other way around. The language of class itself in Europe drew on a range of images and metaphors that were racialized to the core ... . How the hierarchies of race and class played off one another had profound consequence ... [C]lass – for whites – was being made into a relationship of co-optation and alliance while race became a line of exclusion far clearer than it had been before.[11]

But these interconstitutive dynamics went beyond the linkages between race and class. Gender and sexuality were integral to the laws, policies and administration of colonial regimes, the discourses that constituted imperial knowledge, and the tropes in which colonial relations were represented, all of which helped to shape definitions of masculinity and femininity in Europe itself. Such tropes were shifting and polyvalent; the imperial power could be characterized in either maternal or paternal terms, invoking differently gendered notions of authority. European colonizers were cast in gendered terms in their relations with colonized others, such that colonial rulers and by extension Europeans in general could be represented as wiser, more responsible and self-disciplined, characteristics seen as masculine, while the colonized were cast as sensual, childlike and irresponsible, and hence were feminized.

Yet gender could cut across the metropolitan/colonial divide, so as to stigmatize European and colonized women simultaneously in differently effective ways. For example, masculinist resistance to first-wave feminist movements in Europe led some Europeans to decry modern European women as unsexed while seeing colonized women as more passive and feminine, and therefore as an exotic repository of traditional gender relations that were under threat in the metropole.[12] Sexual practices and codes of sexual morality were integral to the construction of gender, even as they were shaped by racial ideologies. Here too Ann Stoler's analysis is incisive, this time from her book *Race and the Education of Desire*:

> [T]he racial obsessions and refractions of imperial discourses on sexuality have not been restricted to bourgeois culture in the colonies alone. ... Bourgeois identities in both metropole and colony emerge[d] tacitly and emphatically encoded by race. Discourses of sexuality [did] more than define the distinctions of the bourgeois self; in identifying marginal members of the body politic, they have mapped the moral parameters of European nations. These deeply sedimented discourses on sexual morality could redraw the 'interior frontiers' of national communities, frontiers that were secured through – and sometimes in collision with – the boundaries of race.[13]

Stoler's work has focused on Southeast Asia, especially the Dutch East Indies and French Indochina, but her insights are pertinent across the European empires. As Julia Clancy-Smith and Frances Gouda argue in the introduction to their anthology *Domesticating the Empire: Race, Gender, and Family Life in French and Dutch Colonialism*, it is important both to identify the dynamics that were common to the European empires, and to examine 'the differences and similarities in national styles and in the particular sensibilities that infused almost every colonial state'.[14]

My choice to limit this project to the British Empire is at once a practical decision about limitations, and a recognition that different imperial administrations, while bearing common structural features, also had particular characteristics, policies and styles that were linked to specific metropolitan economies, political values and cultural practices. Thus, while I wish to underscore the significance of the pan-European impact of colonialism on the metropole, this book focuses on the operation of gender within and across British imperial possessions and between them and the British Isles. Demonstrating that very interconnectedness is one of its main contributions. Because most scholars of the empire have essentially been students of one colony or region, or of that colony or region's interconstitution with the British Isles, historians have not often read across geographical boundaries. While I am very aware of the enormous debts I owe to the many scholars on whose work I rely in this project of synthesis, I hope to repay those debts by drawing connections that only such a project allows. One of my goals is for my own cross-field reading to point others toward directions and topics pertinent to their own work, of which they may have been unaware. Further, by identifying the ways in which gender ideologies linked diverse parts of the empire, I hope to provide fresh insights into the historical construction of gender, not least the role of colonialism therein.

The book's chapters focus on major episodes and topics in the modern history of the British Empire that reveal the operation of gender, and in which the crucial importance of gender as a shaping historical force is clear. My first topic is that of women in the systems of unfree labour that were central to the empire in the eighteenth and nineteenth centuries, including the last stages of the imperial slave trade, its abolition in 1807, the subsequent 1833–1834 abolition of slavery itself in British territory, convict transportation to the Australian penal colonies and the escalation of indentured labour in the wake of slavery. By the mid-eighteenth century Britain was the major slave-trading power in the world. Enslaved Africans were the labour force that sustained Britain's sugar industry in the West Indies, and the slave trade itself was a lynchpin of Britain's enormous maritime trade. In British colonies in the Caribbean, slave women's lives were shaped by gendered divisions of labour and by sexual exploitation by their owners. But gender ideologies shaped the British movement for the abolition of slavery too, not only through issues surrounding women's participation (and subsequent invisibility) in the movement, but through the very arguments made to show the wrongs of slavery itself. Moreover, in early- and mid-nineteenth-century Cape Colony, South Africa, emancipation itself was shaped by gender ideologies, so that freedwomen faced legal and social inequalities.

Gender similarly saturated the structures and changing cultures of other unfree labour systems in the British Empire. Historians have debated for decades whether the convicts sent out to Australia from 1788 to 1868 were innocent village Hampdens, victims of the harsh social changes that accompanied industrialization, or were moral reprobates and criminals. Recently, feminist historians have been at pains to redress the neglect of women convicts in earlier histories, to challenge received images of them as depraved 'whores', and to document their profound contributions to the establishment of Australian society and economy. Gender and sexuality were central to official views of convict women at the time and to accounts by historians since. In the wake of the abolition of slavery, and even as convict transportation to Australia was being questioned there and in Britain both in the 1830s and 1840s, the practice of indentured labour escalated. Between 1837 and 1917 hundreds of thousands of Indian men and women migrated to the British Caribbean, but men significantly outnumbered the women. This sex ratio imbalance, along with gendered divisions of labour and the ideology of domesticity, would powerfully shape migrants' lives, those of both women and men. Slavery, convict transportation and indentured labour were foundational structures of the eighteenth and nineteenth-century empire. Focusing on women enables us to observe their workings and trajectories. Comparing these systems of unfree labour allows us to see the racially justified difference in treatment of women slaves compared to women convicts, but also the ways in which emergent gender ideologies connected all three systems. Racialized and class-based ideas of gender forged in the colonies inflected shifting gender definitions in the metropole, even as metropolitan definitions underlay changing treatment of slaves, convicts and indentured labourers. This chapter points to the ways in which racialized notions of feminine respectability and unrespectability, as well as comparably racialized notions of the independent masculine breadwinner, flowed between British slave colonies before and after emancipation, the abolitionist campaign in Britain, the penal colonies in Australia, and the system of indentured labour that escalated in the wake of slavery. These historically evolving gender definitions were a conduit of changing imperial culture; they underscore the value of looking for external as well as local sources of change.

Chapter 2 looks at cultural dimensions to imperial rule from the mid-nineteenth to the early twentieth century by examining narratives of interracial sexual assault deployed as justifications for violent acts of territorial conquest, reprisal and repression. The imperial circulation of narratives of interracial sexual assault presents evidence of historical change from early modern captivity narratives, in which men's fears of sodomy and circumcision outweighed fears of sexual assault on women. A turning point occurred in the early nineteenth century in the captivity narratives in white-settler colonies such as the Eliza Fraser and White Woman of Gippsland stories in 1830s and 1840s Australia, in which the spectre of interracial sexual assault became determinant. The chapter focuses on two major episodes of revolt, the Indian 'Mutiny' or Revolt of 1857 and after, and the 1865 uprising in Morant Bay, Jamaica, and the violent suppression of it ordered by Governor Edward John Eyre. What concerns me here about the Indian 'Mutiny' or the First War of Independence, as some Indian historians have renamed it, is not so much the events of 1857 and afterwards, but the narrative forms in which those events were told both by contemporaries and succeeding generations. In the uprisings by sepoys of the Indian Army, at Kanpur (Cawnpore) and elsewhere, British officers and their families were indeed murdered. But as feminists scholars have demonstrated, scores of British and Anglo-Indian writers cast the events of 1857 as primarily an episode in which Indian men raped and mutilated English women. Interracial sexual assault, and outrage against British womanhood, was the narrative that was told, retold, embellished and legitimized by fiction writers and others for decades. Jenny Sharpe argues that the fears that galvanized Anglo-Indians after the revolts were responsible for the repressive nature of British rule in India, and the particular taboos on interracial sex that lasted as long as the Raj itself – an argument well illustrated by E.M. Forster's 1924 novel *A Passage to India*.[15]

While constructions of colonized men's sexual aggression and white women's vulnerability shaped colonial rule in India, definitions of official English masculinity were at stake in the controversy that followed the 1865 Morant Bay riot in Jamaica. Apprehensive of the whole black population rising against the whites whom they vastly outnumbered, Governor Eyre ordered severe martial repression, in which hundreds of black and mixed race people were killed, more flogged, and still more had their houses burnt. As news reports reached England, debate slowly gained steam over the propriety of Governor Eyre's actions. The government set up a Royal Commission to investigate, and public opinion coalesced on both sides. The Commission decided not to prosecute Eyre, but in the meantime, according to historian Catherine Hall, the two sides in the debate had mobilized competing definitions of English manhood. Prior to becoming Governor of Jamaica, Eyre's colonial experience had included both New Zealand and South Australia, thus his behaviour reflected on British administration across the empire. The critics of Eyre, led by John Stuart Mill, contended that English manhood depended upon the rule of law, which Eyre had violated, and that all people existed in equal relation to each other, so that neither women nor black people should be subservient to white men. Eyre's supporters, who won over public opinion, defended him as a national hero who had acted to maintain order at a moment of crisis, securing English dominance in the empire and a conservative order at home. Thus a particular definition of dominant English middle-class masculinity emerged victorious in a debate that stretched between Jamaica and the metropole.[16]

A fresh look at the evidence presented by Eyre in his own defence to the Jamaica Royal Commission reveals his reliance on the notion of white woman-hood being threatened by nonwhite men during the uprising. One of Eyre's defenders drew explicit connections to the Indian 'Mutiny', and petitions signed by thousands of Jamaican women colonizers claimed that he had preserved them from a fate worse than death. In contrast to the fears of sexual subjection of British *men* contained in seventeenth- and eighteenth-century captivity nar-ratives, these nineteenth-century stories of violent encounter position British women as the vulnerable sex, in need of the protection of their men. Such nar-ratives would reappear around the empire, from South Africa in the 1880s and again in 1912, to Amritsar in north India in 1919, to Papua (New Guinea) in the 1920s, and the north of Australia in 1938. Taken together, the narratives of interracial sexual assault that characterized these crises reveal a remarkable shift in imperial gender ideologies towards racialized notions of white feminine virtue and colonized men's barbarity. They show how racialized narratives of sex and gender lay at the core of imperial politics, and how they were invoked to explain the appropriation of land from indigenous peoples in white-settler colonies as well as extreme measures of reprisal in colonies of rule.

Imperial dimensions to masculinity more broadly form the subject of Chapter 3. Here I show how late-nineteenth and early-twentieth-century understandings of masculinity drove African 'exploration' and conquest, and were related to some particularly egregious episodes in that epoch of imperial history. I consider as well how constructions of masculine imperial adventuring became part of the fabric of popular culture, and how they played out in impe-rial wars and territorial annexation. Connotations of British masculinity that included militarist power, unapologetic racism, 'heroic' action and imperialist adventuring proliferated in the late nineteenth century. Several writers have recently interrogated the conception of the heroic European explorer in late-nineteenth-century Africa, questioning legends of intrepid discovery and map-making on 'the Dark continent', and establishing in their place evidence of aggressive geographical claims and ruthless bloodshed. 'American' (actually Welsh-born) Henry Morton Stanley (of 'Dr. Livingstone, I presume?' fame) now appears to have been a sensation-currying, brutal, even murderous oppor-tunist, for all of his adulation in England as a conquering hero. Looking closely at the record of adventuring by Stanley and others, Stanley's connection to Joseph Conrad's contemporaneous novel *Heart of Darkness*, and the wider his-tory of British conquest in Africa in the last decades of the nineteenth century, allows us to identify the ways in which 'heroic' definitions of British masculinity – the very stuff of public school culture and the sporting ethos in England – were implicated in rapid imperial expansion and jingoism. Such definitions were popularized in the hugely influential adventure literature for boys read around the world, and the Boy Scout movement that was founded at the turn of the twentieth century. The empire played a role in shaping not only these dominant versions of masculinity, but variants as well, such as muscular Christianity (notions of the masculine missionary), the rise of male homosexuality as an identity, and suburban notions of domestic masculinity and companionate marriage. A lesser-known aspect of the ways in which imperial exploring shaped masculinities and sexualities are the connections between explorers like Sir Richard Burton, the evolution of learned geographical and anthropological circles in Britain and the circulation of pornography with explicitly colonial and racist dimensions.

Imperial adventuring in late-nineteenth-century central Africa was quickly overtaken by the outbreak of the South African War in 1899, Britain's blatant effort to wrest control of the valuable Transvaal from the Afrikaners. Notions of imperial masculinity were adopted in troop recruitment. Less than a generation later, the European conflagration sparked in 1914 became a global war, drawing troops from around the British, French and other empires. Recent scholarship has shown that Indian and African soldiers were not treated equally with white soldiers, their freedom and masculinity both circumscribed. Definitions of masculinity were deployed in and generated by the war, from compelling men to volunteer, to becoming the stuff of exotic legend in the postwar figure of Lawrence of Arabia, and to being linked to emergent myths of nationhood in Australia, New Zealand and Canada. Martial race theories, which held that men from particular races within the empire were born to be soldiers, became powerful interpretations of masculinity. They were related to empire-wide contests over masculine physical prowess with weapons, which in turn were related to the elite manly sport of big-game hunting. From the mid- to late nineteenth century, then, to the 1920s, definitions of masculinity impelled and were produced by the major expansions and crises that the empire faced.

Chapter 4 takes up the topic of how gender was integral to structures of colonial administration and to quotidian colonial practices, from the late nineteenth to the mid-twentieth centuries. Even in peaceful times shifting constructions of gender mediated relationships between colonizers and colonized. Historian Mrinalini Sinha has shown how contests over masculinity were at the nexus between colonizer and colonized, between colonialism and nationalism, and between India and metropolitan Britain in the late nineteenth century. Rudyard Kipling's 1919 story of the construction of a bridge over the River Ganges compels us to consider how the huge engineering projects of colonial modernity shaped relations of masculinity between employer and employed. And Joyce Cary's moving novel *Mister Johnson*, based on his experience in the British colonial service in Nigeria from 1913 to 1919, shows notions of manliness as central to the quest of a black colonial service clerk for acceptance by his white superiors. Further, a proliferating body of work on the history of sport shows how cricket especially became a highly visible arena for the competitive performance of masculinity between and among colonial and metropolitan men.

Racially differentiated constructions of femininity mediated relations among women under colonialism. Scholars have disagreed over just how complicit white women missionaries, feminists, doctors, teachers and mistresses were in the subordination of colonized women in India, and in Indian women's appropriation for their own ends by white women in Britain. Similar issues have been raised about relations between white women and colonized indigenous and nonwhite women in contexts that range from latter nineteenth-century British Columbia, to late-nineteenth and early-twentieth-century Fiji, to early- to mid-twentieth-century Nigeria, and to twentieth-century Australian domestic relations and Australian feminist activism of the interwar decades. Gender mediated more than relations between the individual colonizers and colonized. It structured administrative hierarchies; social institutions; cultural representations, appropriation and adaptations; and, as Timothy Burke has evocatively shown of postwar Zimbabwe, even commodity culture under colonialism. Women's bodies were often the site of these struggles in debates over *sati* and child marriage in nineteenth-century India, child servant bondage in early-twentieth-century Hong Kong, and female genital excision in East Africa from the 1920s. Recent scholarly literature on interracial sexuality shows the ways in which it breached the structures and boundaries set up by colonial regimes, and produced new, creole societies. This literature has been central to recent feminist, postcolonial work. Focusing on interracial sexuality, perhaps more than any other topic, shows the hierarchies and contradictions of daily life in colonial societies. Here too fiction complements documentary sources, such as George Orwell's searing 1934 novel *Burmese Days*, based on Orwell's time as a member of the colonial police force, and in which the English colonizer's abuse of his Burmese mistress leads to his own undoing.

Especially for the twentieth century, anti-colonial nationalist movements and mythologies are a dominant theme in world history. Chapter 5 considers the centrality of gendered symbolism, and the contributions of women as well as men, to nationalist and anti-colonial movements in widely separated colonies. These shared connections compel us to consider links between gender, colonialism and political modernity, as women's relationships to the nation-state and citizenship were variously debated in diverse contexts, at the same time that mythologies of male citizenship were constructed. The chapter covers nationalist and anti-colonial movements in colonies including India, Ireland, Kenya, South Africa, Canada and Palestine from the late nineteenth to the mid-twentieth century. Gendered mythologies fuelled nationalist movements and assertions of autonomy from Britain across the colonies and dominions, and within the British Isles, in Ireland. It is impossible to understand the history of feminism in late-nineteenth and early-twentieth-century Ireland without realizing its intimate interconnections with the Irish nationalist movement, from the Land League to Sinn Fein, and its alternate ties to the Unionist movement. In the white-settler colonies, women have been constructed as bold pioneers, whether in the context of 'roughing it in the bush' in frontier Canada or, in New Zealand, as the first women in the world to be granted national suffrage rights. Nationalism was spurred in the white-settler dominions by their massive participation in the First World War, with enormous losses, in the wake of which masculinist national identities were built on images of soldiers' courage and sacrifice. In Canada, both before and after the First World War, women sought inclusion in the national pantheon through, for example, the popular construction of Madeleine de Vercheres and Laura Secord as venerable historical figures and national icons.

If nationalism in the dominions was mostly a matter of slowly growing autonomy within continuing constitutional links to Britain, anti-colonial nationalist movements elsewhere dramatically forced the process of decolonization in the middle decades of the twentieth century. In a fashion similar to the way scholars of gender and war have been reinserting women into histories of warfare, historians and others have revised accounts of nationalist movements to show that women were important participants. A whole body of scholarship now exists on women and nationalist movements in India, from the ways in which nineteenth-century nationalists reimagined ancient Indian women, and women participated in mid-twentieth-century peasant struggles, to women's participation (and its limits) in Indian nationalist debates of the 1920s and the 1930s. And in relation to the very bloody anti-colonial nationalist struggle in Kenya, the Mau Mau war of the 1950s, Tabitha Kanogo, Cora Ann Presley and others have shown the importance and contradictions of women's participation. As gender ideologies and practices structured colonial cultures, so too did they shape the historical forces that precipitated the end of formal colonial rule. A survey of these various colonial sites shows how central issues of gender were to emergent nationalisms, in this critical phase of imperial history.

The final chapter, despite its position in this roughly chronological book, argues that colonialism and its gendered dimensions were always already part of the British Isles, and that post-Second World War migration from South Asia and the West Indies only made them impossible to overlook. The empire had, since the late sixteenth century, been a focus of high politics. By the late nineteenth century, parliament and Whitehall were consumed by the administration and challenges of the empire. But the imbrication of the empire was far more subtle and pervasive than just government. Imperialism saturated modern British society, cultural representations, trade and economy, and colonial hierarchies shaped domestic British class, race and gender relations. English country houses had been built from the profits of colonial trade and plantations, English fiction was stocked with characters who washed up on British shores from the colonies or quickly disappeared to them, and British shops and advertising were filled with goods from the empire and (gendered) images of them. While English schoolboys were being trained for the responsibilities of empire on the playing fields of Eton, British housewives were urged to consider the empire when shopping for their families, and the propaganda of migration societies and schemes sought to lure men to the colonies with promises of wide, open spaces, and women through prospects of matrimony.

Amongst this web of imperial signification in British towns and cities, colonial subjects travelled, some for short periods and others for the rest of their lives. Expectations of gender shaped the circumstances from which colonial subjects of all races travelled to the metropole, and their motivations for going, then mediated their movements within it. And as Annie E. Coombes and others have shown, racialized images of both masculinity and femininity were produced by the material spectacles of empire, in both museums and exhibitions, so popular in England either side of the turn of the twentieth century. This chapter, then, argues for the significance of identifying the interconstitution of the empire and 'home', the pervasive ways, both overt and subtle, in which the empire and structures of colonialism were imbricated in domestic British culture, the ways in which gender figured therein, and the linkages between colonialism and gender ideologies and practices.

Looking across the diverse colonies of the British Empire, through the lens of almost a generation of feminist and postcolonial scholarship, provides an altered view of imperial history from the late eighteenth to the twentieth centuries. Several scholars recently have argued that it is no longer adequate to envision the empire as a set of peripheries shaped from the imperial centre. Whether we identify what Alan Lester has called the 'circuits of empire' in which colonies were directly connected, or adopt Tony Ballantyne's similar metaphor of the empire as a spider web, we need to recognize the dense connections among imperial sites, and the multivalent forging of imperial culture.[17] Changing conceptions and practices of gender must be identified as central. The British Empire was a connected if always shifting and changing entity, in which ideologies, stories and people all circulated, and colonial rule both depended on and was shaped by racialized conceptions of masculinities and femininities.

Notes

1. Mrinalini Sinha, 'Mapping an Imperial Social Formation: A Modest Proposal for Feminist Historiography', *Signs* vol. 25, no. 4 (Summer 2000): 1077–82.
2. Catherine Hall, 'Gender Politics and Imperial Politics: Rethinking the Histories of Empire', in Verene Shepherd, Bridget Brereton and Barbara Bailey (eds), *Engendering History: Caribbean Women in Historical Perspective* (Kingston: Ian Randle Publishers, 1995), p. 51.
3. Philippa Levine (ed.), *Gender and Empire*, volume in *The Oxford History of the British Empire* series edited by Wm. Roger Louis (Oxford: Oxford University Press, 2004).
4. Perhaps the closest has been Margaret Strobel's 1991 book *European Women and the Second British Empire* (Bloomington: Indiana University Press) but as is evident from the title Strobel focused only on British women in particular roles in the colonies.
5. Moira Ferguson (ed.), *The History of Mary Prince, A West Indian Slave, Related by Herself* (Ann Arbor: University of Michigan Press, 1993).
6. Malia B. Formes, 'Beyond Complicity Versus Resistance: Recent Work on Gender and European Imperialism', *Journal of Social History* 28 (Spring 1995): esp. p. 635.
7. Jane Haggis, 'Gendering Colonialism or Colonising Gender? Recent Women's Studies Approaches to White Women and the History of British Colonialism', *Women's Studies International Forum* vol. 13, nos. 1/2; (1990): 113.
8. Robert Johnson, *British Imperialism* (Houndmills, Basingstoke: Palgrave Macmillan, 2003), p. 127.
9. For example, Antoinette Burton (ed.), *After the Imperial Turn: Thinking With and Through the Nation* (Durham: Duke University Press, 2003).

10. Kathleen Wilson, *The Island Race: Englishness, Empire and Gender in the Eighteenth Century* (London: Routledge, 2003).

11. Frederick Cooper and Ann Laura Stoler (eds), *Tensions of Empire: Colonial Cultures in a Bourgeois World* (Berkeley: University of California Press, 1997), pp. 9–10.

12. On this, see Julia Clancy-Smith and Frances Gouda (eds), *Domesticating the Empire: Race, Gender, and Family Life in French and Dutch Colonialism* (Charlottesville, VA: University of Virginia Press, 1998), pp. 16–17.

13. Ann Laura Stoler, *Race and the Education of Desire: Foucault's History of Sexuality and the Colonial Order of Things* (Durham: Duke University Press, 1995), pp. 7–8.

14. Clancy-Smith and Gouda (eds), *Domesticating the Empire*, p. 4.

15. Jenny Sharpe, *Allegories of Empire: The Figure of Woman in the Colonial Text* (Minneapolis: University of Minnesota Press, 1993).

16. Catherine Hall, *White, Male and Middle Class: Explorations in Feminism and History* (New York: Routledge, 1992).

17. Alan Lester, 'British Settler Discourse and the Circuits of Empire', *History Workshop Journal* Issue 54 (Autumn 2002): 25–48; Tony Ballantyne, *Orientalism and Race: Aryanism in the British Empire* (Houndmills, Basingstoke: Palgrave, 2002), pp. 14–15.

1

Women and Unfree Labour in the Eighteenth and Nineteenth Centuries: Slavery, Convict Transportation, Emancipation and Indentured Labour

Several interconnected systems of unfree labour were central components of the British Empire from the seventeenth to the twentieth centuries. Looking at gender relations within these systems, particularly in the period from the later eighteenth to the mid-nineteenth century, permits us to see how they were driven by far more than economic imperatives. Slavery, convict transportation and indentured labour were shaped by contemporary cultural attitudes, racial ideologies and social hierarchies, and laid the bases for relations of power within the empire. If colonial labour and employment patterns have traditionally been the subject of economic and labour history, it is now clear that gender and racial hierarchies were fundamental to systems of unfree labour. Studying gender, sexuality and the family from the perspectives of cultural history thus can shed light on imperial economic structures, indeed on the wellsprings of the British Empire's wealth, as well as its disciplinary and punitive regimes. The operation of gender as a changing ideological system interconnected with racial and class hierarchies, and the daily practices that shaped relations between women and men in historically and culturally specific ways, allow us to see these systems at work and thus to examine the very fabric of the empire. Reading across fields and geographical locations that have usually been studied separately permits us to contemplate the question of whether or how these systems inflected one another, which in turn raises the issue of ideas and practices circulating within the empire rather than being confined to disparate imperial locations.

Women in Caribbean slavery

The status and lives of women slaves show how gender ideology in this period was fundamentally shaped by racial assumptions. Those who practised and advocated slavery contradicted dominant European notions of femininity in relation to the women they exploited, even as changing ideas of femininity were class contingent as well as racially based. In the seventeenth century, plantation owners in the West Indies purchased many more male slaves than female, partly because more male slaves were available in Africa and partly because of a belief that men were better able to perform the physical labour they required, although plantation labourers also included indentured Europeans, both men and women. By the latter eighteenth century, however, workers were all enslaved rather than indentured and women slaves comprised more than half of the field hands, the gangs of labourers who worked the fields on sugar and other plantations.[1] The shift towards enslaved African-born and Creole women as the basic labourers on plantations reflected the growing influence of racist beliefs that nonwhite women were essentially different from white women. In Britain in the late eighteenth century, women's work in agriculture was being curtailed. Whereas women had performed much the same labouring tasks as men, the introduction of machines, the effects of land enclosure and new agricultural techniques created a context in which women were pushed to the margins of agricultural production. Women of the labouring classes were confined to particular areas of work while middle-class women's lives were increasingly shaped by an ideology of domesticity that defined them as fragile, dependent and vulnerable. At the same time, in British colonies in the Caribbean, higher proportions of enslaved women worked just as long and hard as men in the sugar cane fields. Until the late eighteenth century, under British slave law in the West Indies women were subject to the same punishments and abuse as men, even during pregnancy, and were given no protection from sexual abuse. Like men, women slaves were punished by being put in stocks and being whipped, as well as being kicked and beaten at the whim of their masters and mistresses.[2]

Defenders of slavery justified harsh treatment by describing enslaved women and men in racist terms that likened them to animals and that purported that they were less sensitive than Europeans. Racially contingent ideas of female strength and capability were particularly delineated in the Caribbean, where white women's status was defined by their avoidance of physical labour and their supposed delicacy exacerbated by the tropical climate. In contrast, not only were black women assumed to be hardier, but their endurance and survival under slavery was considered proof of their inferiority. A British woman commenting on black women in Antigua in the 1840s, soon after the ending of slavery, asserted that many 'are so very masculine' that it was difficult to tell to which sex they belonged. This masculinization had occurred, she continued, due to their treatment during slavery. Their workload and punishment had 'rendered them callous, and in the end, divested them of all those principles of modesty which are so great an ornament to the feminine character.'[3] Whereas for white women pregnancy was considered a state requiring extraordinary consideration and protection, until late in the period of slavery pregnant slaves were given no relief from work and were flogged, punished and sexually abused even late in their terms.[4]

An invaluable account of a slave woman's life is *The History of Mary Prince*. Mary Prince was born a slave, around 1788 on a farm in Bermuda. After decades of physical, verbal and emotional abuse from several different owners, in 1827 Prince was taken to London by her owners as their washerwoman and child-nurse. In London Prince escaped, and eventually found her way to the Anti-Slavery Society. The society's secretary Thomas Pringle took her into his own household, where she narrated the story of her life to an anti-slavery sympathiser. Prince's story was carefully framed, in its transcribed and printed form, as a narrative calculated to hit the right moral tone and elicit a strong anti-slavery response. Hence we need to read it carefully, but the evidence it contains tells us much about the conditions of women's lives under British slavery in the late eighteenth and early nineteenth centuries. One of the most horrifying episodes involves 'a French Black called Hetty, whom my master took in privateering from another vessel, and made his slave'. A teenager newly sold and terrified by her circumstances, Prince was in awe of and grateful to Hetty, who took time to care for Prince despite her enormous workload. Hetty's work included looking after the livestock, milking the cows, cooking supper, housecleaning and childcare. Despite her prodigious efforts, Hetty was regularly whipped by Captain I – for not doing enough. Prince herself attributed to Mrs. I – her own learning of 'the exact difference between the smart of the rope, the cart-whip, and the cow-skin, when applied to my naked body by her own cruel hand'. Late in Hetty's pregnancy, because a cow for which she was responsible got loose, the master had Hetty stripped naked, tied to a tree in the yard, and then he person-ally whipped her 'till she was all over streaming with blood'. Hetty went into premature labour and had a stillbirth. Although she apparently recovered from the birth, she was again repeatedly whipped by both master and mistress. Soon Hetty suffered from a condition of severe bodily swelling, and died. For Prince this was a traumatic lesson in her own vulnerability as a slave.[5]

Focusing on gender ideologies and practices within British slavery in the Caribbean especially in the eighteenth and nineteenth centuries compels us to identify the contradictions at the heart of the institution of slavery. Most domes-tic slaves were women, who were considered fortunate to be among the rela-tively privileged group of slaves who did not have to work in the fields. Yet if domestic slaves had lighter work, they were even more subject to tantrums and physical abuse by both masters and mistresses, and to sexual abuse by their mas-ters, than field hands. In the latter stages of Caribbean slavery, most field slaves were women. Thus women performed the hardest labour, while the elite and relatively autonomous positions of skilled and semi-skilled artisans, and most of the positions as slave drivers and overseers available to slaves, were reserved for men. Probably the closest that women came to this kind of privileged position was as housekeepers and washer women, yet these positions were not as high in status or as well rewarded as the best positions available to men. Another con-tradiction or paradox central to slavery in the British West Indies is the fact that, although the offspring of slaves were their masters' property, for most of the period of slavery reproductive rates were so low that the slave population had to be sustained by fresh importations of slaves, and declined after the end of the slave trade.[6] As historian Barbara Bush has convincingly argued, low fertility rates were a result of multiple factors: harsh labour regimes, poor nutrition, physical abuse of women slaves, lack of incentives for women to reproduce, the effects of psychological trauma, and women's own control of their reproduction through abortion and infanticide.[7]

Nevertheless widespread sexual intercourse between white men and enslaved women, both African-born and Creole, resulted in a mixed-race population. The offspring of any slave were legally defined as slaves and the property of the slave's owner, yet some masters viewed their offspring by women slaves with affection, and treated them as heirs. Some 'mulattos' therefore lived a contradictory existence shaped by slavery, but privileged in various ways that slaves were not. Some children thus born were manumitted (i.e., their freedom was granted or purchased) while others remained legally enslaved but were educated or raised to occupations not available to most slaves.

Sexual relations between white men and black women, perhaps more than any other aspect of slave society, show the contradictions within slavery in stark relief. Sexual assault of slaves by owners and overseers was ubiquitous, as were prostitution and concubinage. While some slaves earned small amounts of money through prostitution, female slaves, particularly in towns, were forcibly prostituted by their masters and mistresses who took the proceeds as their own income.[8] Because of the power relationship between white men slave owners and overseers, on the one hand, and enslaved women on the other, the threat of punishment and coercion meant that women had little option to resist unwanted sexual advances. Yet such relationships, particularly longer-term relations between a master and a favoured concubine, could be complex. The fact that such relationships often combined sexuality, reciprocal favours, affection, and at times violence and coercion, reveals the complicated nature of slavery itself. Some longer-term relations could result in manumission for the woman, or at least small amounts of property, but women often worked hard and endured a good deal for such benefits.[9]

A striking case in point is the thirty-three-year-long relationship between Thomas Thistlewood, an English overseer on a Jamaican sugar plantation called 'Egypt', and Phibbah, the plantation's Creole slave housekeeper who apparently held an unusual degree of respect from both white and black people. We know a great deal about this relationship thanks to the detailed diary, amounting to about 10,000 pages, that Thistlewood kept during his thirty-six years in Jamaica. Thistlewood and Phibbah first met in 1751 when he arrived as the plantation's new chief overseer; by the end of 1753 Thistlewood was referring to her as his 'wife', and the relationship lasted until his death in 1786. In the will he made shortly before he died, Thistlewood arranged for Phibbah's manumission and bequeathed her a house, land, money and slaves. Their relationship had produced a son, named John after Thistlewood's brother in England. John was raised as Thistlewood's heir and was the object of both parents' affection. He was educated, apprenticed as a carpenter, and became a free coloured man, but died suddenly at age 20. In 1767 Thistlewood acquired his own 160-acre property, and hired Phibbah from her owner so that she could live with him.

Phibbah became a seamstress, earning a steady income, and Thistlewood regularly borrowed money from her. Some diary entries show that when Phibbah was ill at night Thistlewood looked after her. These pieces of evidence suggest an affectionate relationship that provided mutual comfort and reciprocal practical assistance.

Yet throughout their relationship Thistlewood constantly engaged in sexual intercourse with other women slaves, occurrences he recorded in his diary. Most of these slaves he had direct power over, and the sex was thus coerced despite the fact that he often gave them small amounts of money in payment. Between 1751 and 1754, for example, he recorded 265 sexual encounters with over 45 slaves; of these more than 45 encounters were with Phibbah in 1754. In 1759–60 he recorded having sex with 27 women: 160 times with Phibbah, and as many as 29 times with Egypt Susanah and 24 times with Mazerine.[10] Phibbah was aware of at least some of this sexual activity with other slaves, and its often coercive nature. Thistlewood easily mixed sex and violence. In 1771, for example, Thistlewood recorded 39 instances of sex with his domestic slave Abba, whom he also repeatedly flogged for what he considered substandard work. His exercise of what he considered proprietorial sexual rights in disregard of slaves' physical well-being is revealed by one of his sexual encounters with Abba, in May 1775, which occurred less than two weeks before she gave birth.[11] Thistlewood refers to numerous instances of Phibbah being upset with him, and even refusing his sexual advances, perhaps out of anger, jealousy or disapproval. Diary entries such as 'Phibbah did not speak to me all day' and 'Phibbah denied me' reveal the ways in which Phibbah could and did exert her will.[12] Thistlewood also reveals his suspicions that Phibbah's owner Mr Cope has sexual liaisons with her, an exercise of power that Thistlewood seems to feel he can do nothing about. It is evident from Thistlewood's diary that enslaved women and the white men who sexually abused them were constantly reinfecting each other with venereal disease; both symptoms and treatments are regular features in his diary entries. The abundant detailed evidence of Thistlewood's diary shows that his constant sexual abuse of slaves was typical; indeed, he seems to have been more moderate in both his sexual abuse and violence than other masters and overseers who populate his pages.[13]

The relationship between Phibbah and Thistlewood illustrates the contradictions of slavery: even a long-term relationship that involved affection was corroded by the abuse of power, specifically both Thistlewood and Cope's sexual and physical abuse of slaves.[14] As Trevor Burnard has argued, Phibbah exemplifies the possible benefits for a slave of accommodating to the system, and thus reveals the anomalies within the system. By astutely identifying sources of comfort and privilege, working very hard, and managing her relationship with Thistlewood carefully, Phibbah eventually secured her own freedom and accrued material possessions.[15] But even if Thistlewood spared Phibbah the physical abuse he meted out to other slaves, it is clear that physical violence and sexual abuse were interwoven around her. Thistlewood's punishments of his slaves included having one slave defecate into the mouth of another slave after the latter was flogged.[16] Phibbah received material benefits from her relationship with Thistlewood, especially after his death, and she herself exercised power over – indeed, finally owning – other slaves, but she patently suffered much over the years, including living with the knowledge of his treatment of the other slaves.[17]

Even women's participation in the various levels of island economies shows the hybrid nature of slave societies. While women's productive and reproductive labour for their masters was uncompensated, many were permitted some ground around their houses to grow their own produce and keep smaller livestock. Slaves produced a good deal of their own food in this way, which was necessary because the rations provided by masters were often sorely inadequate. But they also produced marketable goods, participated actively in local markets especially on Sundays, and would sell services such as sewing and other craft work, or even provide dances with food for other slaves and charge an entrance price. In these ways enslaved women engaged in the local economy and were able at times to accumulate a few savings. Thistlewood, for example, often borrowed money from Phibbah and even other women slaves, at the same time that he would give them small amounts of food and other items, besides the small payments for sex. Market and service activities were one part of slaves' creation of their own creole cultures, built within the constraints of slavery, yet autonomous and distinctive.

As chattel slaves, women were the property of their masters and could be sold at will, as could their children. They could not marry without their owner's permission; indeed, slaves' own marriages were often disregarded by their owners, and it was only in the later stages of Caribbean slavery that Christian marriages were encouraged, although enslaved women widely rejected the gendered contract within these. Hence it was difficult for many women to maintain a marriage or relationship of cohabitation, and their children and other family members could be and often were sold away. Despite these great obstacles to family relationships, women slaves sometimes managed to sustain not only kin relationships but friendships and a wider sense of community. Women's contributions to black community bonding and survival could be more central than men's where there was networking among women, and because of their determined maintenance of relationships with their children even against the odds. Mary Prince's mother, for example, was able for some years to create a sense of family for her children despite the fact that Prince's father was an enslaved carpenter living at some distance from the house where she was a domestic slave. When Prince was twelve, her mistress died and her master decided that she and two of her sisters would be sold. Prince's description of her sale and parting from her mother is suffused with bitterness and grief. Prince's new owner beat her severely; when this first occurred she ran away and went back to her mother who hid her and brought her food, but her father insisted that she had to go back to her master. Years later she and her mother were briefly reunited when Mary was forced to do gruelling salt pond labour on Turk's Island and her mother was also brought there. The splitting up of her family by sale meant that she lost contact with her seven brothers and three sisters, and was far from both parents at the times of their deaths – although the slave network was such that she eventually learned of these and some news of her siblings.[18]

A particular nexus of the contradictions within slavery were relations between white and black women. White men's constant sexual traffic with black women, not surprisingly, provoked jealousy on the part of white women, whose sexual possibilities were more limited due to racist and patriarchal attitudes that proscribed sex between white women and black men. Such jealousy within a household could incite harsh and violent treatment of women slaves by their mistresses.[19] At the same time, there is limited evidence that occasionally a mistress might be more lenient and humane than the master. Mary Prince recalled great affection for her first mistress: 'I was truly attached to her, and, next to my own mother, loved her better than any creature in the world.' She described this mistress, Mrs. Williams, as 'a kind-hearted good woman' who 'treated all her slaves well' when the master was away, which, as he was a merchant ship captain, was most of the time. When he was home Captain Williams abused both his slaves and his wife, to such an extent that 'all her slaves loved and pitied her'. Mrs. Williams died when Prince was twelve. She and her mother both wept and grieved for their mistress, partly from foreboding about their own fates.[20] This is not to suggest any inherent bonding between women across the lines of race and slavery. Rather, it reflects how severely abusive slave-holding men could be, corrupted by a patriarchal system in which being white and male meant enormous privilege, and by the profit motives of plantation slavery. But these structures corrupted white women too, as is suggested by evidence that at least one newly arrived mistress was critical of the abusive treatment creole mistresses meted out to their slaves.[21]

Enslaved women's daily lives and actions provide us with insight into the power dynamics of slavery itself, through their subtle and intimate forms of resistance, as well as their overt participation in rebellions and renegade communities such as the Maroons. Women's refusal of masters' sexual advances (such as Phibbah's occasional refusals of Thistlewood, and Mary Prince's occasional refusals of her owner's orders to wash him naked in the bathtub) and their sporadic rejection of masters and mistresses' demands and abuse, constituted daily resistance against the oppression of slavery.[22] Maintenance of slavery as a system depended on the authority of masters and owners in all capacities; minor acts of resistance required courage because they were often punished violently, and they undermined the system. Evidence of recurrent minor and often intimate acts of resistance shows slaves' constant rejection of their own enslavement.

Feminist theory underscores the centrality of sexuality to social relations of power. Because the personal and intimate are political, and because gender relations are structured by sexuality and vice versa, scholarship on gender has revealed sexuality as foundational to social relations in slavery. The sexual abuse of women slaves by white masters was central to the social, racial and gendered hierarchies of slave society; indeed, it created and sustained those hierarchies. While male slaves were subject to physical violence and on rare occasions even sexual coercion, sexual abuse overwhelmingly characterized the lives of slave women more than those of slave men.[23] White masters and mistresses' rationalization of this abuse, through representations of black women as sexually promiscuous and wanton, produced a staple racist stereotype that has permeated Western culture for centuries, with a damaging legacy still. As historian Hilary McD. Beckles has pointed out, it was not only that white men exhibited sexual desire, even preference, for nonwhite women. The evidence of white men's sexual behaviour in British slave colonies in the West Indies suggests that it was women's very enslavement that they found sexually enticing.[24] Men claimed their rights to sexual intercourse with enslaved women in their houses (often under the noses of their wives) and in the fields. The power that slavery and racial hierarchies gave them over subjugated women provided a dimension of sexual mastery that they apparently relished, at the same time that women's abilities to resist them were severely constrained. If the profit motive was integral to both the plantation economy and chattel slavery, so too was sexual mastery a reason that Caribbean planters fought against the ending of slavery as long as they could, resisting vociferously the movement that outlawed the slave trade in British territory in 1807 and finally prohibited slavery itself in 1833–34.

Connections between slavery and convict transportation

Recent scholarship has pointed to the connections between systems of unfree labour in the centuries when the British Empire was ascendant. In the seventeenth century, the indenture of white labourers preceded the rise of the British slave trade and the full flourishing of the plantation economy in the British West Indies. Indentured white workers were soon joined by enslaved Africans; together they constituted the early West Indian labour force. It is crucial to recognize the historical entrenchment of racial hierarchies, and the ways in which, from the latter seventeenth to the nineteenth centuries, blackness and otherness came to mark degraded, menial and enslaved status within European colonialism. Hierarchies of colour shaped the practise of slavery and relations between colonizer and colonized in British colonial possessions. At the same time, categories of unfree labour were not completely segregated, but overlapped and can be seen as existing on a continuum, with slavery at one terrible extreme.[25] It is instructive, for example, to recognize the historical relationship between slavery and indentured labour. Having coexisted in the Caribbean in the seventeenth century and in the Cape Colony right up to abolition, the ending of slavery in the nineteenth century was rapidly followed by the rise of indentured labour in colonies including the West Indies, Cape Colony, Mauritius, Fiji and Queensland. Labour suppliers took advantage of extreme poverty in places such as India and China, and deployed both kidnapping and ruse there and elsewhere such as Melanesia, to provide plantocracies with labour at rates below those of the open market and where labour was short.

One interesting component in this developing picture of interconnected systems of coerced labour are the threads connecting convict transportation to both indentured labour and slavery. Earlier in the eighteenth century, in British North America indentured labour, convict transportation and slavery all coexisted as conduits of labour to the colonies. But above and beyond that connection we now know, thanks to the work of several historians, that not all of the convicts transported to the Australian penal colonies between 1788 and 1868 were from the white labouring classes or political radicals of Britain. Convicts in Australia included slaves, former slaves and free blacks from the Caribbean, free blacks and former slaves from Britain, indigenous Africans sent from the

Cape Colony and via Britain, African-Americans, and Malagasy slaves, former slaves, Indian convicts and Indian and Chinese indentured labourers transported from Mauritius.[26] Ian Duffield, a pioneer in this field of research, and James Bradley have put the total number of nonwhite convicts as probably under one thousand.[27] Yet this long-overlooked group complicates historical understanding of early colonial Australia, and indeed of the progenitors of modern Australia. Moreover, the fact that transportation to Australia was employed as a punishment and putative deterrent in multiple imperial sites suggests the importance of interconnections between these various systems of unfree labour. The belief by colonial rulers that banishment or exile to Australia was a severe punishment for those who had experienced indentured labour and even slavery tells us about the role of both those interconnections and the penal colonies in the imperial imagination.

Evidence suggests that nonwhite convicts sent to Australia overwhelmingly were men. But there were some women, and we even know something of their stories. These stories too provide us with some evidence of the particular circumstances and cultural associations of women under slavery. In March 1831 Theresia arrived in New South Wales, having been convicted in and sent from Mauritius. Born in Madagascar, in Mauritius she was enslaved. Her convicted offence was striking her master's daughter with intent to kill; she was caught holding a hoe over the ten-year-old's head. Theresia's treatment by her master had been so brutal that he had been placed under police surveillance and prohibited from punishing his slaves without prior permission. Interestingly, when her master intervened in her apparent attack on the daughter, Theresia jumped on him and grabbed his testicles; two other slaves rescued him. Attacking her master by grabbing his testicles at least raises the possibility that the treatment which had sent her over the edge included sexual abuse – a possibility that suggests treatment of women slaves in Mauritius was similar to that in other slave colonies.[28] Several stories of enslaved females who were transported to Australia involve the offence of attempted poisoning of masters and mistresses. Slaveholders often feared the possibility of poisoning by women slaves, partly because as domestics women had access to masters' and mistresses' food and drink, and partly because of women's assumed roles in African religious practices (often called 'obeah' in the West Indies). For example, Priscilla, a housemaid and cook in Jamaica was sent to New South Wales in 1836 for putting arsenic in her master's family's food; she had been tried and convicted in 1831 before the abolition of slavery.[29]

stop

Convict women in Australia

Contemporary discourse and official attitudes regarding convict women in the Australian penal colonies reveal ways in which class difference was related to racial attitudes, even as racial assumptions meant real differences between the treatment of convict women and enslaved women. Like slaves, convict women were frequently described as being of such a low order of humanity that they were indistinguishable from animals. Significantly, some such descriptions claimed women convicts were more bestial than convict men. In 1837 James Mudie, an officer formerly in New South Wales, derided women convicts in extreme terms: 'Their open and shameless vice must not be told. Their fierce and untameable audacity would not be believed. They are the pest and gangrene of the colonial society – a reproach to human nature – and lower than the brutes, a disgrace to all animal existence.'[30] Other commentators too likened women convicts to animals, or described them as 'savages'. Such terminology dehumanized women convicts in a fashion not dissimilar to early-nineteenth-century commentary that dehumanized Aboriginal people, both men and women, by describing them as 'savages', uncivilized and animal-like. Aboriginal people, however, often could be marginalized and overlooked when not the objects of removal or violence, whereas convict women were part of the colonial *raison d'être* and the official responsibility of colonial administrators. Their control and reform was central to the colonial mission. Viewing them as incorrigible and even inhuman was a way of deflecting responsibility for their salvation.

The actual labour expected of convict women bore a superficial resemblance to the labour of enslaved women. In the 1820s at the Emu Plains settlement near the Blue Mountains in New South Wales, for example, convict women engaged in some light field work. Both on government and private assignment, women convicts were expected to perform domestic service, washing, cooking, cleaning, and care of children and the sick. Yet this resemblance is deceptive, because the hours of convict labour were more regulated, convicts could appeal to colonial officials if they believed themselves hardly done by, and convict servants were not supposed to be beaten by masters or mistresses. Differences in physical punishment between men and women convicts, moreover, illustrate the intersections of gender and racial ideologies: women convicts benefitted from emergent definitions of femininity denied to enslaved black women. Even after the early 1820s legislation that prohibited the flogging of women slaves in some parts of the British Caribbean (following similar legislation in Britain in 1817), this practice continued; some planters asserted women slaves needed flogging even more than men. The fact that men and women slaves were treated equally harshly, expected to perform equally arduous labour and punished in the same ways, whereas convict men and women were not, shows that black women were considered beyond the application of definitions of feminine delicacy.

Women convicts, for all the harsh rhetoric, were not subject to the same degree of physical punishment as slaves, or as men convicts. Women convicts were flogged too in the first years of the Australian penal colonies, but received fewer lashes than men, and were not flogged after 1817. More arduous labour was demanded of convict men than women, they continued to be flogged after women were not, and men were more subject to such physical punishments as being put in irons and sentenced to hard labour.[31] In the early period women were also punished by labour, both public and in the factories, but by the 1820s their punishments had moved towards time in the factory and solitary confinement.[32] But there was another form of physical punishment implemented from the 1820s for convict women, that of head shaving. Head shaving was applied to men prisoners too in British prisons, but it was adopted in the penal colonies as a particular punishment for women convicts with multiple gendered meanings. After 1817 women were no longer flogged because flogging was now considered too harsh for white women even of the dissolute lower orders. But it was clearly understood that head shaving was an effective form of punishment for women because, not only were they humiliated and branded as prisoners, but they were robbed of a fundamental symbol of their femininity. Convict women strongly resented and resisted head shaving. Not only was it a way of marking the convict body, it was understood to reduce women's sexual attractiveness and therefore their options.[33]

Both contemporary commentators and historians in recent decades have centrally defined convict women through their sexuality. Both at the time and in recent historical works, women convicts have been described as deviant, polluting, corrupt, depraved, degraded 'whores'.[34] Historian Kay Daniels has suggested that both the contemporary and the historical debate have been dominated by 'the priapic male', who has considered men's sexual activity as quite natural, women's sexuality only in terms of their response to male desire, and women sexually active outside marriage as immoral, corrupt and indeed 'whores'.[35] Evidence suggests that contemporary male officials often found convict women threatening, which was a key factor in their tendency to describe them as 'shameless', 'untameable' and bestial. Early histories of the penal colonies readily condemned convict women as prostitutes. More recent statistical analysis has put the proportion of transported women who were prostitutes in Britain as less than a third. Moreover, we know now that many women of the poorer classes in eighteenth- and nineteenth-century Britain lived precarious economic existences. Women who defined themselves as domestic servants, maids, dressmakers, milliners, factory workers and dairywomen might at times turn to prostitution out of desperation, as a survival strategy. Women moved in and out of prostitution depending whether they could find other work. Further, analysis of convict records shows that even women who were prostitutes in Britain, after transportation became settled and respectable women in Van Diemen's Land.[36] Therefore earlier historians' assumptions that women convicts were often morally corrupt women who preferred prostitution to honest labour and were a degrading influence on the colonies have been belied by historical evidence.

Recently feminist historians, such as Kay Daniels and Joy Damousi, have suggested that contemporary condemnations of convict women as whores were indictments intended to control women, whose expression of their own sexual desire was seen as disorderly and threatening. Not only did some convict women choose to cohabit with or have sexual relations with men outside marriage, but by the 1840s particularly in Van Diemen's Land lesbianism in convict women's factories was regarded by officials as a problem. Convict women's homosexuality represented an autonomous subculture, a rejection of dominant definitions of respectable heterosexual femininity, and was clearly linked to acts of resistance and subversion of authority.[37] Other factors also complicate the old picture of convict women as dissolute whores, such as evidence that some instances of prostitution were officially instigated (e.g., at the Colonial Hospital in Launceston in 1831), and that women convicts were coerced into commercial sex.[38]

While enslaved women were blamed for interracial sexuality in the Caribbean by being represented as lustful, promiscuous and amoral, convict women were blamed for disorder in the penal colonies and held morally responsible for sexual activity regarded as natural for men. Convict women were subject to some sexual coercion because of the power colonial officials and assigned masters held over them, yet the degree of sexual abuse was significantly worse for women slaves. In Britain in the late eighteenth and early nineteenth centuries, gender definitions were changing. New definitions of respectable bourgeois masculinity and femininity were linked to industrialization, capitalism and commerce. An ascendant middle class defined itself in opposition to both the corrupt aristocracy and the chaotic poor at home, as well as enslaved and exotic others in the colonies. Women convicts were represented as an extreme instance of the necessity to impose new definitions of respectable femininity on the lower orders. Bourgeois femininity was increasingly linked to physical, moral and spiritual purity, and was held up as the standard to which all other women should aspire. With asexuality now a touchstone of respectable femininity, colonial authorities contended that convict women's extramarital and especially homosexual activity demonstrated the need for their moral uplift and regimes of reform. The contemporary focus on convict women's sexuality and the enterprise to reform disorderly women was one instance of gender definitions and redefinitions moving back and forth between colony and metropole.

Gender, families and the abolition of slavery

As several scholars of slavery have pointed out, any consideration of the gendered dynamics of the anti-slavery movement must begin with the recognition that enslaved Caribbean women resisted, opposed and subverted slavery in multiple ways. Women slaves were importantly involved in maroon communities and slave revolts, but to focus only on such overt acts of rebellion is to miss the pervasive and subtle ways that women undercut the system. They did so by occasionally refusing sexual advances, suppressing their reproduction, being intransigent in the face of work demands and running away. Individual women slaves were cultural, spiritual and political leaders of their communities, while some practised traditional forms of medicine and intimidated Europeans with their knowledge of herbs and poisons. Many enslaved women carved out limited pieces of economic and cultural autonomy through their commercial production and marketing activities. Some deliberately entered sexual relations with white men in order to improve their condition and even leverage the possibility of manumission.[39] Beside these continual and pervasive forms of subversion on the behalf of large numbers of women slaves, here too we need to recognize the contribution of Mary Prince. It was Prince's own idea to tell her autobiography, so that people in England could read a first-hand account by a slave of the horrors of the system. Repeatedly throughout her story she positions herself as a spokeswoman for other slaves, and condemns slavery in strident terms. The publication of her story was an effective contribution to the anti-slavery campaign, and Prince needs to be identified as not just a slave who opposed the system in courageous ways, but an anti-slavery campaigner in the metropole.[40]

A powerful vector through which gender ideologies circulated in the empire and intersected with slavery was the abolition movement of the late eighteenth and early nineteenth centuries. Although the most celebrated abolitionists were men and the national abolition organizations in Britain were run by men, women constituted significant numbers of grass-roots members and a few of the key strategists were women, especially in the movement's political shift around 1830 from advocating gradual emancipation to demanding immediate abolition. More importantly, the abolition movement emerged simultaneously and in tandem with new definitions of gendered probity, the definitions just mentioned that were linked to economic change and the expansion of the middle class. According to these prescriptions for appropriate behaviour, women were the particular representatives and guardians of the domestic realm. Supposedly, their activities should be confined within or linked to the household, while men's activities embraced the public and political realms. This cultural script placed women as the moral guardians of home and family because of their purportedly more spiritual, pious and refined natures. New class-based notions of gender shaped the dynamics of the abolition movement at the same time that they provided the stuff of many of its arguments. Both abolition and gender ideologies were connected to this period's evangelical Christianity, which produced sects and societies committed to missionary work both at home and abroad. Middle-class British women took inspiration from evangelicalism to give their support to the abolition movement. In response to any suggestion that being involved with such a cause was transgressing their domestic boundaries, women argued that proper feminine qualities led naturally to opposition to slavery; women naturally felt pity for those who suffered. Feminine virtues of delicacy and modesty led women, they claimed, to care strongly about issues of humanity and justice. Moreover, women abolitionists used women's supposed natural concern with the family to justify their protests about the suffering of slave women and the disruption of family life under slavery. They contended that it was an extension of British women's domestic duties to object to the flogging of other women, their sexual abuse and degradation, and the separation of mothers and children.[41]

Eighteenth-century Britain had witnessed the rise of both industrialization and consumerism; the growing consumption of sugar in Britain was directly linked to the expansion of British sugar plantations and hence to slavery in the Caribbean. One of the gendered strategies of the abolition movement drew upon women's domestic role as household managers and consumers to persuade them to bring their moral sensibilities to their purchasing power. Women were urged to boycott sugar in protest against slavery, and thus to sway men to the same end. In these various ways, middle-class women's location in the domestic realm was implicitly extended to the public realm. Abolitionist women largely worked within these ideological constraints, but through their activism helped to lay the groundwork for what would become the mid-nineteenth-century women's movement. Scholars have demonstrated the complex ways in which feminism was implicated in British imperialism, connections that were already foreshadowed in the abolition movement. Charlotte Sussman has suggested that abolitionist tracts that urged Englishwomen to abstain from buying West Indian sugar represented them as having finer sensibilities than the women of any other nation, contributing to English cultural superiority both through their sympathy for slaves and their safeguarding of the English home from such immorally produced goods.[42] Moreover, women anti-slavery activists contrasted the terrible lot of women slaves with the superior condition of British women, representing themselves as an ideal of femininity that should be extended to less fortunate women. They portrayed black women as helpless, and themselves as offering benevolent help to women who were much more vulnerable, and on whose behalf they spoke. Women abolitionists believed in the imperial mission, appealed to planters as fellow Christians, and argued for the extension of Christianity and the enlightened principles of British government to the colonies. In all of this, they assumed the superiority of Christianity, British culture and their own gendered position.[43]

In the same period, a few political radicals such as Mary Wollstonecraft and some Owenite socialists drew analogies between the position of women in Britain and the position of slaves. In her 1792 treatise, *A Vindication of the Rights of Woman*, Wollstonecraft repeatedly refers to white middle-class British women as slaves, at the same time that she indicts British slavery in the colonies, elicits pity for the condition of slaves, and argues that slaves and women both have rights to natural liberties.[44] Both the contrasts drawn by evangelical abolitionist women between the terrible plight of women slaves in the colonies and their own idealized position as British women, and radical suggestions that the two positions of female subordination were more similar than different, invoked colonial gender constructions as yardsticks for metropolitan gender relations. Such invocations were one way in which gendered hierarchies in one colonial site operated to construct gendered hierarchies in another.

Conceptions of gender moved at the same time from metropole to colonies. A clear instance of this was the ways in which the notions of appropriate spheres and familial roles for men and women, elaborated by abolitionists and colonial officials, entered colonial societies before and after the abolition of slavery. We know from the work of Pamela Scully that in the Cape Colony, South Africa, notions of separate spheres for men and women, and of patriarchal relations in the family, shaped ameliorative legislation in the 1820s, the period of apprenticeship from 1834 to 1838, and then the postemancipation period. So convinced were white colonizers of the intertwining of freedom and gender relations, that on 1 December 1838, the day emancipation took effect, the *South African Commercial Advertiser* celebrated freed men's ability to claim the privileges of patriarchy:

> The Freeman becomes the Head of a Family. ... The Father, however poor, however overlooked or despised by the world, is now an object, in one place at least, not only of love but of *reverence*. There is now a circle where, if he chooses, he may reign as a King not only over the outward actions, but in the souls and hearts, in the thoughts and affections of his sincere and willing subjects.[45]

Scully shows, however, that the profound social transitions that occurred in the wake of abolition, while influenced by such bourgeois British notions, were far more complicated. Until the changes of the 1820s, Cape slavery had incorporated a division of labour more marked by gender than slavery in the

West Indies. Enslaved and indentured men had largely performed the labour required by the farms that were the economic base of the western Cape, while women laboured inside the households. Emancipation thus entrenched preexisting notions of gender-appropriate work. But freed women also used their new status to avoid domestic labour for white farmers as far as possible, preferring to stay in their own homes and perform their own household labour, produce goods for market, or sell their labour through laundry or seasonal agricultural work. By the late 1840s the lack of availability of land plots for black farmers and uneven economic conditions meant that some freed women were forced to resort to domestic service for white farmers. Their desire to avoid such work was based less on gendered notions of women not performing paid labour than on their knowledge that domestic service meant sexual vulnerability to white men.

The limited opportunities for freed people in postemancipation society meant that any aspirations to the ideal nuclear family were undercut by realities such as men having to leave home to find work elsewhere. The lived reality of freed families, then, often did not match British, missionary and white-settler ideologies, despite legal and policy measures to impose it. The Masters and Servants Ordinance of 1842, for example, made women workers subject to the authority of their husbands, and white farmers sought to shore up the authority of freed men as heads of families so that they, the employers, could have access to black wives and children as cheap labour. Undergirding reconfigured postemancipation society was a legal culture which reified women's subordination in newly cross-racial ways. Black women were refused proper legal protection against rape by white and even black men, for example, in a masculinist solidarity built upon sexual access to black women's bodies.[46]

In Jamaica too the postemancipation period was marked by attempts to inculcate a new gender order, as Baptist missionaries and colonial officials sought to encourage Christian marriages and to curb illicit sexual unions, although missionaries and officials had different reasons. The missionaries, who had actively contributed to the abolition movement, as in the Cape Colony saw freedom as directly linked to the nuclear family. The father would be the bread-winner and head of the household, while women would take a subordinate and domestic role. Parents and children would no longer be torn asunder and men would now be able to protect their wives from the planters' physical and sexual abuse. Godly villages would be places of sexual order and propriety. Colonial officials, on the other hand, were more interested in establishing a social order where, unlike slave concubinage, paternity would be acknowledged and registered. This would mean that men would take economic responsibility for children, and conversely, elderly men could be supported by their own children.[47] Patriarchal family arrangements were also assumed in land settlement schemes in the latter part of the nineteenth century, although women heads of households asserted their own claims.[48] Despite a wave of enthusiasm for Christian marriage after emancipation, and a brief revival period in the early 1860s, missionaries' hopes were largely dashed as black Jamaicans chose extra-legal forms of cohabitation. Jamaican peasants sought as far as they could to live off their own plots of land and in their own villages rather than remain subject to planters. Poor women avoided domestic service as far as possible, just as women in the Cape Colony did, opting to sustain themselves through cultivating and marketing various foodstuffs.[49] From the mid-nineteenth-century black Jamaicans established lives and communities that were resistant to missionary and official social and gender prescriptions.[50]

Indentured labour in the Caribbean

Just how various were the purposes that the ideology of the male-headed family could serve is illustrated by the disparate stakes in the contests over gender ideology for Indian indentured labourers in the mid- to late-nineteenth-century Caribbean. Planters in the British Caribbean colonies responded rapidly to slave emancipation by seeking cheap labour in the form of indentured immigrants from India. Indentured labourers were sent to British Guiana as early as 1838, and to Trinidad and Jamaica from 1845. Reflecting attitudes that they had held until the late stages of slavery, planters thought that natural reproduction of labourers in the Caribbean would be expensive and messy, and preferred to rely on continued importation of labour. Especially in the first stages of this new system of Indian indentured labour, the labourers were not viewed as permanent settlers with familial, emotional and cultural needs but simply as a temporary solution to an economic dilemma for planters. For these reasons, and because they thought women would be physically less able workers, employers chose to import far more male labourers than female. From the inception of Indian indentured labour until its termination in 1917, the issue of a severely imbalanced sex ratio would be at the base of tensions relating to gender and sexuality in colonies from the West Indies, to Fiji and Mauritius. In Trinidad, for example, the first boat to arrive with Indian labourers in 1845 brought 206 men and 21 women; and in the decade from 1871 to 1881 there were 2143 Indian men for every thousand women.[51] It would seem that concern about the nuclear family, at least for Indian labourers, was remarkably absent from the thinking of colonial officials, planters and immigration agents. In the very early years of Indian indentured migration, the Anti-Slavery Society was the only group to object to this underrepresentation of women,[52] and it is probably an index of the waning authority of evangelicals in Britain that missionary opinions were relatively muted in later debates about Indian labourers in the colonies.

As debate about this disparity between men and women waxed and waned over the decades of Indian indenture schemes, the British Government in India tried to control the problem by restricting the proportions of men to women allowed to leave. Thus the permitted ratio approved by emigration officials in India varied from one woman for every two men, to one woman to every four men, but it was never equal at any point in the period. When questions were raised or complaints made, emigration agents in India consistently reported that they could not find greater numbers of women migrants of a 'better class'. Inherent in the discourse surrounding Indian labour migration were complaints about the low order of women who migrated, complaints that echo a similar discourse surrounding the women convicts transported to Australia. When colonial officials or Caribbean planters complained that the Indian women sent were immoral, emigration agents responded that only lower caste women were willing to migrate, and that even if they could induce higher caste women to do so, they would be completely unsuitable for plantation labour. As with women convicts, this discursive construction of the immoral Indian migrant woman was linked to issues of women's autonomy. Even though later representations of Indian women in the Caribbean emphasized docile and subservient wives, evidence pertaining to indentured migrants shows that around two-thirds of the women went on their own, not with husbands. The single women migrants included widows, women running away from their husbands, women who had been deserted, and those for whom the only likely occupation if they remained in India was prostitution.[53] For Indian women, then, indentured labour represented a strategy to escape difficult circumstances in India, and to try to start a better life.

On Caribbean sugar, cocoa, coconut and banana plantations, Indian women labourers faced arduous field work and rates of pay that were only about half to two-thirds those of men.[54] Marriage and co-habitation were integral to women's survival strategies, and women who had left harsh circumstances in India often proved willing to make matches that were most strategic for their own needs. Given the sex ratio imbalance, women often found themselves able to move from one partnership to another that offered greater comfort or pleasure. Contemporary observers, however, often equated such relationship mobility with lack of morality. Sarah Morton, a missionary in Trinidad, reported the following conversation with an Indian woman in the 1870s:

> 'I said to an East Indian woman, whom I knew to be a widow of a brahmin [*sic*]. "You have no relatives in Trinidad I believe." "No Madame", she replied, "only myself and two children; when the last immigrant ship came in I took a *Papa*. I will keep him as long as he treats me well. If he does not treat me well, I shall send him off at once; that's the right way, is it not." '[55]

What could well be interpreted as striking pragmatism was used as evidence that Indian women were degrading the moral tone of their communities. Such interpretations were discursively linked to evidence of high levels of violence against women amongst Indian immigrants.

In colonies including Fiji, Mauritius, and the Caribbean, communities of Indian labourers in the nineteenth century witnessed extraordinarily high levels of the murder of women by men, and also suicide by men.[56] Statistics show that the women murdered were mostly the wives or partners of the murderers. For example, in Trinidad between 1872 and 1879 the reports of murders among Indian immigrants showed 102 total murders, of which 76 victims were women, including 59 wives or partners of the murderers.[57] As these high levels of violence continued, colonial officials responded in various ways. One was to increase the rates of commission offered to women recruited in India, such that by the early twentieth century women were offered substantially more than men. Higher rates, it was hoped, would mean greater numbers of women migrating, which would alleviate the sex ratio imbalance. Countervailing this measure, however, was a continuing concern that the women recruited needed to be of the right moral character. The recurrent accusation that women migrants were dissolute worked to lay a good deal of the blame for the murders with the women themselves; the suggestion was that their sexual behaviour incited the violence.[58] Blaming Indian women belied in Fiji, at least, contemporary commentary showing one source of sexual jealousy and violence to have been the sexual harassment and assault of Indian women by white overseers.[59]

The other way in which colonial officials responded shows a coalescence of interests among officials, planters and Indian men labourers. In a cumulative fashion, regulations and policies worked to strengthen the family and the authority within it of men over women. Marriage ordinances applying to Indian immigrants were increasingly codified, and came to include provisions such that there were sanctions for what were seen as offences against marriage. One such provision allowed a manager or overseer to transfer elsewhere a worker leading a woman astray from her husband. When this provision seemed inadequate to control what was often represented as women's fickleness, a later provision introduced punishments for harbouring a wife, a provision which meant that a woman could not even seek refuge with others from a violent husband. In the debate surrounding these provisions and in their enactment it was clear that the husband's interests and prerogatives outweighed those of the wife.[60] In Trinidad in the last decades of the nineteenth century, these legal measures were augmented by land allocations to Indian peasants, so that Indian families could engage in small-scale sugar cane production as well as subsistence farming. This system worked to tie peasants to the larger estates through men's wage labour, while creating a separate sphere of household labour for women, who also served as a supply of extra labour at harvest time. Women were thus increasingly defined by their reproductive and domestic labour, a move widely regarded as helping men to entrench their patriarchal authority.[61]

As Madhavi Kale has suggested, male commentators ranging from British officials to Indian nationalists deployed women as symbols and vessels in the decades-long debate over indentured labour, rather than focusing on women labourers as people with hopes and needs.[62] Yet indentured labour represented a survival strategy for Indian women, and the social effects of sex-ratio imbalances could provide them with limited choices.

* * *

In looking at these interconnected forms of unfree labour through the impact of gendered and racialized conceptions on women, I do not want to suggest that women were simply victimized alike by these various but overlapping imperial systems. Nor am I suggesting that we should see a single global structure at work, along the lines of Immanuel Wallerstein's world systems theory. Rather, I would propose that bringing these systems together into a frame of analysis allows us to see the centrality of gender ideology and sexual relations to structures often viewed in economic and legalistically political terms. It reveals as well the constitutive role of racial conceptions in ideas and practices of sex and gender, and the ways in which these conceptions and practices were shaped at once in both the British metropole and diverse colonies. Such dynamics, of course, were not limited to the British Empire. It is important to recognize what

Penny Edwards has called 'this connective tissue of colonial ideology.'[63] As she suggests, racial and gender ideologies moved across the boundaries between European empires, and need to be seen as circulating globally. But I wish to draw attention to the ways in which they moved *within* the British Empire and their effects. Moreover, I would underscore that the colonies under consideration here included both white-settler colonies and colonies of exploitation, which calls into question the usual separation of the two categories.

Conceptions of gender travelled within the British Empire, shifting and reproducing in protean fashion, shaping power relations and being invoked in order to exert or sustain power over others. We can see how racial and class-based slurs against women were used to justify their sexual abuse and to attribute responsibility to the women rather than men. Focusing on sexual and domestic relations and inequalities compels us to see how these systems of unfree labour shaped the private worlds of women and men, and how intimate matters were directly connected to the public faces of labour regimes. Women labourers and enslaved women negotiated the odds against them both night and day. Notions of respectable femininity emergent in late-eighteenth and early-nineteenth-century Britain were applied in limited ways to women convicts and arguably alleviated their suffering by the 1820s. The application by missionaries and abolitionists of conceptions of femininity, such as modesty and maternal affection, to enslaved women may have helped to hasten abolition, although it did little to impact the treatment of women under slavery. The arguments and tactics of abolitionists and radicals reflect the ways in which gender relations under slavery shaped gender definitions in the metropole, while convict women were considered exemplars of female moral depravity and its costs. Ascendant bourgeois definitions of the nuclear family and patriarchal authority were invoked as the ideal to which newly emancipated men should aspire in the Cape Colony and Jamaica, and similar definitions were employed in the West Indies to help Indian labouring men to assert authority over Indian women.

All of these contestations show that subordinate gender conceptions coexisted with and challenged dominant conceptions. They show as well the shifting racial and class inflections of gender definitions. Examining the circumstances of women under slavery, convict transportation and indenture impels us to recognize the importance of women's productive and reproductive labour to the basic structures and enterprises of the empire. Such an examination reminds us simultaneously of the diversity of Britain's colonies in this period, and the fact that they were connected by cultural ideologies, capitalist enterprises, punitive judicial systems, administrative regulations and practices, the movement of people among them, and not least by the imperial imaginary. Beside recognizing such connections between diverse imperial sites, we need also to see the cumulative significance of women's acts of resistance, subversion and transgression. In these various colonial locations, slaves, convicts, freed people and indentured labourers sought to recreate familial structures in new circumstances. Women negotiated sexual and other relationships, albeit frequently temporary or compromised, even as they endured abuse. Those who survived within these harsh labour systems often sought to create emotional and practical networks, and sought stability in order to be able to reproduce. There is a transcendent pattern here of women parrying with contingent racialized gender ideologies of British and settler cultures, as they devised strategies to survive. Enslaved women, women convicts, freedwomen and women indentured labourers bartered with and against men in the same categories as themselves, as well as other women and men, to secure their own lives. Women under duress reinvented their own reproductive and familial systems, creating new structures that became integral to creole societies and cultures.

Notes

1. Hilary Beckles, *Afro-Caribbean Women & Resistance to Slavery in Barbados* (London: Karnak House, 1988), pp. 14–17; Rhoda Reddock, 'Women and the Slave Plantation Economy in the Caribbean', in S. Jay Kleinberg (ed.), *Retrieving Women's History: Changing Perceptions of the Role of Women in Politics and Society* (Oxford: Berg and Unesco, 1988), p. 108.
2. Barbara Bush, *Slave Women in Caribbean Society 1650–1838* (London: James Currey, 1990), pp. 42–5.
3. Quoted in Bridget Brereton, 'Text, Testimony and Gender: An Examination of some Texts by Women on the English-speaking Caribbean from the 1770s to the 1920s', in Verene Shepherd, Bridget Brereton and Barbara Bailey (eds), *Engendering History: Caribbean Women in Historical Perspective* (New York: St. Martin's Press, 1995), p. 88.
4. Beckles, *Afro-Caribbean Women*, p. 23; Bush, *Slave Women*, p. 45.
5. Moira Ferguson (ed.), *The History of Mary Prince, A West Indian Slave, Related by Herself* (Ann Arbor: University of Michigan Press, 1993), esp. pp. 55–7.
6. Beckles points out that Barbados was an exception in this regard, and that pronatal policies resulted in natural population growth of slaves in Barbados by 1800. Hilary McD. Beckles, 'Taking Liberties: Enslaved Women and Anti-Slavery in the Caribbean', in Clare Midgley (ed.), *Gender and Imperialism* (Manchester: Manchester University Press, 1998), p. 142.
7. Barbara Bush, 'Hard Labor: Women, Childbirth, and Resistance in British Caribbean Slave Societies', in David Barry Gaspar and Darlene Clark Hine (eds), *More Than Chattel: Black Women and Slavery in the Americas* (Bloomington: Indiana University Press, 1996), pp. 193–217.
8. Hilary McD. Beckles, *Natural Rebels: A Social History of Enslaved Black Women in Barbados* (London: Zed Books, 1989), pp. 141–3.
9. Bush, *Slave Women*, pp. 114–17.
10. Hilary McD. Beckles, *Centering Woman: Gender Discourses in Caribbean Slave Society* (Kingston: Ian Randle Publishers, 1999), ch. 3 'Phibbah's Price: A Jamaican "Wife" for Thomas Thistlewood', esp. pp. 44–5.
11. Douglas Hall, *In Miserable Slavery: Thomas Thistlewood in Jamaica, 1750–86* (London and Basingstoke: The Macmillan Press Ltd., 1989), pp. 184–7.
12. Hall, *In Miserable Slavery*, p. 67.
13. On this, see Trevor Burnard, 'Theater of Terror: Domestic Violence in Thomas Thistlewood's Jamaica, 1750–1786', in Christine Daniels and

Michael V. Kennedy (eds), *Over the Threshold: Intimate Violence in Early America* (New York: Routledge, 1999), pp. 237–53; and 'The Sexual Life of an Eighteenth-Century Jamaican Slave Overseer', in Merril D. Smith (ed.), *Sex and Sexuality in Early America* (New York: New York University Press, 1998), pp. 163–89.

14. While Thistlewood's diary is extraordinary, Thistlewood is a fair representative of the behaviour of overseers and slaveowners. Despite being more intellectually active than the generality of his peers, in most ways he was typical; the normativity of his behaviour is reflected in his descriptions of others, the regard in which he was held, and by other sources. Trevor Burnard, 'Thomas Thistlewood Becomes a Creole', in Bruce Clayton and John Salmond (eds), *Varieties of Southern History: New Essays on a Region and Its People* (Westport, CT: Greenwood Press, 1996), esp. pp. 101–2. Moreover, Jamaica was the largest single British West Indian slave society. See Trevor Burnard and Kenneth Morgan, 'The Dynamics of the Slave Market and Slave Purchasing Patterns in Jamaica, 1655–1788', *The William and Mary Quarterly* vol. 58, no. 1 (Jan. 2001): esp. p. 205.

15. Trevor Burnard, especially latter part of the chapter 'Adaptation, Accommodation and Resistance: Thistlewood's Slave Women and Their Responses to Enslavement', *Mastery, Tyranny, and Desire: Thomas Thistlewood and His Slaves in the Anglo-American World* (Chapel Hill, NC: University of North Carolina Press, 2004).

16. Hall, *In Miserable Slavery*, pp. 71–3.

17. Beckles, *Centering Woman*, ch. 3; and Barbara Bush, ' "Sable Venus", "She Devil" or "Drudge"? British Slavery and the "Fabulous Fiction" of Black Women's Identities, c. 1650–1838', *Women's History Review* vol. 9, no. 4 (2000): 761–89.

18. Ferguson (ed.), *The History of Mary Prince*, pp. 50–4, 60, 66.

19. Bush, ' "Sable Venus", "She Devil" or "Drudge"?', p. 773.

20. Ferguson (ed.), *The History of Mary Prince*, pp. 47–9.

21. Maria Nugent, wife of the Governor of Jamaica 1801–06, criticized creole mistresses' treatment of their domestic slaves; Beckles, *Centering Woman*, p. 97, and Brereton, 'Text, Testimony and Gender', p. 79.

22. Ferguson (ed.), *The History of Mary Prince*, pp. 9–10, 67–8.

23. Trevor Burnard discusses rare evidence of sexual abuse of slave men, in his chapter 'Adaptation, Accommodation and Resistance: Thistlewood's Slave Women and Their Responses to Enslavement', *Mastery, Tyranny, and Desire*.

24. Beckles, *Centering Woman*, p. 41.

25. On this, see Ian Duffield, 'Daylight on Convict Lived Experience: The History of a Pious Negro Servant', *Tasmanian Historical Studies* vol. 6, no. 2 (1999): 31; Ian Duffield and James Bradley (eds), *Representing Convicts: New Perspectives on Convict Forced Labour Migration* (London: Leicester University Press, 1997), pp. 2–4.

26. As well as the two works by Duffield above, see, for example, Ian Duffield, 'From Slave Colonies to Penal Colonies: The West Indian Convict Transportees to Australia', *Slavery and Abolition* vol. 7, no. 1 (May 1986): 25–45; Clare Anderson, 'Unfree Labour and its Discontents: Transportation

from Mauritius to Australia, 1825–1845', *Australian Studies* vol. 13, no. 1 (Summer 1998): 116–33; Ian Duffield, 'The Life and Death of "Black" John Goff: Aspects of the Black Convict Contribution to Resistance Patterns During the Transportation Era in Eastern Australia', *Australian Journal of Politics and History* vol. 33, no. 1 (1987): 30–44; Ian Duffield, ' "Stated This Offence": High-Density Convict Micro-Narratives', in Lucy Frost and Hamish Maxwell-Stuart (eds), *Chain Letters: Narrating Convict Lives* (Carlton South, Vic.: Melbourne University Press, 2001), pp. 119–35; Leslie C. Duly, ' "Hottentots to Hobart and Sydney": The Cape Supreme Court's Use of Transportation, 1828–38', *Australian Journal of Politics and History* vol. 25, no. 1 (April 1979): 39–50; V.C. Malherbe, 'Khoikhoi and the Question of Convict Transportation from the Cape Colony, 1820–1842', *South African Historical Journal* vol. 17 (November 1985): 19–39; V.C. Malherbe, 'South African Bushmen to Australia? Some Soldier Convicts Investigated', *Journal of Australian Colonial History* vol. 3, no. 1 (April 2001): 100–124 and Portia Robinson, *The Women of Botany Bay* (Sydney: Macquarie Library, 1988), p. 156.

27. Duffield and Bradley (eds), *Representing Convicts*, pp. 2–3.
28. Anderson, 'Unfree Labour and Its Discontents', pp. 119–20. This possibility of sexual abuse is supported by the 1838 testimony of 'Bibee' Zuhoorun, an Indian woman and former indentured servant in Mauritius, who told a parliamentary committee of her sexual harassment by her employer there. Quoted in Jane Samson (ed.), *The British Empire* (Oxford: Oxford University Press, 2001), pp. 111–12.
29. Duffield, 'From Slave Colonies to Penal Colonies', pp. 26, 34.
30. Quoted in Joy Damousi, *Depraved and Disorderly: Female Convicts, Sexuality and Gender in Colonial Australia* (Cambridge: Cambridge University Press, 1997), p. 37.
31. Robinson, *Women of Botany Bay*, pp. 166–7.
32. Damousi, *Depraved and Disorderly*, pp. 17, 31.
33. Damousi, *Depraved and Disorderly*, chapter 4 'Defeminising Convict Women'.
34. Damousi, *Depraved and Disorderly*, pp. 35–6; Kay Daniels, *Convict Women* (St. Leonards, NSW: Allen & Unwin, 1998), p. x.
35. Daniels, *Convict Women*, p. 157.
36. Daniels, *Convict Women*, pp. 186–92.
37. Daniels, *Convict Women*, pp. 175–83; Damousi, *Depraved and Disorderly*, pp. 69–72.
38. Daniels, *Convict Women*, pp. 200–4.
39. Hilary McD. Beckles makes a strong case for historiographical revision to embrace such acts as anti-slavery resistance in 'Taking liberties', pp. 137–57.
40. Clare Midgley, *Women Against Slavery: The British Campaigns, 1780–1870* (London: Routledge, 1992), p. 89.
41. Midgley, *Women Against Slavery*, pp. 94–7.
42. Charlotte Sussman, *Consuming Anxieties: Consumer Protest, Gender, and British Slavery, 1713–1833* (Stanford, CA: Stanford University Press, 2000), pp. 126–7.

43. Midgley, *Women Against Slavery*, pp. 98–103.
44. Moira Ferguson, 'Mary Wollstonecraft and the Problematic of Slavery', *Feminist Review* no. 42 (Autumn 1992): 82–102.
45. *South African Commercial Advertiser*, 1 December 1838, quoted in Pamela Scully, *Liberating the Family? Gender and British Slave Emancipation in the Rural Western Cape, South Africa, 1823–1853* (Portsmouth, New Hampshire: Heinemann, 1997), p. 1.
46. Scully, *Liberating the Family?*, especially pp. 2–11, 34–46, 81–4, 170–5.
47. Catherine Hall, 'In the Name of Which Father?' *International Labor and Working-Class History* no. 41 (Spring 1992): 23–8.
48. Joan French, 'Women and Colonial Policy in Jamaica after the 1838 Uprising', in Saskia Wieringa (ed.), *Subversive Women: Women's Movements in Africa, Asia, Latin America and the Caribbean* (London: Zed Books, 1995), pp. 125–6.
49. Persis Charles, 'The Name of the Father: Women, Paternity, and British Rule in Nineteenth-Century Jamaica', *International Labor and Working-Class History* no. 41 (Spring 1992): 4–22.
50. Thomas C. Holt, 'Gender in the Service of Bourgeois Ideology', *International Labor and Working-Class History* no. 41 (Spring 1992): 32–4.
51. Rhoda Reddock, 'Indian Women and Indentureship in Trinidad and Tobago 1845–1917: Freedom Denied', in Hilary Beckles and Verene Shepherd (eds), *Caribbean Freedom: Economy and Society from Emancipation to the Present* (Princeton, NJ: Markus Wiener Publishers, 1996), pp. 225, 232.
52. Reddock, 'Indian Women and Indentureship', p. 225.
53. Reddock, 'Indian Women and Indentureship', p. 227; Verene Shepherd, 'Emancipation Through Servitude: Aspects of the Condition of Indian Women in Jamaica, 1845–1945', in Beckles and Shepherd (eds), *Carribbean Freedom*, pp. 245–6.
54. Shepherd, 'Emancipation Through Servitude', p. 246.
55. Sarah Morton, *John Morton of Trinidad* (Toronto: Westminster Company, 1916), p. 342 quoted in Prabhu P. Mohapatra, ' "Restoring the Family": Wife Murders and the Making of a Sexual Contract for Indian Immigrant Labour in the British Caribbean Colonies, 1860–1920', *Studies in History* vol. 11, no. 2 n.s. (1995): 243.
56. Brij V. Lal, 'Labouring Men and Nothing More: Some Problems of Indian Indenture in Fiji', in Kay Saunders (ed.), *Indentured Labour in the British Empire 1834–1920* (London: Croom Helm, 1984), pp. 148–9; Clare Anderson, 'Unfree Labour and Its Discontents', pp. 126–7.
57. Mohapatra, ' "Restoring the Family" ', p. 232.
58. Reddock, 'Indian Women and Indentureship', p. 229.
59. John D. Kelly, *A Politics of Virtue: Hinduism, Sexuality, and Countercolonial Discourse in Fiji* (Chicago, IL: University of Chicago Press, 1991), pp. 31–41.
60. Mohapatra, ' "Restoring the Family" ', pp. 249–59.
61. Reddock, 'Indian Women and Indentureship', pp. 231–2.

62. Madhavi Kale, *Fragments of Empire: Capital, Slavery, & Indian Indentured Labor in the British Caribbean* (Philadelphia: University of Pennsylvania Press, 1998), p. 166.

63. Penny Edwards, 'On Home Ground: Settling Land and Domesticating Difference in the "Non-settler" Colonies of Burma and Cambodia', *Journal of Colonialism and Colonial History* vol. 4, no. 3 (2003): 2.

2

Narratives of Interracial Sexual Assault and Crises of Imperial Rule

Stories of colonial misadventure were avidly consumed in nineteenth- and early-twentieth-century Britain, especially narratives that were driven by fears of British or 'white' women's vulnerability to the violent predations of indigenous men. This particular aspect of imperial culture constitutes a significant topic for a broad analysis of gender and empire because of the diversity of colonial locations of such stories, and because of evidence that the metropolitan publishing industry and market influenced their shaping and circulation from one colony to another. The popularity of captivity narratives, from the seventeenth to the nineteenth centuries, and narratives of sexual assault, in the nineteenth and twentieth centuries, reflected both colonial and metropolitan fascination with the dangers of the colonies. In the latter period, the particular focus of interest was the perceived potential of the colonies and the 'frontier' contact zone for violent interracial sexual abuse. Moreover, as I hope to show, narratives of interracial sexual assault by men against women came to anchor colonial and imperial justifications for what most historians now view as egregious instances of repressive rule.

Captivity narratives

The fascination of nineteenth-century imperial popular culture with narratives of virtuous white women's sexual vulnerability to lascivious and violent nonwhite indigenous men needs to be seen as a historical development, one that illuminates shifting imperial dynamics of the nineteenth century. There is now a substantial body of scholarship on the captivity narratives that constituted a major popular print genre in Europe, North America and other European colonies from the seventeenth to the nineteenth centuries. Early modern Europeans' experience of kidnappings by Barbary corsairs and their enslavement in North Africa (Algiers, Tunis, Tripoli and Morocco) was a fraught cultural encounter that highlighted Europeans' vulnerability and their struggle for ascendancy over non-Christian others. With ransoms driving much of this kidnapping and a relatively high rate of return of the captives to Europe, stories of captives' fears, abuse, suffering and redemption became a familiar genre in the seventeenth and eighteenth centuries. From the late seventeenth century, stories of Barbary captivity were augmented by narratives emanating from North America. These had as their core, not enslavement and fear of Islam, but captivity in the wilderness and physical and spiritual degradation at the hands of pagan 'savages' and, seemingly even worse, Indians who had converted to Catholicism under French occupation. Linda Colley's work on early modern British captivity narratives demonstrates that, for the British audience, in the late-eighteenth and early-nineteenth-century North African and North American stories were further augmented by those from Asia, by-products of British military adventuring and the capture of British troops and their families especially by Muslims.[1] The growing popularity of captivity narratives occurred, of course, in the same period as the rising enslavement of Africans in the Americas. It is important to keep this juxtaposition in mind, partly to be aware of the captivity stories *not* finding publication and an audience in Europe, while the stories of Europeans held captive gripped public imagination.

Much of the work in this field documents the pivotal role of London, the British publishing industry, London editors and British audiences in the popular rise of the captivity narrative genre and its commercial success. Literary critic Joe Snader, for example, points to the metropolitan origin of this genre in English, and indeed the influence of the British tradition on the American narrative as it emerged.[2] Historically based captivity narratives became very popular, and were supplemented by a plethora of captivity fiction, such that the boundary between the two was often blurred. Interest in the captivity phenomenon was sparked by its prevalence, its reach (including the coasts of England, Wales and Ireland), the dramatic and harrowing experiences of those who fell captive, and their testimony to British, European and Christian people's vulnerability to foreign and especially non-Christian powers.[3] The captivity narrative became such a familiar cultural artifact that by 1842, British captives in Afghanistan, Colley demonstrates, spent much of their time in captivity writing their narratives in an atmosphere of mutual competition, even embellishing their stories in hope of being among those who would be published in London.[4]

As Kay Schaffer and D'Arcy Randall have shown, by the nineteenth century captivity narratives had garnered a global market with rapid circulation. Schaffer and Randall's research shows the plasticity of such narratives and their commercial manipulation by shrewd publishers. A good example of this appropriation is the Eliza Fraser story, the first captivity narrative located in Australia, based on events that occurred in 1836 off the coast of what is now the northeastern Australian state of Queensland. Fraser's story had such international circulation that it was even published in New York in 1837 and 1838 in the guise of an American captivity narrative, with the names of the main characters and elements of the story based on the historical events, but transposed to an American landscape, and a native people 'with "squaws", "papooses", "tepees" and "tomahawks" '. But the New York version of the Eliza Fraser story was itself a product of the story's popularity in London.[5]

The London versions of the story were embellished and sensationalized. As Kay Schaffer has shown from her careful research, the historical Eliza Fraser was the wife of a Scottish sea captain who accompanied her husband on a trip to New South Wales. On the return journey, in May 1836, their ship the *Stirling Castle* was wrecked during a storm off the island that takes its name from this episode, Fraser Island. Frightened by stories of 'cannibals', Captain Fraser ordered the survivors to remain in leaking lifeboats for weeks. Some of the crew rebelled, and finally the captain, his wife and four remaining survivors landed on the island, where they were taken in by the indigenous people, who included Ngulungbara, Badtjala and Dulingbara groups. The survivors were not so much held prisoner, but rather incorporated into the local communities and expected to contribute labour. Eliza Fraser was compelled 'to nurse lice-infected infants, dig for fern roots in the swamps, and harvest honey from honey-ant nests in the treetops'.[6] The captain and the first mate died. Meanwhile several of the other survivors of the shipwreck made it to another island, and made contact with a British officer from the Moreton Bay penal settlement, what is now Brisbane. An official rescue party was organized, including particularly a convict, John Graham, who had previously absconded, lived among the indigenous people of the island for around six years, and learned a local language. Graham led the rescue of first two crew members and finally Fraser herself. His rescue of Fraser involved an overnight journey during which he may have raped her, but she was delivered to Moreton Bay, went back to Sydney, and finally returned to England. There was no evidence that she was raped or assaulted by any indigenous man, although she clearly suffered great physical hardships.

What we know of the Eliza Fraser story is based on the accounts given by Fraser and the two surviving crew members, but Fraser herself contributed to its sensationalization for her own material ends. Her versions varied between the first official report she gave in Moreton Bay, the story she told in Sydney and the account she gave to the British press. In Sydney, Fraser had received four hundred pounds and two trunks full of clothes from public donations to her. When she returned to England in July 1837, she was married to another merchant ship captain, Alexander Greene, but she and her new husband hoped for further financial gains from public sympathy. Fraser presented herself to English authorities as an impoverished widow, and peddled her story to the press. In August 1837 versions of Fraser's 'captivity' story were published in three London newspapers, and Fraser became a celebrity. These versions were melodramatic depictions of 'a white woman "held in bondage" by murderous Savages'.[7] While Fraser had embellished her own tale, there were further editorial additions designed to appeal to public appetite. Eventually Fraser's fraudulent representation of her own marital and financial status was made public and she was impugned, but the story took on a life of its own, and the mythical Eliza Fraser became part of the British, North American and colonial public imagination of empire. The adaptations of the tale distorted the historical events, and became part of the popular literature of captivity, featuring distinctively nineteenth-century innuendos of violent sexual assault of a white woman by indigenous men.[8]

Immediately on the heels of the Eliza Fraser narrative came the myth of the White Woman of Gippsland. Thanks to the work of Kate Darian-Smith and Julie Carr in particular, we now have a sense of how this second famous Australian captivity story emerged. Its foundational narrative, the report by Scottish settler Augustus McMillan, instantly suggests the circulating operation of such myths. McMillan's framing of his eye-witness testimony of an encounter with an Aboriginal encampment indicates his expectation that his audience will be predisposed to captivity stories. On 28 December 1840 McMillan published in the *Sydney Herald* a report of an expedition he had recently undertaken in what is now the state of Victoria, to find a way from the Gippsland interior to the coast – a coastline that had been the site of several shipwrecks. He and his party startled a camp of twenty-five Kurnai people, mostly women they thought, who immediately ran away leaving behind their material possessions, including a size-able quantity of European goods. Sifting through the camp, McMillan and the men with him created a detailed inventory of items including blood-stained clothing, a lock of a European woman's hair, hand towels, a purse, a thimble, bottles, English and Scottish newspapers, a bible, some insurance and medical documents, and the body of a European two-year-old boy. Immediately after listing this inventory to establish tragic circumstances involving Europeans (implying shipwreck, massacre or both), McMillan reverts to the Indigenous people running away on their arrival, and notes that the women were driven away by the men brandishing spears. He reports that his party noticed one of the women 'constantly looking behind her, at us, a circumstance which did not strike us much at the time, but on examining the marks and figures about the largest of the native huts we were immediately impressed with the belief that the unfortunate female is a European – a captive of these ruthless savages'.[9] McMillan's ordering of his story – first the detailed inventory including blood-stained clothing and European women's accoutrements, then the image of the white woman looking back helplessly across the spear-wielding black men to the white men – indicates a familiarity with the captivity narrative formula. In particular, the denouement of his story, 'the unfortunate female' being 'a captive of these ruthless savages', managed pithily to elicit the key elements: the spectre of a white woman being held as a sexual prisoner by black men.

The work of recent scholars has turned up no evidential basis to the White Woman myth, but it documents the power of the myth both contemporaneously and in recent local culture. Rumours of the White Woman recurred in the early 1840s, and then in the mid-40s the *Port Phillip Herald* led a campaign for a government investigation. In 1846–47 three official search parties and one private expedition set out to find and rescue the White Woman, all failing, despite strategies such as distributing handkerchiefs and mirrors printed with messages to her. Regardless of the absence of the woman herself, the reach of the myth was imperial if not international. Reports of the White Woman and the searches for her appeared in Sydney and London newspapers, and were discussed in the New South Wales Legislative Assembly. By the 1870s she had been inscribed in two novels, one novella, and several poems.[10] The fact that the commercial potential of the myth was quickly recognized, no doubt due in part to the Eliza Fraser story, is evident from the fact that the editor of the *Port Phillip Herald* led the campaign for a search expedition, and obtained exclusive publishing rights to the public expedition's reports.[11] The printed discourse surrounding the myth repeatedly constructed the White Woman as a sexual captive through descriptions such as the woman who is ' "compelled to yield to the disgusting passions and desires of a set of black cannibals" '.[12] As Darian-Smith and Carr both argue, the timing of the myth in relation to white settlement in the Gippsland area is key to understanding its ideological dimensions. British settlers invaded Gippsland to use it as grazing country beginning in 1839, and McMillan was central in its early exploitation. By 1847 it was clear that the Europeans had won the battle for the land. The bloodiness of the battle was recorded in such local place names as Boney Point, Butcher's Creek and Slaughterhouse Gully.[13] The White Woman had served at once to deflect attention from the massacres of Kurnai people, and to justify them because of the imagined threat that Kurnai men represented to white women settlers.

Captivity narratives like those of Eliza Fraser and the White Woman shaped metropolitan British conceptions of indigenous peoples in North America, the Australian colonies and elsewhere, and were an element in the popular British construction of racial hierarchies, in which Indigenous Australian people were ranked towards the very bottom. The sexual charges made in such stories, which focused on interracial sexual assault but not on the inter-European assault for which there is some evidence in the Fraser case, became integral to empire-wide understandings of interracial relations, and a cornerstone of the widespread view that the colonies were no place for a white woman. The allegations contained in such stories of physical and sexual abuse, as well as murder, perpetrated on Europeans by indigenous peoples, became part of the justification for the conquest of indigenous lands and for colonial rule. At the same time, by inversion, they contributed to the emergent nineteenth-century European bourgeois definitions of respectable masculinity that emphasized reason, self-control and protective behaviour towards bourgeois women, even as knowledge of 'white' men's actual behaviour in the colonies often had to be sanitized for domestic consumption. Simultaneously they helped shape European bourgeois definitions of respectable femininity as delicate and vulnerable, a colonial source of nineteenth-century European gender ideology that has until recently been largely overlooked.

Importantly, the dimensions of interracial sexual assault in these nineteenth-century Australian captivity narratives stand in dramatic historical contrast to seventeenth- and eighteenth-century captivity narratives from the Barbary coast, North America and Asia. Women's purity and safety was *not* at the centre of early modern anxieties as revealed in captivity narratives. Rather, the great wellspring of early modern fear of captivity was the possibility that European *men* might be subject to physical abuse that included the sexual, specifically circumcision and sodomy. Contemporary accounts reveal the subjection of male captives in North Africa to both, and in Asia at least to circumcision. The fear of circumcision reflected its powerful religious significance. To early modern Christians, circumcision was the mark of the old covenant, having been replaced by baptism as the mark of the new covenant. Being circumcized represented a rejection of the gospels, and thus a very serious state of religious apostasy.[14] Circumcision was felt by many British men as a loss of their physical integrity; a violation akin to rape that some even imagined as a form of castration; and a loss of their religious and national identity. Both circumcision and sodomy clearly signified vulnerability to non-European, non-Christian others, and emasculation.[15] The prevalence of male-related sexual fears stemmed in part from the fact that women were a small minority of captives in both North Africa and Asia, but it reflected far more than that. Some European and British women *were* taken by hostile men in each arena, and fell sexual victims, but their stories were not emphasized in captivity literature, indeed at times they were ignored.[16] A few early North American captives, such as the late seventeenth-century victim Mary Rowlandson, explicitly denied that sexual assault had occurred, while other early captivity narratives and fiction make clear that the rape of European women was not a particular concern.

There was, however, a significant shift that began in the late eighteenth century and is manifest by the early to mid-nineteenth century. By the mid-nineteenth century North American captivity narratives stressed white women's vulnerability to sexual assault from predatory Indians. In North America this shift in representation apparently correlates with historical evidence that suggests little evidence of interracial rape in early New England, but its occurrence during the westward expansion of European Americans to the plains and western regions in the mid- to late nineteenth century.[17] But the freight of such narratives exceeded their correlation to specific occurrences. Captivity narratives, aimed at a transatlantic metropolitan audience, could include political messages about the relationship between colonies and central imperial administration, such as the desirability of colonial political autonomy.[18] In both American westward expansion and Australian land grabbing, early to mid-nineteenth-century race relations could have been a lightning-rod for unwanted scrutiny at a time when humanitarian movements in the British metropole had led to the abolition of slavery within the empire and the formation of the Aborigines Protection League. Although public opinion and its effects are difficult to measure, it is possible that captivity narratives helped to blunt humanitarian intervention.

In the nineteenth century, newly articulated fears of white women's vulnerability to lustful indigenous men reflected a growing confidence on the part of British men as to their own ability to defend themselves against sexual assault, and the ascendant naval might of the British Empire. They show the waning of concern about attacks by foreign powers and religious struggles, and a new emphasis on the expansion of imperial territory and stable imperial rule. This narrative shift of focus correlates to the expansion of British settler colonies, in Australia, New Zealand, southern Africa and Canada, the strains of which added to the burdens of imperial government alongside crises of rule in the older established colonies of India and Jamaica. British settlers locked in battles for land with indigenous peoples had reasons to fear for their physical safety, yet newly articulated gender ideologies of manly engagement with the public sphere and feminized domesticity prohibited the expression of much fear on the part of men. Gender prescriptions that circulated between metropole and colony worked instead to locate European women's supposed particular vulnerabilities as an admissible site of settlers' fears. At the same time, concerns about biological reproduction in fledgling settler communities and desires to erect racial boundaries made European women's sexuality a matter of cultural anxiety. Protecting their supposed purity became a culturally scripted imperative that at once justified their 'defence' no matter how bloody and violent the acts entailed.

Stories of the Indian 'Mutiny'

I suggest that we should see a pattern of historical emergence and change, a genealogical linkage connecting the captivity narratives in early modern Europe and colonial America, the commercialization of the Eliza Fraser and White Woman stories set in mid-nineteenth-century colonial Australia, and the later eruption of sensationalized stories of sexual violence by colonized men against white women in the 1857–58 war in India. Crucially, the metropolitan market was the lynchpin, the major publication clearing house, audience and conduit for such stories. We know from the work of scholars such as Jenny Sharpe and Nancy Paxton that, during and after the series of anti-British uprisings in 1857–58 that were inscribed in British history as the Indian 'Mutiny', a dominant narrative emerged in which the rape and torture of Englishwomen was a key trope. These stories came to undergird violently repressive measures by the British government in India, both in quelling the uprising and during the rest of the Raj. In fact, while British men, women and children were indeed killed during the revolts, there is little evidence of rape by Indian men of English women. Subsequent official investigations found no evidence of systematic rape or torture even in the notorious massacre at Kanpur.[19]

The retrospective retelling of Mutiny stories through the lens of sexual assault and torture of white women is illustrated in the memoirs of Harriet Tytler, written decades later, just after the turn of the twentieth century. Tytler was married to a British army captain, was forced to flee Delhi at the beginning of the uprisings, but returned with the British troops that besieged Delhi for three months and retook it. Recalling her experiences on the first dramatic day of the uprising in Delhi, when she had to abandon her house and hide in a tower with other Europeans, Tytler noted: 'I had to give up the idea of ever expecting to see my darling husband again and prepare myself for death. I thought they would have shot me or cut me down, but thank God I never supposed that I could have met a worse death, which I afterwards learnt was meted out to so many poor women.'[20] These sentences indicate that at the beginning of the uprisings Tytler did not consider herself a target for particular violence or sexual assault as an English woman. Yet the stories that circulated from the first day soon raised this fear, even though Tytler was aware that not all reports were reliable. During the siege on Delhi, she narrates, 'we began to get news of all that was transpiring in other stations and the horrors of Cawnpore', which she immediately qualifies with 'though of course we could not tell how much of it was true'.[21] Despite her uncertainty, she asks her husband to procure a bottle of laudanum for her to have on hand, that she might administer to her children and take herself, in the event of an attack.[22] Tytler's narrative is packed with unflinching detail concerning the violent deaths of people she knew, and scenes of carnage and destruction that she witnessed. But the stories of sexual assaults on women are almost all innuendo, such as in an account of two young unmarried Englishwomen who were killed in Delhi on the first day of the war. Tytler reports that 'Many stories were current ... as to the way these poor girls met their death. The one generally believed was that ... the two poor girls in their terror hid themselves under their beds and were dragged out and thrown out of the window on to the pavement below, a merciful death compared to what might have been their fate.'[23] The vagueness of stories of sexual assault on women, in contrast to other details in Tytler's narrative, reflects the general lack of substantiation for what became formulaic accounts of 'the Mutiny'.

Rape stories evolved as rumours and were picked up and circulated by multiple sources especially including the metropolitan press. Typically, these accounts relied upon the eyewitness evidence of someone other than the narrator, and were printed without corroboration. One famous example was a letter from a clergyman describing events in Delhi in which forty-eight English women and girls were raped, stripped and exposed naked in the streets, tortured and left to die. This letter was reprinted in several newspapers including *The Times*, but Karl Marx, then a reporter for the *New York Daily Tribune*, noted what others had failed to, that this letter was written by a clergyman in Bangalore, Mysore, more than a thousand miles from Delhi.[24] It was later exposed as a fraud. The stories were reminiscent of captivity narratives in that they involved, variously, abduction, torture, humiliation and subjection of Europeans by non-Europeans, but they centred on the sexual violation of white women for the lascivious and barbaric pleasures of native men. They appeared not only in metropolitan newspapers, but also in theatrical productions, and in personal letters and diaries.

Rape narratives became integral to the ways in which the metropolitan public perceived the events of the 'Mutiny' at the time, and represented them for decades to come. Indeed, between 1857 and 1947 there were more than eighty novels written in English about the events of the uprisings.[25] These stories commonly enacted in their plot the very concept of 'a fate worse than death'. Proper English heroines chose death rather than the possible fate of falling sexual victim to an Indian man. As Paxton points out, the racialized gender ideology of the day prescribed that a true Englishwoman would either die trying to preserve her honour or commit suicide afterwards, so any woman who survived such an assault was considered morally suspect.[26] One typical novel, for example, had its heroine make the hero promise that he would kill her rather than let her fall into the hands of the enemy, a promise he fulfills by shooting her during the British retreat from 'Cawnpore' in the face of invading Indian forces.[27] The notion that pure English womanhood in India had to be protected from the lustful behaviour of uncivilized colonized men became foundational to the repressive tightening of the Raj in the decades following this early anti-colonial war. Colonial government in India was reorganized and expanded. Specific measures included the adoption in 1861 of a new criminal code with a more straightforward and encompassing definition of rape than existed in England at the time.[28] But there were ramifications in Britain too. The rape stories of 'the Mutiny', so popular in Britain, worked to entrench definitions of femininity that cast women as being in need of male protection and as under the threat of sexual assault, thus effectively policing women's sexuality and countering moves towards their social autonomy. The anti-feminist agenda of 'Mutiny' rape novels is made particularly clear by the fact that there was a whole new wave of them in the 1890s in response to the escalation of the women's movement in that decade, the publicity it achieved, and the gains women were making in education and employment.[29] Thus, in the modern period, debates about, and historical shifts within, gender definitions in Britain itself cannot be comprehended without identifying the cultural and ideological impact of the empire.

Edward John Eyre and the Morant Bay Massacre

The spectre of interracial sexual assault in the colonies was invoked, as well, in highly publicized debates in Britain over the proper manly conduct of a British public servant and gentleman. In Jamaica in 1865, not long after the Indian uprisings, a riot in Morant Bay was put down violently through the proclamation of martial law and extreme official reprisals. Under the orders of the British Governor, Edward John Eyre, the reprisals were so harsh that 439 black and mixed race people were killed, 600 men and women were flogged and over 1000 huts and houses burnt. At first the government response in Britain was support for Eyre, but as criticism emerged a royal commission was conducted and Eyre finally returned to Britain amid great controversy. As Catherine Hall has shown, the debate which raged around Eyre in England in 1866–67 involved arguments about masculinity. Each side of the debate had as a champion one of the eminent public intellectuals of the day, with Thomas Carlyle supporting Eyre and John Stuart Mill leading the charge against him. While issues of race were central, they were interwoven with those of gender and sexuality.

In Carlyle's view, Eyre had not only saved the lives of English men from the violent rampages of the Jamaican blacks, but had protected Englishwomen, 'a crucial aspect of independence and manliness'. An Englishman should be the clear ruler of his domain, whether domestic or colonial, with recognized authority over women, servants and blacks, and protection was a corollary of authority. Mill, on the other hand, defined manhood not as a natural or inevitable state specific to white men but as an achieved social rank, a state of being marked by individuality and independence, a state to which he argued men of other races and women could both aspire and should be able to achieve, given the requisite education and opportunities. To Mill, the privileges of manhood were those of full personhood, and all should be able to aspire to them and to overcome dependence on others. Mill believed strongly in civil liberties and the rule of law, and argued against Eyre on the basis of Eyre's abrogation of the rule of law and implementation of martial law in response to the uprising. The purchase of each of these competing definitions of manhood was sufficiently strong that in the end Eyre was neither prosecuted for his actions nor reinstated as governor.[30]

Eyre was an appropriate focus for such a debate because he stood for the masculine possibilities and responsibilities of mid-nineteenth-century empire. The son of a clergyman who arrived in Australia in 1833 as a 17-year-old without a great deal of money, he had pitted himself against the opportunities of empire, acquired a reputation as a heroic explorer through his expeditions into the arid inland of southern Australia, and eventually risen to the status of colonial governor. Thus he had shown that an Englishman could make himself by meeting the challenges of the empire. Moreover, Eyre had won a reputation, early in his colonial career, as a progressive and a humanitarian in his interactions with Aboriginal people in South Australia and Maoris in New Zealand. In his famous expedition from Adelaide to Albany in 1840–41, according to his published journals, he had scrupulously avoided conflict with Aboriginal people as much as possible, prevented sexual abuse of Aboriginal women by the men in his party, and expounded on the sovereignty of Aboriginal people over their land and even their rights to defend themselves against Europeans with violence when necessary.[31]

This humanitarian position on Aborigines was put to the test, when, in good part because of his perceived ability to treat Aboriginal people well, he was appointed resident magistrate and protector of Aborigines at Moorundie on the River Murray from 1841 to 1844. This newly created position helped shape his reputation as a humanitarian with an unmatched knowledge of the Australian Aborigines. In an area where there had been interracial conflict because of the overland route of settlers moving from the eastern colonies to South Australia, he reportedly brought temporary peace. But his self-proclaimed solution to the problem of racial coexistence involved the containment of Aborigines, and the clear assertion of authority by and rights to land of Europeans.[32] His notion of childlike Aborigines becoming dependent upon their British rulers, and gradually, generationally, learning their Christian work ethic, depended upon deeply held assumptions of the racial and cultural superiority of Europeans. His next colonial post in 1847 was as Lieutenant Governor in New Zealand, serving with Governor George Grey, also from South Australia and also a humanitarian committed to 'improvement' of the native races. Together, they sought to nurture amicable relations with the Maori people within a British legal and cultural framework, but were fundamentally committed to the expansion of European settlement by force when necessary. The eruption of the Maori wars in 1860 showed the intractable nature of the conflict they had hoped to manage in British interests.[33]

Work on the Morant Bay massacre and the Eyre controversy has framed the debate around issues of masculinity imperially defined, domestic politics in Britain and the significance of Eyre's shift from defending the colonized to oppressing them. The spectre of Eyre's biographical trajectory from the vaunted progressive humanitarian of South Australia and New Zealand to the repressive governor of Jamaica has raised thorny questions historians have sought to answer. Catherine Hall argues that there were both circumstantial and historical factors at work. When Eyre was in Australia and first in New Zealand, an influential humanitarian discourse on racial equality that had impelled the abolition of slavery in 1833 and the formation of the Aborigines Protection Society permeated imperial culture and influenced colonial administrations. In the 1830s and 1840s Eyre himself was influenced by this discourse and by the atmosphere of optimism in the white settler colonies. After 1850 an insidious ideology of white racial superiority gained ground in Britain and elsewhere, an ideology that would receive the spurious imprimatur of 'science'. For Eyre, this shift in imperial culture coincided with the culture shock he received on his appointment as colonial administrator in the West Indies, first to St. Vincent in 1854, then Antigua in 1859 and Jamaica in 1861.

Significantly, of course, the Indian 'Mutiny' reinforced this ideological shift and compounded Eyre's own fears of the vulnerability of white colonizers in colonies with large nonwhite majorities. In the West Indies, Eyre's humanitarianism towards 'native races', which had always been founded on premises of European superiority, evaporated in the face of his desire to establish white authority and military security, and his growing belief in the inability of Caribbean blacks to engage in self-rule or to absorb European cultural values. Feeling increasingly insecure and with a growing conviction that Caribbean blacks were 'savages', he convinced himself that brutal repression would save British lives and, according to one of Eyre's subsequent defenders, save British women from ' "the murder and the lust of black savages" '.[34]

Julie Evans, while not disagreeing with Hall, insists that we must look to specific material and power relations in particular colonial contexts in order to understand Eyre, as well as to the metropolitan and broader imperial political discourses. She pinpoints a critical shift in Eyre's discursive constructions of Indigenous people as occurring during his time as protector at Moorundie. Through a close reading of his second volume of writings about his time in South Australia, his 1845 *Account of the Manners and Customs of the Aborigines*, Evans argues that Eyre muted his earlier defence of Aboriginal rights to sovereignty. Instead, he advocated a system in which Aboriginal people would be confined to reserves and compensated for their loss of land by handouts of food. The generations should be segregated so that the young would be imbued with a work ethic and the values of 'civilisation'. Eyre's vision included the use of the colony's police force to impose this arrangement. Central to his scheme was the idea that only the elders were truly 'authentic' Aborigines and had any claims to sovereignty. By curtailing their power over the young, and thus 'authentic' Aboriginal culture itself, as they passed away this scheme would result in harmonious relations between black and white. As Evans points out, Eyre's scheme reflects the fact that by 1845 South Australia's imagined promise as a humane settler colony had foundered. While Eyre still emphasized settlers' responsibilities towards Indigenous people, by the time he left South Australia his insistence on European authority and control was paramount. Such insistence would only become starker and more emphatic in the context of 1860s Jamaica, where Europeans were in a small minority and freedpeople openly challenged their own economic oppression.[35]

I find Evans's argument persuasive, but I would add that Eyre's changing definitions of Aboriginal sovereignty, and the marked shift in his views on black–white relations, correlate to a shifting articulation of his own masculine station. As the renowned explorer of 1840–41, Eyre was a daring, heroic, liminal figure who redrew the cartographic boundaries of British Australia. In suffering great privations, risking his life, and depending on the counsel of Indigenous people for survival, Eyre's claims to imperial masculinity were centred in his own person and his individual abilities to communicate and negotiate. As the Protector of Aborigines at Moorundie, in contrast, his success, and therefore his manhood, depended instead on his exercise of official, colonial authority. Instead of pushing boundaries, now he had to fortify them. Because his masculine authority was now identified with that of the state, it was more in alignment with settler interests and European rule.

Eyre raises troubling questions, such as: Did the entrenched power of white men within colonial regimes foster any susceptibility towards the imposition of authority, and violence? And how did the corruption of individual men in specific colonial contexts play out in imperial politics and culture? If such questions skirt dangerously close to essentialist notions of gender, we can at least trace the deployment and operation of particular discursive tropes, such as that of vulnerable white womanhood in need of protection against lustful colonized nonwhite men.

Evidence presented to the 1866 Jamaica Royal Commission suggests that Eyre's main motives in ordering harsh reprisals were to re-establish white control, to prevent the uprising spreading and to punish the offenders in a severe fashion. He seems to raise the concern over white women's sexual vulnerability as something of an afterthought in his own defence, a concern that was easily digested by a British public with an appetite recently whetted by the 'Mutiny' rape narratives. But if it was not in the forefront of his mind during the events themselves, it is a recurrent script in the testimony he presented to the commission. A few witnesses called before the commission claimed that in the events leading up to and during the uprising, black men threatened sexual assault of white women. Eyre himself, drawing on such testimony, claimed that during the insurrection 'threats to kill all the white and coloured men, and to reserve the ladies and estates for themselves, had been freely indulged in.'[36]

The testimonies presented to commissioners contain some countervailing evidence, such as that comparable threats were made to black women who did not support the uprising, and that many black women were active participants and were considered at least as responsible as the men.[37] There is also evidence that white and mixed-race women had their lives threatened.[38] In one instance, a 'mulatto' woman whose husband had been killed, had her life spared when she convinced her assailants, who stripped her for confirmation, that she was indeed a woman and not a man in women's attire. She was forced to act in a submissive and humiliating way towards her assailants, and in her own words was 'struck and maltreated'. She tells the story of a young woman in her neighbourhood who was taken into 'the bushes' and 'so severely and brutally maltreated and injured, that she is now in a dying state'. It is unclear whether this witness meant the word 'maltreated' to connote rape.[39]

If the evidence of actual rape of white or mixed-race women is unclear, and the numbers of women implicated small, Eyre and his supporters repeatedly alluded to the threat of such sexual assault in Eyre's defence. Dr Edward William Major, in a statement submitted by Eyre, made the connection to the Indian 'Mutiny' explicit:

> I believe there has not been one lady killed, but the purpose for which they were spared makes the rebellion still worse than the Indian mutiny, and it is now admitted that orders were given by the leaders to kill all the males and to save the females as they would take them for themselves. How truly thankful we all ought to be to

Almighty God for frustrating the wicked designs of such brutish demons, and I need not tell you how his Excellency the Governor is blessed by every right-minded person in the Island for having been the means, with God's blessing, of rescuing our wives and daughters from the horrible fate intended for them.[40]

Jamaican women, both elite and 'poor', actively participated in the construction of this narrative strand. Amongst the documents Eyre submitted to the commission are several petitions of gratitude he received from Jamaican women thanking him for 'saving' them. The 'Ladies of Port Antonio and Manchioneal' asserted that: 'As women we must ever pray for your Excellency's welfare, for if the men return thanks for their lives alone, we return ours to you for saving us from every indignity a female most dreads.' Similarly, the 'Ladies of St. Elizabeth' believed themselves indebted to Eyre because his actions had prevented 'a fate worse than death [that] awaited ourselves', while 'certain Poor Women of the Parish of St. Catherine' thanked Eyre for 'our narrow escape from the horrible cruelties to which our sex ... were exposed during the late rebellion'. Eyre supported the sentiments expressed in these letters (one of which was signed by over two thousand women and others by hundreds) in his letters of reply, expressing his pride at having made the right decisions, while also asserting that it was due 'to the merciful over-ruling of an allwise God' that 'the Colony [was] saved from a succession of horrors and atrocities which can better be imagined than described'.[41] Eyre's invocation of the imagination is telling. Claims of interracial sexual threats are only one of Eyre's justifications for killing hundreds of black and mixed-race Jamaicans, but the role they play shows the prominence of the rape narrative in imperial culture and the imperial imaginary, especially in the wake of the 'Mutiny'.

Colonial panics and circulating narratives of assault

The Eyre controversy was not the last time that a debate about appropriate, manly official behaviour in the colonies would rage in England. Decades later, in 1919, after the Amritsar massacre in the Punjab in northern India in which around 400 unarmed people were killed by British troops because of their participation in an illegal but peaceful gathering, a similar public debate occurred over the orders of the officer in charge, Brigadier-General Reginald Dyer. In the British parliamentary commission established to investigate the events, and the metropolitan public debate surrounding them, some of the greatest contention was over Dyer's response to the violent assault upon an English woman missionary, Marcella Sherwood. During the unrest preceding the massacre, Sherwood had been knocked off her bicycle by a street mob, severely beaten, and left for dead. She was picked up by some Indian people, received medical attention and survived. Dyer's specific response to her beating was to close the street on which it occurred, to force any Indian man who entered it between certain hours to do so only on all fours, and to order an investigation of the involvement of residents of the street that included the violent abuse (though not rape) of women residents.[42] As we know from the official statement he made in his own defence, Dyer claimed that the attack on Sherwood was 'probably the most dastardly outrage in the whole rebellion', and that the crawling order was intended not as a racial insult but to mark the spot of her assault as 'holy ground', as a place of 'special sanctity'.[43] In short, he implied that the attack on Sherwood had been sexual, despite absence of any evidence, and argued that his actions had been intended as a defence of the purity and sanctity of English womanhood.

While many in Britain were horrified by the Amritsar massacre, publicly protested it and criticized Dyer, others in Britain and India declared Dyer the hero of the Punjab, and paid tribute to him as a saviour of the Raj with a large public subscription and a 'sword of honour', which it is tempting to read as signifying his masculine prowess.[44] Here too competing definitions of English masculinity were at work, this time against the backdrop of a Britain which had lost enormous numbers of young men and was coming to terms with wounded and shell-shocked soldiers in its midst. In such a context, and with evidence of growing anti-colonial unrest, militarist manhood held appeal for some because they associated it with national and imperial strength. Not surprisingly, the British community in India, including British women, were among the most vociferous supporters of Dyer, fearful as they were of the rising tide of anticolonial nationalism there.[45]

Just as the narratives and code words of interracial sexual assault circulated from colony to colony in the nineteenth century, early twentieth-century episodes picked up key phrases and tropes with transnational currency. In the 1912 'Black Peril' scare in South Africa that Timothy Keegan has explicated, discourse surrounding inflated fears of the sexual threat black men supposedly presented to white women included references to British India, and also to the Deep South. Extremist proponents of white vigilante tactics invoked the rise of lynching in the late nineteenth-century US South as an example of what could happen if the legal system was not harsh enough on putative black offenders. Keegan shows the South African 'imagined pandemic of sexual assaults by black men on white women' to have been rooted in white male anxieties about economic turbulence and dislocation, urbanization, female freedoms in urban spaces, and, specifically, the prevalence of 'houseboys' as domestic servants in the industrial areas of the Rand.[46] The panic, fanned by sensationalist newspaper reporting and based mostly on incidents in which the actual charges were vague, was built upon venerable and multipurpose euphemisms such as 'outrage' and 'unspeakable acts'.[47] Its political effects included helping to maintain white racial and masculine supremacy in the new Union of South Africa with its evolving industrial and urban dimensions.

The 1912 'Black Peril' scare in South Africa was but one of a spate of such moral panics over the largely imagined spectre of interracial sexual assault in Southern Africa in the late nineteenth and early twentieth centuries. In the late 1860s and early 1870s, there was an unfounded panic in Natal,[48] a panic which recurred in very similar form albeit with a shorter span in December 1886. In the 1886 panic, one of the underlying fears was concern about black male servants performing feminized domestic work in intimate proximity to white women who, some contemporaries suggested, behaved inappropriately in relation to these servants and thus provoked their violent behaviour.[49] In Southern Rhodesia too there was a spate of comparable panics from 1902 to 1916, with recurrences up to the mid-1930s, described at the time as driven by fears of 'Black Peril'. Historian Jock McCulloch shows that these Southern Rhodesian panics, in which twenty African men were executed and two hundred more were imprisoned and flogged, were likewise founded on flimsy evidence and trials were prosecuted shoddily. McCulloch argues that each wave of panic was historically contingent and that we must understand these phenomena as complex events, produced by the fragility of the early colonial Rhodesian state. Significantly, these episodes of 'Black Peril' reflected, besides fraught race relations, the numerical imbalance between white men and white women, and white women's attempts to increase their own economic, social and political power. White women argued that white men's sexual relations with indigenous women were an immediate cause of black men's presumptions towards white women. White men, in turn, here too accused white women of failing to manage properly their black male domestic servants and of acting in such a way as to incite assault. Racial, class and gender tensions, McCulloch shows, were tightly interwoven as white British men colonizers scrambled in the chaotic conditions of colonialism to secure their hegemony.[50]

Then in turn, when a similar panic erupted in Australian-ruled Papua (New Guinea) in the mid-1920s, a key phrase was 'Black Peril'. Just as in the earlier southern African episodes where this phrase arose, a central fear was the supposed threat posed by black male domestic servants. Amirah Inglis demonstrates in her pioneering work on the 1926 White Women's Protection Ordinance in Papua, that this extraordinary piece of colonial legislation was enacted at a time when there had been very few assaults on white women. Yet it instituted the death penalty 'for any person convicted of the crime of rape or *attempted* rape upon a *European* woman or girl'.[51] Inglis argues, moreover, that while previous historians blamed white women in Papua for demanding such legal protection, in fact it was white men who were primarily responsible for its enactment. The European fears that produced this violent and extreme measure were based in a changing colonial culture, particularly in the capital Port Moresby, where urbanized and Europeanized indigenous men were felt to be challenging white supremacy.[52]

Stories of white women's vulnerability to sexual assault by nonwhite colonized men constituted a cultural script that held enduring appeal in nineteenth- and early twentieth-century imperial culture. Such narratives contributed to the construction of racial hierarchies in which white British people were the natural rulers and colonizers because of white men's supposed self-control compared to nonwhite men's ascribed uncontrolled lustful and barbaric behaviour. Focusing on nonwhite men's alleged sexual aggressions obfuscated, for the metropolitan and white colonial publics, white men's actual sexual behaviour in the colonies. Moreover, the myth of white men's self-control served to mask the high rates of prostitution both in Britain itself and in the colonies, and, from the 1860s, the involvement of the British government in the regulation of prostitution both at home and in the colonies through the domestic and colonial contagious diseases acts.[53] Notions of white women's vulnerability in the colonies were integral to the domestic construction of respectable femininity, a gender ideology that in the early-mid nineteenth century stressed bourgeois women's confinement to a notional private sphere and their supposed incapacity for productive labour, education, professional work or political citizenship. By the late nineteenth century, when the first women's movement flourished and began achieving legal and social victories in Britain, the anti-feminist mobilization of such scripts was very apparent.

As with any such historical phenomenon, there were, not surprisingly, variations and counter-discourses. Mary Procida, in her book on Anglo-Indian culture and politics in the interwar period, presents a body of fiction and non-fiction by Anglo-Indian women rejecting the traditional gendered account of the 'Mutiny'. In stories published in the late nineteenth and early twentieth centuries, Anglo-Indian women authors re-wrote the dominant narrative by showing women as valiant actors during the events of 1857–58, including stories that cast women as the protectors and saviours of British men. Anglo-Indian women, Procida argues, used this counter-narrative to reject the traditional notion of women as hapless victims of racial politics in India, and to show themselves as active defenders of the empire.[54] In another very symbolic inversion of the Mutiny rape script, Nancy Paxton has identified a small corpus of late-nineteenth and early-twentieth-century novels written by Anglo-Indian women that incorporate plots of interracial romance. The plots in this fiction populated by New Women encompass a range of ideologies and unhappy endings, but they do include potential challenges laid by both colonizing women and colonized men to the cultural and social power of British men, reflecting the rise of both feminism and anti-colonial nationalism.[55]

*   *   *

Narratives of violent interracial sexual encounter on colonial frontiers are an example of the dynamics through which intra-imperial connections constituted both metropolitan and imperial culture. As Mrinalini Sinha has suggested with her concept of an imperial social formation, to understand Britain – or any other European imperial power – in the modern period, it is crucial to apprehend the ways in which colonies and metropole were interdependent, economically, politically and legally among other dimensions.[56] The category of gender is a particularly useful analytical tool that helps us to identify these interconnections, and also to use them to track historical shifts in British society and culture. Looking at gender as an imperial, rather than only domestic, set of shifting ideologies permits us insight into the transnational – or transcolonial – operation of culture, and the circulation of gendered representations with powerfully political meanings.

A comparison of early-modern captivity narratives with nineteenth-century narratives of interracial sexual assault, and indeed the linkage between them of the shifts within early-mid nineteenth-century captivity narratives in white settler colonies, reveals changing imperial contours and their reflection in imperial popular culture. The centrality of the sexual abuse and circumcision of European men in early-modern captivity narratives, and its subsidence within nineteenth-century equivalents, is an index of growing military, religious and cultural confidence. Britons abroad were no longer fearful of being forced into religious apostasy by Islamic, pagan or Catholic captors. British territorial expansion and naval ascendancy by the mid-nineteenth century reassured British males in foreign parts that they were sufficiently safe themselves that they could now position themselves as protectors of their own womanhood, a role that demonstrated their manly authority. Rather than European men fearing their own humiliating physical or sexual subjection, the culturally scripted fear became that of European women's supposed vulnerability. This new script at once demonstrated the superiority of European civilization by fetishizing white women's honour and delicacy in contrast to nonwhite women's imputed lack of such qualities, and positioned white men as the guardians of their women who could and would contain nonwhite men with their primitive and lustful behaviour. This cultural script perhaps represented the more popular and commercially successful end of a spectrum of eroticized, gendered and racialized colonial representations. Lisa Sigel has pointed to the connections between pornography and anthropology in late nineteenth-century London, specifically the writings and anonymous pornographic publications of the London Anthropological Society from the 1860s to the 1880s. The prurient sexual interests of these leading Victorian 'men of science', she shows, tie together imperial power, technologies of colonial rule, racialized gender ideologies and eroticism.[57]

An important factor of continuity was the role of London and the British metropole as the locus of the main publishing houses, audience and conduit for these narratives. But London was just one base, if in some ways the lynchpin, for a circulating and shifting imperial culture that itself worked to shape the narratives that emerged and travelled from colony to colony. Tony Ballantyne, in his book on the nineteenth-century concept of Aryanism, argues that the metaphor for empire of a spoked wheel with lines of contact radiating out from London to the colonial peripheries, is no longer adequate. He suggests instead the metaphor of a spider's web, showing that empires were at once fragile and dynamic, always being reworked, and were complex networks connecting many disparate points, including direct links between colonies.[58] In as far as one metaphor for empire is useful, I see many advantages to Ballantyne's suggestion of the web. To some extent, the subject of narratives of captivity and assault supports the idea of the web, because these narratives circulated around the empire, and stories from one colony can be seen to have shaped the telling of events in another. Yet at the same time the role of the publishing industry, firmly centred in London and the capitalist enterprise through which these stories circulated in commercial form, lends continuing validity to the image of the spoked wheel. Perhaps what we need to recognize is a dynamic tension between capitalist and administrative structures that channelled the empire through London, on the one hand, and on the other hand the more chaotic nature of imperial culture with the movement of peoples and ideas across boundaries and directly between diverse sites.

Finally, these interconnected but historically changing narratives mirror shifts in imperial imperatives. The expansion of British settler colonialism in the nineteenth century, combined with crises in older established colonies of rule, proved a crucible for the rise of a new set of colonial anxieties that often pivoted on fears of interracial sexual assault. With the emergence of racialized bourgeois gender ideologies that cast European women as the delicate vessels of European morality, threats to their purity were easily conceived and of intense cultural interest. If early modern captivity narratives highlighted Britain's vulnerabilities and underwrote its desire to compete with 'other' powers, from the mid-nineteenth-century narratives of interracial sexual assault became an official reflex, a tried-and-true way of shoring up imperial authority in times of conquest, crisis, moral panic or when the actions of a colonial official were under close scrutiny. They show, yet again, the cultural currency of racialized ideas of gender, or conversely, gendered and eroticized ideas of race in this period of empire. For the imperial public, such narratives served a larger and more confident empire by justifying territorial expropriation, harsh measures of rule and the suppression of revolt.

Notes

1. Linda Colley, *Captives* (New York: Pantheon Books, 2002).
2. Joe Snader, *Caught Between Worlds: British Captivity Narratives in Fact and Fiction* (Lexington: University of Kentucky Press, 2000), esp. p. 4.
3. Robert C. Davis has estimated that 'between 1530 and 1780 there were almost certainly a million and quite possibly as many as a million and a quarter' Europeans taken captive on the Barbary coast. Their fates often included hard labour in public works, agriculture, and ships' galleys. Davis, 'Counting European Slaves on the Barbary Coast', *Past & Present* no. 172 (August 2001): 118.
4. Colley, *Captives*, pp. 350–4.
5. Kay Schaffer and D'Arcy Randall, 'Australian Shipwrecks and Texan Captivities: The History and Dissemination of Two Interrelated Tales from the English and American Frontiers in the 1830s', unpublished paper, pp. 14–15. My thanks to Kay Schaffer for allowing me to read and cite this paper. Some of the same material is covered in Kay Schaffer and D'Arcy Randall, 'Transglobal Translations: The Eliza Fraser and Rachel Plummer Captivity Narratives', in Graeme Harper (ed.), *Colonial and Postcolonial Incarceration* (London: Continuum, 2001), pp. 105–23.
6. Schaffer and Randall, 'Australian Shipwrecks and Texan Captivities', unpublished ms., p. 5.
7. Schaffer and Randall, 'Australian Shipwrecks and Texan Captivities', unpublished ms., p. 13.
8. These paragraphs summarize key parts of the arguments made by Schaffer and Randall in their article 'Australian Shipwrecks and Texan Captivities'. For further detail on the Eliza Fraser story and its continuing resonance in Australian culture, see Kay Schaffer, *In the Wake of First Contact: The Eliza Fraser Stories* (Cambridge: Cambridge University Press, 1995) and Ian J. McNiven, Lynette Russell and Kay Schaffer (eds), *Constructions of Colonialism: Perspectives on Eliza Fraser's Shipwreck* (London: Leicester University Press, 1998).

9. Julie E. Carr, *The Captive White Woman of Gipps Land: In Pursuit of the Legend* (Carlton South, Vic.: Melbourne University Press, 2001), pp. 4–5.

10. Kate Darian-Smith, 'Capturing the White Woman of Gippsland: A Frontier Myth', in Darian-Smith (ed.), *Captive Lives: Australian Captivity Narratives*, Working Papers in Australian Studies Nos. 85, 86 and 87 (Sir Robert Menzies Centre for Australian Studies, Institute of Commonwealth Studies, University of London, 1993), p. 15.

11. Julie Carr, 'In Search of the White Woman of Gippsland', *Australasian Victorian Studies Annual* vol. 1 (1995): 41–2.

12. Letter to the *Sydney Morning Herald*, 10 October 1846, quoted in Carr, 'In Search of the White Woman', p. 43.

13. Carr, 'In Search of the White Woman', p. 45.

14. On this, see Margo Todd, 'A Captive's Story: Puritans, Pirates, and the Drama of Reconciliation', *The Seventeenth Century* vol. 12 (1997): 37–56.

15. Colley, *Captives*, pp. 128–30, 288–9; Snader, *Caught Between Worlds*, pp. 102, 148, 162, 166; Ralph Bauer, 'Creole Identities in Colonial Space: The Narratives of Mary White Rowlandson and Francisco Nunez de Pineda y Bascunan', *American Literature* vol. 69, no. 4 (Dec. 1997): 676.

16. Colley, *Captives*, pp. 59, 128, 356; Davis, 'Counting European Slaves on the Barbary Coast', p. 120.

17. June Namias, *White Captives: Gender and Ethnicity on the American Frontier* (Chapel Hill: University of North Carolina Press, 1993), pp. 43, 89, 99, 102.

18. Bauer, 'Creole Identities in Colonial Space', p. 672.

19. Jenny Sharpe, *Allegories of Empire: The Figure of Woman in the Colonial Text* (Minneapolis: University of Minnesota Press, 1993), p. 64.

20. Anthony Sattin (ed.), *An Englishwoman in India: The Memoirs of Harriet Tytler 1828–1858* (Oxford: Oxford University Press, 1986), pp. 122–3.

21. Sattin (ed.), *An Englishwoman in India*, p. 160.

22. Sattin (ed.), *An Englishwoman in India*, p. 160.

23. Sattin (ed.), *An Englishwoman in India*, p. 119.

24. Sharpe, *Allegories of Empire*, pp. 66–7.

25. Nancy L. Paxton, *Writing under the Raj: Gender, Race, and Rape in the British Colonial Imagination, 1830–1947* (New Brunswick, NJ: Rutgers University Press, 1999), p. 111.

26. Paxton, *Writing Under the Raj*, pp. 8, 11.

27. Paxton, *Writing Under the Raj*, pp. 6–7.

28. Paxton, *Writing Under the Raj*, pp. 112–14.

29. Paxton, *Writing Under the Raj*, p. 127.

30. Catherine Hall, *White, Male and Middle Class: Explorations in Feminism and History* (New York: Routledge: 1992), pp. 278–86.

31. Kay Schaffer, 'Handkerchief Diplomacy: E.J. Eyre and Sexual Politics on the South Australian Frontier', in Lynette Russell (ed.), *Colonial Frontiers: Indigenous-European Encounters in Settler Societies* (Manchester: Manchester University Press, 2001), pp. 134–50; Julie Evans, 'Beyond the Frontier: Possibilities and Precariousness along Australia's Southern Coast', in Russell (ed.), *Colonial Frontiers*, pp. 151–72.

32. Evans, 'Beyond the Frontier', pp. 165–8.
33. Catherine Hall, 'Imperial Man: Edward Eyre in Australasia and the West Indies, 1833–66', in Bill Schwarz (ed.), *The Expansion of England: Race, Ethnicity and Cultural History* (London: Routledge, 1996), pp. 142–8.
34. Hall, 'Imperial Man', p. 163. See also Catherine Hall, *Civilising Subjects: Metropole and Colony in the English Colonial Imagination 1830–1867* (Chicago: University of Chicago Press, 2002), pp. 23–65, 421–4 and 434–41.
35. Julie Evans, 'Re-Reading Edward Eyre: Race, Resistance and Repression in Australia and the Caribbean', *Australian Historical Studies* vol. 33, no. 118 (2002): 175–98.
36. British Parliamentary Papers, *Colonies. West Indies, Vol. 5. Minutes of Evidence and Appendix to the Report of the Jamaica Royal Commission 1866*, Eyre's evidence to commissioners 21 March 1866, p. 1013.
37. British Parliamentary Papers, *Colonies. West Indies, Vol. 4. Jamaica Royal Commission 1866. Papers Laid Before the Commission by Governor Eyre*, p. 6; British Parliamentary Papers, *Colonies. West Indies, Vol. 5*, for example pp. 988, 994, 997.
38. British Parliamentary Papers, *Colonies. West Indies, Vol. 4*, pp. 72–3.
39. British Parliamentary Papers, *Colonies. West Indies, Vol. 4*, Statement of Mrs. Captain Hitchins, pp. 82–3.
40. British Parliamentary Papers, *Colonies. West Indies, Vol. 4*, Statement of Dr. Edward William Major, p. 74.
41. British Parliamentary Papers, *Colonies. West Indies, Vol. 4*, pp. 478–82.
42. See Vinay Lal, 'The Incident of the "Crawling Lane": Women in the Punjab Disturbances of 1919', *Genders* no. 16 (Spring 1993): esp. pp. 47–53.
43. *The Amritsar Massacre, 1919: General Dyer in the Punjab* (1920; London: The Stationery Office, 2000), p. 137.
44. Derek Sayer, 'British Reaction to the Amritsar Massacre 1919–1920', *Past and Present* no. 131 (May 1991): 158. Stanley Wolpert describes it as 'a jewelled sword inscribed to the "Saviour of the Punjab" ', *A New History of India* 2nd Edition (New York: Oxford University Press, 1982), p. 299.
45. Mary A. Procida, *Married to the Empire: Gender, Politics and Imperialism in India, 1883–1947* (Manchester: Manchester University Press, 2002), pp. 118–19.
46. Timothy Keegan, 'Gender, Degeneration and Sexual Danger: Imagining Race and Class in South Africa, ca. 1912', *Journal of Southern African Studies* vol. 27, no. 3 (Sept. 2001): 460, 468.
47. Keegan, 'Gender, Degeneration and Sexual Danger', p. 471.
48. Norman Etherington, 'Natal's Black Rape Scare of the 1870s', *Journal of Southern African Studies* vol. 15, no. 1 (Oct. 1988): 36–53.
49. Jeremy C. Martens, 'Settler Homes, Manhood and "Houseboys": an Analysis of Natal's Rape Scare of 1886', *Journal of Southern African Studies* vol. 28, no. 2 (June 2002): 379–400.
50. Jock McCulloch, *Black Peril, White Virtue: Sexual Crime in Southern Rhodesia, 1902–1935* (Bloomington: Indiana University Press, 2000).

51. Amirah Inglis, *'Not a White Woman Safe': Sexual Anxiety and Politics in Port Moresby 1920–1934* (Canberra: Australian National University Press, 1974), p. viii.
52. Inglis, *'Not a White Woman Safe'*, p. 11.
53. On this, see for example Philippa Levine, 'Venereal Disease, Prostitution, and the Politics of Empire: The Case of British India', *Journal of the History of Sexuality* vol. 4, no. 4 (1994): 579–602; and 'Orientalist Sociology and the Creation of Colonial Sexualities', *Feminist Review* no. 65 (Summer 2000): 5–21.
54. Procida, *Married to the Empire*, chapter 4 'Re-Writing the Mutiny'.
55. Paxton, *Writing Under the Raj*, chapter 6 'Mixed Couples'.
56. Mrinalini Sinha, 'Mapping an Imperial Social Formation: A Modest Proposal for Feminist Historiography', *Signs* vol. 25, no. 4 (Summer 2000): 1077–82.
57. Lisa Z. Sigel, *Governing Pleasures: Pornography and Social Change in England, 1815–1914* (New Brunswick, NJ: Rutgers University Press, 2002), chapter 2 'Sexuality Raw and Cooked: Empirical and Imperial Pornography'.
58. Tony Ballantyne, *Orientalism and Race: Aryanism in the British Empire* (Houndmills, Basingstoke: Palgrave, 2002), pp. 14–15.

3
Masculinities, Imperial Adventuring and War

Conceptions of masculinity that were closely linked to episodes of imperial adventuring and war saturated the popular culture of the Victorian and Edwardian British Empire. Forms of boyhood and manhood that supported imperial annexation, expansion, aggressive posturing, and outright warfare became dominant, although at the same time they were challenged by divergent and oppositional notions. By drawing together work on boys' literature and popular culture, analyses of the heroic cultural status of the Victorian explorer and scholarship on the imperial construction of 'the martial races' as well as hunting, physical feats and sports, we can chart the interconnections among racialized masculinities, imperial adventuring and war.

Foregrounding these connections demonstrates the manifold ways in which definitions of manhood fed imperial wars by prescribing militaristic qualities as integral to British masculinity. British, colonial and colonized boys and young men supported militaristic cultural prescriptions, yet paid heavy prices because of them, as they volunteered for or were coerced into imperial campaigns that took their health, limbs and lives. While it was politicians, military leaders, merchants and imperial strategists who typically provoked and welcomed invasions and battles, millions of ordinary subjects of the empire were caught up in them. It comes as no surprise that jingoistic and imperialist narratives in popular culture spurred military recruitment and popular support for war. Yet the sheer pervasiveness of such tropes, and the connections they forged between areas of culture from the juvenile to the scientific, present a powerful picture of a culture prepared to sacrifice its members, especially young men of the middling and labouring classes, for imperial gain and expansion, at the same time that it engaged in vast bloodshed of the colonized.

young boys gave lives for the imperial gain.

Books for boys

When G.A. Henty died at the age of sixty-nine in November 1902, *The Times* sadly predicted that his death 'will be deeply felt by a multitude of youthful admirers'. 'For many Christmas seasons', the newspaper continued, 'no books have been so eagerly expected and so gladly welcomed by boys. ... We understand that the circulation of "With Buller in Natal," one of the latest of the trinity of stories which invariably appeared towards Christmastide, surpassed that of any of his previous books.'[1] It was significant that *The Times* linked Henty's passing both to the effect on book sales for boys at Christmas, and to the popularity of his latest adventure story set amidst the recently ended South African War. Henty was perhaps the most popular of a whole cohort of writers of imperial adventure stories aimed at British boys, from the mid-nineteenth century through the Edwardian period, part of the rise of the mass literature industry. Within this popular cultural phenomenon, the nuances of heroic boyish and manly behaviour shifted over time. Nevertheless, for well over half a century boys' fiction put imperial wars and territorial annexations at the heart of domestic and empire-wide culture. These stories imparted to the rising generations of soldiers, colonial administrators, and citizens of both colonies and metropole a visceral sense of the excitement and importance of the empire.

Colonial readers were a numerically substantial constituency for this fiction. For white-settler boys, such stories helped them to locate themselves as part of the empire.[2] Adventure stories constituted arguably the most powerful cultural vehicle for inculcating notions of imperial mission and purpose. That they did so while purveying a shifting complex of notions of admirable British and colonial boyhood and manhood was so culturally accepted that it was considered natural. Generations of British and white-settler boys learnt from such stories that the empire proffered an amazing array of exciting places where they could test their mettle and prove their worthiness to family, God and country. Colonized boys, some of whom would have been among the readership for the same stories, would have absorbed a very different set of lessons: about the very compromised position they occupied in imperial hierarchies, and their own problematic prospects. It was apt that *The Times* should lament Henty's passing in relation to Christmastime, the traditional season for family and friends to endow British and white-settler boys with presents of stories that would inculcate notions of imperial adventure and manliness. And it was particularly significant that Henty's death coincided with the height of his popularity at the conclusion of the South African War, an episode which had demanded jingoistic support from British citizens in the face of international criticism of imperial rapacity and scandal surrounding the conduct of the war. It was arguably the high water mark for dominant cultural support of British imperial expansion.

As was true of other prominent writers of boys' adventure stories, like R.M. Ballantyne who entertained generations of boys with stories set in the Canadian wilderness, and Ernest Favenc who specialized in the Australian outback, Henty's stories drew on his own experience and observations. Henty had been born in 1832 to a middle-class English family, and was educated at Westminster School and Cambridge. During the Crimean War he and his brother Frederick both volunteered for active service. Despite his brother's death from cholera at Scutari, Henty began a career that combined military adventuring and journalism. He held administrative posts in the British army in various locations, before leaving the military to assist his father with running a Welsh colliery. His subsequent war journalism took him to the wars of Italian unification in the 1860s; Abyssinia; the Suez Canal; the Franco-Prussian War in 1870–71; the Russian conquest of Khiva in 1873; Lord Wolseley's expedition to

Ashanti in 1873–74; guerrilla warfare in 1874 Spain; the Prince of Wales's tour of India in 1875 and the war between Turkey and Serbia in 1876.[3]

It was this breadth of travel and observations of soldiering and combat in a variety of geographical settings that fuelled his fictional imagination. The British imperial public came to believe that '[h]is stories were always fundamentally trustworthy'.[4] Patrick A. Dunae has argued that although Henty's stories feature military officials and adventures, his primary concern was actually with economic affairs and the commercial success of the empire, and it was for that reason that his stories include young men 'with mining companies, on planta- tions, or in trading establishments'.[5] Especially in the late nineteenth century, there were direct links between economic interests in the empire, territorial acquisition and military power. It is quite consistent, then, that Henty was concerned about trade and investments, while centring his stories on military adventures. Joseph Bristow points to the detail in which Henty intentionally described matters like the handling of weapons, the obeying of orders and army codes of conduct, such that '[p]assages of his prose read like instructions for the cadets corps'.[6] Given Henty's popularity, which, according to Bristow out- stripped even Rider Haggard's with total sales of Henty's books numbering somewhere in the vicinity of twenty-five million, British boys' absorption of his representations of the military excitement to be found in colonial escapades was a major component of Victorian and Edwardian culture.[7]

Henty ranged widely through centuries of history for settings and plots for his hundred or so boys' stories, from ancient and early modern times to contemporary wars. Many, however, concerned the empire's engagements and battles from the mid-nineteenth century and thus his opus constituted a politi- cal history of the Victorian empire that shaped popular conceptions. His *Jack Archer: A Tale of the Crimea* was written in the 1880s, but served to justify Britain's imperial interest in thwarting Russian ambitions towards the Ottoman Empire in the 1850s. No doubt his analysis of the war was coloured by his own experience of volunteering and fighting in it, and losing his brother. In *Jack Archer*, in 1854 Jack leaves school early to become an officer in training in the hastily enlarged naval fleet, while his older brother Harry obtains a commission in the army. Their father, sending them off proudly and patriotically, explains Britain's position. Britain, in alliance with France, must protect Turkey's independence and prevent any part of it, especially Constantinople, from falling under Russian dominion. Partly, this is because of Britain's interest in maintain- ing its presence in the eastern Mediterranean. More importantly, 'Egypt is rapidly becoming our highway to India, and many men think that in the future our trade with that great dependency will flow down the valley of the Euphrates. Consequently, it is necessary to prevent Russia, at any cost, obtaining a footing south of the Black Sea.'[8] In Henty's view, then, the Crimean War was an instance of military intervention necessary for the protection of British trading interests – specifically, its imperial trade with India, which was envisaged as being re-routed through the Middle East even before the Suez Canal was constructed in the 1860s.

For fifteen-year-old Jack Archer, it is a dream come true to become 'a mid- shipman in her [*sic*] Majesty's service'. It is all the more wonderful that he will serve at a time of war: 'Oh, father, I have so wished to go to sea, but I have never said much about it because I thought you did not like it, and now to think of my getting it when I had quite given up all hope, and just at a time, too, when there seems to be a chance of a row.'[9] Jack's delight at enlisting and sailing for 'the East' is sharpened by his unhappiness at school: he has just been castigated by his master for writing the worst Latin verses in his class. In a class-based definition of British masculinity that values physical hardiness and bravery over classical education, Jack's father assures his lieutenant that Jack is 'active and intelligent' despite having 'not shone greatly at school' especially in Latin. 'He will make none the worse sailor for that', the lieutenant laughs.[10]

The plot bears out the lieutenant's prediction that Jack's shortcoming at Latin will be irrelevant to his career in the navy. In fact, Jack evinces an awareness of the importance of contemporary languages (as opposed to dead languages) and a facility at picking up Russian while he is held captive. More importantly, Jack's courage, physical strength, quickwittedness and strong allegiance to the gentlemanly code of honour are his sterling attributes, and ensure his survival and ultimate fortune. He and his new best friend Dick Hawtry, for example, save the lives of sixteen ordinary sailors during a terrible storm that kills hundreds. Jack saves Dick's life in an honourable act that results in their both being taken prisoner by the Russians. Although they have, prior to this, both killed more than their share of the enemy, their captivity turns out mostly to be in the lap of luxury while their shipmates suffer through a terrible Crimean winter. Having been marched north by their captors, they are quartered upon a Russian count and his Polish wife on a grand estate and treated according to the code of conduct for officers. Not least, the count and countess have three attractive daughters who turn captivity into social pleasure. Jack and Dick's allegiance to the code of gentlemanly honour transcends national hatreds; the count is a reformer who is persecuted by the local governor, and the English boys save him and his family from banishment through their wits and bravery. Escaping with the count's help, the young men make their way through Poland, where they are caught up with a band of nationalist forest guerrillas. Here too they lend their talents to the local cause, one that Britain supports, and again are rewarded for their honour and daring. Jack eventually rejoins his ship at Sebastopol, and continues to heap military honour upon himself. Unlike Henty's own brother Frederick, Jack's brother Harry survives his wounds. After the war, Jack joins another ship headed for China, which is eventually sent to Calcutta after the outbreak of the 'Indian Mutiny'. Here too Jack participates in the central fighting of a critical imperial struggle, particularly at Lucknao. Jack returns to Britain as a twenty-three-year-old lieutenant, but his real reward comes when he is reunited in Paris with the family of the Russian count. He marries the youngest daughter, Olga, whose fortune allows him to retire from the sea and to purchase a 'handsome estate in Sussex',[11] the landed idyll to which every ambitious English boy should aspire. The youthful readers of *Jack Archer* thus learnt that classical education did not count as much as bravery, honour, and national and imperial service. By committing themselves to the imperial cause, English boys could have breathtakingly exciting adventures in all sorts of foreign places, prove their worth, become men honoured by all around them, and ultimately be rewarded with wealth, social status and happiness. A decent, adventurous lower middle-class boy, thanks to the rewards attainable through the empire, could have it all, without having to suffer through endless Latin.

Major imperial campaigns inspired Henty to write more than one story about them. Beside *With Buller in Natal* (1901), the South African War engendered *With Roberts to Pretoria* (1902). Henty explained in the preface to the latter that they represented different stages of the war, the first with 'desperate fighting in Natal' and strong Boer resistance, and the second marked by a larger British force staging marked success with less Boer opposition.[12] British expeditions in Sudan in the 1880s and 1890s were of such popular interest that Henty devoted two stories to them, *The Dash for Khartoum: A Tale of the Nile Expedition* (1890s) and *With Kitchener in the Soudan: A Story of Atbara and Omdurman* (1903). The historical and political detail with which Henty laced his stories served to explicate British interests and justify imperial actions. Both Sudan novels indict in the most stringent terms the failure of the British government to send an expedition soon enough to save General Gordon at Khartoum in 1885. Henty's descriptions of the actions of the Mahdi and his supporters work to vindicate Gordon's refusal to abandon Khartoum to them, yet as with Henty's other novels the heroes learn to judge friend and foe carefully according to the code of honour.

In *The Dash for Khartoum*, Edgar Clinton befriends the Arab sheikh who enslaves him when he is captured. The plot harks back to the captivity narratives of an earlier epoch: Edgar endures his status as a 'white slave' but refuses his new master's invitation to convert to Islam to gain his freedom. Vowing fidelity to his own religion and country, Edgar carefully honours his obligations to the sheikh, saves the sheikh's life through his own bravery, and purchases his own freedom with a large ransom. Needless to say, despite this connection to the sheikh and his tribe, Edgar is unconcerned about the deaths of large numbers of indigenous people throughout the story. As in *Jack Archer*, Edgar's facility with a living language, despite his lack of brilliance at school, combines with his bravery, endurance and honour to save him and earn his secure future.[13] Edgar Clinton and Jack Archer also have in common extraordinary strategic skills, on which their comrades rely, even those who are much older. The plots of both Sudan novels centre around confused identities of the young heroes, involving claims to social status and landed estates in Britain; in both stories, the heroes' skills and bravery constitute a moral claim to their patrimony that is rewarded at each novel's end.[14] Here too Henty sees the empire as shoring up Britain's class structure, and underscores that the ownership of land is integral to true British manhood.

While valorizing the social order, and the virtues of friendship, family, school and sports (especially cricket and football, prowess at which seemingly was evidence of suitability for the military), Henty's juvenile fiction did not focus on religion. Adherence to Protestant Christianity was assumed, even considered necessary, but not dwelt upon. In this, Henty's work represents the direction boys' fiction took in the last decades of the Victorian period. Earlier, evangelism had been a wellspring for boys' papers. The *Boy's Own Paper* was founded in 1879 by the missionary Religious Tract Society as an antidote to the 'penny dreadfuls' that Christian organizations felt were leading boys astray. Dunae argues that, by the late 1880s, the *Boy's Own Paper* had toned down its reports of missionary activities, and moved towards the kind of fiction that Henty came to exemplify: a genre that included the school as context but featured imperial adventure stories.[15] There were many such boys' story papers, with differing editorial agendas, whose heyday overlapped with the high period of empire, and a number of the major boys' fiction writers appeared in their pages.[16] Henty either edited or wrote for several, including the *Union Jack, Boys' Own Magazine* and *Camps and Quarters*.[17] Henty's interest in the empire was catholic, encompassing not only the colonies of conquest but those of settlement. Emigration frequently occurred as a possible path for his ambitious and restless boy heroes. His titles included *With Wolfe in Canada: or, The Winning of a Continent; Maori and Settler: A Story of the New Zealand War;* and *A Final Reckoning: A Tale of Bush Life in Australia* the last of which Henty described in the preface as 'a story of adventure in Australia, in the early days when the bushrangers and the natives constituted a real and formidable danger to the settlers'.[18]

Explorers

The qualities that boy heroes exhibited in Henty stories were comparable to those required of explorers. Like explorers, Henty's heroes travelled long distances, endured enormous physical hardship, developed stamina, adapted to local customs and learnt local languages, and paid much attention to the landscape and its features. Such qualities were standard fare for stories by other writers set in the white-settler colonies. Robert Michael (R.M.) Ballantyne was a popular writer of the mid-Victorian period who specialized in stories set in Canada. A Scotsman, he served as an apprentice to the Hudson's Bay Company for five years in the 1840s. After he returned to Scotland, he turned to writing, first a memoir of his years in Canada, then fiction; he became a frequent contributor to *The Boy's Own Paper*. Significantly, his later career included performing in Scotland and England as 'the brave Mr. Ballantyne' in a fur-trader's outfit, singing songs and telling stories of the Canadian wilderness.[19] Imperial masculinity, apparently, could be transparently performative. Richard S. Phillips has argued, in relation to Ballantyne's successful 1856 novel *The Young Fur Traders*, that in boys' adventure stories journeys were often metaphors for the passage from boyhood to manhood. In the novel, the Canadian frontier operates as a liminal space through which the young hero passes, pitting himself against the cold and the outdoors, defining himself in the company of other colonizing men, and the absence of women, against the indigenous men he encounters.[20]

Journeys across little known and charted frontier zones were, of course, the stuff of explorers as well as adventurous young heroes. The connection was foregrounded in Ernest Favenc's 1896 novel *The Secret of the Australian Desert*, which was apparently closely based on Rider Haggard's 1885 African tale *King Solomon's Mines*. Favenc, a Briton who had migrated to Australia in 1863, spent time as an adventurer and explorer in Queensland before settling down in Sydney to write. His nonfiction works centred on history and geography, particularly the history of European exploration of Australia. In *The Secret of the*

Australian Desert, a young Australian, his uncle and a third man set off from the uncle's sheep station to explore the mystery of the Australian central interior. They pass from known landscape into the unknown, pitting themselves against the harsh desert, and Aborigines who are cannibals, and are rewarded by finding gold – satisfying the archetypal quest. The violence in which they engage against hostile Aborigines becomes genocidal: they help to wipe out one whole tribe of 'cannibals'. This genocidal violence is justifiable within the moral parameters of the story, according to Richard Phillips, because the 'explorers' gesture towards the potential of the Australian desert for irrigated agriculture. They indicate that the mysterious centre could become a fertile zone in which British Australians supersede the Aborigines, who are too primitive to deserve to survive. Central to the story is that the three wanderers solve the mystery of the disappearance in 1848 of the historical explorer Ludwig Leichhardt on an expedition through what is now the Northern Territory. The three fictional 'explorers' find an aging survivor of Leichhardt's party, and a journal that provides evidence regarding Leichhardt's death. Thus Favenc wove together history and fiction in a romantic blend that advocated European conquest of the land, represented the imperial potential of Australia's dry centre, and showed adventurous colonial masculinity as achieving both material rewards (the gold) and heroic stature.[21]

Explorers were equally appropriate as material for adventure stories as soldiers, because they too were integral to the larger imperial enterprise of cultural conquest and territorial annexation. Yet, by the turn of the twentieth century the cultural status of explorers had become a matter of contention. Were they the most heroic and patriotic examples of British manhood, the selfless and brave agents of colonial expansion? – or, were they corrupt, arrogant and violent men, to be abjured? The quintessential explorers of Victorian and Edwardian imperial culture were, of course, David Livingstone and Henry Morton Stanley, and it was the latter who was at the vortex of cultural uncertainty about their status by the end of the nineteenth century. There has been an important, if small, body of recent scholarship which has dramatically shattered the lingering myth of Henry Morton Stanley as a heroic figure. Mary Louise Pratt, a scholar of comparative literature, proffered an influential analysis of the language used by European travellers and 'explorers' to document their own journeys and observations. Particularly the British explorers of the mid-Victorian period, like Richard Burton and John Speke who sought to chart the lakes of central Africa, described themselves in a way that Pratt encapsulates as 'the monarch of all I survey'. 'Explorers' cast themselves in this heroic position through rhetorical devices such as stirring and verbose descriptions of moments when they first 'discovered' a particular landmark. Moreover, they implied that their 'discoveries' were achieved single-handedly through their own endurance and ingenuity. They left out or glossed over in their accounts, published for home consumption, the facts of their 'discoveries' resulting from asking the local people of a region about major geographical features, and hiring them to carry their belongings and, at times, themselves to the spot. As Pratt argues, European 'discoveries' consisted of Europeans learning about what indigenous people already knew. By laying claim to be the first European to see a particular feature, and asserting its importance for European imperial interests in a given area, 'explorers' constructed their own magisterial status.[22]

Building on Pratt's work, several scholars and writers have focussed on Henry Morton Stanley. Historical geographer Felix Driver has pieced together evidence about Stanley who, towards the end of the nineteenth century, was lionized in Britain for, it was considered, filling in the map of central Africa. The 'Napoleon of African travellers', as he was described in 1904,[23] was, appropriately enough, an indefatigable self-promoter. Stanley came to prominence when the celebrated missionary-explorer David Livingstone was 'lost' in central Africa. Livingstone was an iconic figure in Britain: an evangelical missionary, anti-slavery crusader, explorer and advocate of a supposedly moral form of British imperialism. His celebrity status was partly the product of the efforts of his sponsors, including the London Missionary Society, the Royal Geographical Society and the government. Livingstone's reports of his central African expeditions in the 1850s and 1860s had been so well publicized internationally that when, while he was searching for the source of the Nile, several years went by with no news from him, he was considered 'lost'. The Royal Geographical Society mounted an expedition to find him, but were beaten by Stanley, then a reporter for the *New York Herald* who 'found' Livingstone at Ujiji on Lake Tanganyika in 1871. An instant celebrity, Stanley presented himself as an American, aided by the fact that he had spent time in the United States during the years of the Civil War (and indeed had fought on both sides of it). In fact, he was born John Rowlands, the illegitimate son of a Welsh pauper, and had grown up in a workhouse in North Wales.[24] Stanley's dubious origins were only one of the controversies that dogged him. Although the map of central Africa became something of a monument to him, with place names like Stanley Pool and Stanley Falls on the River Congo, his role in the establishment of King Leopold's Congo colony, and his proclivity towards violence – what Driver calls his 'exploration by warfare' – made him by the end of the century a lightning rod for public debate about explorers and imperialism in Africa.[25]

Writer Adam Hochschild has elucidated both Stanley's actions in Africa and his singular relationship with King Leopold of Belgium. After the Civil War, Stanley became a journalist in the United States, and was sent by the *New York Herald* to cover the British campaign against Abyssinia. It was this trip which launched Stanley's career in Africa, including his 'discovery' of Livingstone in 1871. Leopold, meanwhile, had a passionate ambition for Belgium to acquire a colony. By the mid-1870s he had cloaked his territorial desire by founding the supposedly humanitarian International African Association. Just as Leopold's ambitions began to focus on the unclaimed Congo-basin area of central Africa, Stanley pulled off the astonishing feat of crossing central Africa from east to west. In a journey of over seven thousand miles and over two and a half years, Stanley filled in crucial blanks on the European map of central Africa, showing that the Congo River comprised an enormous inland waterway with many tributaries, draining an area of well over a million square miles.[26] Stanley's expedition consisted of 356 people, mostly bearers and most of whom died along the way, and had engaged in multiple acts of aggressive violence against people they had encountered.[27] Nevertheless, this self-invented explorer's achievement resulted in his enormous celebration in both Europe and America. Leopold immediately wooed Stanley, and by the end of 1878 Stanley had contracted to work for Leopold in the Congo region for five years at a very handsome salary. Moreover, Leopold undertook to pay for the force that Stanley would need in order to carry out their agreed mission, of establishing a base near the Congo's mouth, building a road around its impassable lower reaches, then establishing a set of trading bases along its vast navigable length.[28] From 1879 to 1884, Stanley dutifully carried out Leopold's wishes: he negotiated on Leopold's behalf bogus treaties with hundreds of Congo chiefs, such that by the time Stanley returned to Europe Leopold claimed a trading monopoly and control over the whole Congo basin.[29] In this vast territory, Leopold's autocratic fiefdom developed through reliance on massive slave labour, for portage of goods and supplies, for service in the colony's military force, and especially in the ivory and rubber trades that produced the profits Leopold so badly wanted.

By 1904 the Congo Reform Association was drawing international attention to the brutal and murderous conditions of enforced labour in Leopold's Congo colony, and by 1908 the Belgian government was forced by international scandal to buy the colony at great expense from their king, in order to introduce reform. Yet questions about the Congo, and Stanley's methods as explorer and imperial agent, had been raised before. As early as 1890, after Stanley's triumphant return to England from a paradoxically failed expedition to rescue the ruler of an embattled southern province of Anglo-Egyptian Sudan, criticisms of Stanley's violent journeying had aired in the press. More significantly in the longer term, in early 1899 Joseph Conrad published his novella *Heart of Darkness*, in which he drew upon his own time in the Congo to present a stark and horrifying portrait of a colonial moral abyss. *Heart of Darkness* has been the subject of controversy and debate in recent years, particularly because eminent Nigerian novelist Chinua Achebe contends that it is racist in its depiction of Africans. It remains, though, a significant text in relation to turn-of-the-century metropolitan perceptions of the Congo and especially of European ivory-trading men there. Millions of readers spanning the twentieth century were shocked by the portrayal of the utterly depraved ivory trader Kurtz, but most would not have known the closeness with which Captain Marlow's narrative was based on Joseph Conrad's own observations during his six months in 1890 as a steamboat officer on the Congo River working for the Société Belge du Haut-Congo. Marlow's descriptions of the treatment, suffering and deaths of African porters, and the gun-happy bloodthirstiness of the trading company's agents, were based on what Conrad saw. Further, Adam Hochschild shows, the character Kurtz was based on several real-life ivory traders whom he came across: a French agent who died on board as Conrad piloted the boat down the river, a Belgian agent known for keeping a 'harem' of African women as well as for his quantities of ivory and another Belgian agent whom Conrad may have met in 1890, and who in 1895 was reported as having decorated his flower bed at the 'inner station' of Stanley Falls with twenty-one African heads. This latter agent, Leon Rom, was a painter, writer and amateur scientist, and was known for keeping African concubines, as well as for his brutality – all attributes of the character Kurtz. Hochschild notes that *The Saturday Review*, a periodical that Conrad always read, printed an article referring to Rom in December 1898, just at the time Conrad began to write *Heart of Darkness*.[30]

Stanley managed to rise above the debate in the 1890s surrounding the morality and politics of African exploration, having achieved huge international celebrity, and making large sums of money from his speaking tours and books, as well as receiving a knighthood and being elected to the British Parliament. His continued celebrity was buoyed by the dominant British public's imperialistic jingoism. He died in 1904, still an international icon, and before the Congo atrocities hit their peak as a cause celebre. Even when they did Stanley was not directly blamed, despite the publicly aired evidence of his trigger-happy and brutal methods in obtaining the Congo for Leopold, perhaps partly because even when he was working for Leopold he had professed his British imperial allegiance. Henry Morton Stanley's celebrity status from the 1870s to the beginning of the twentieth century ensured that a violent, swashbuckling, opportunistic and imperialist version of masculinity continued to be highly visible and influential in British culture.

Heart of Darkness may have been something of a deathknell for the Victorian public's political naivete, but the debate in Britain about the moral status of explorers continued on through the Edwardian period. In June 1908, the year that the Congo became Belgian national property, W. Somerset Maugham's play *The Explorer* was first produced at the Lyric Theatre in London. A drama in four acts, the play reprised some of the same issues as *Heart of Darkness* albeit in a much more reductive form. More importantly, its verdict was different: the explorer emerges as a true patriot and hero, while the play acknowledges that some Britons in Africa behaved badly. The protagonist is Alexander Mackenzie, whose Scots ethnicity is surely a reference to David Livingstone. Prior to the action, Mackenzie had made more than one long trip to East Africa; the second scene is set in the midst of another such trip; and at the play's close he is about to set sail, again, for Zanzibar – Stanley's point of departure for his 1870s trip across central Africa. His trips are explained by recurrent references to his supposedly important role in suppressing the slave trade in East Africa, King Leopold's well-worn humanitarian pretense for his ephemeral associations. These references, seemingly, are such justification for Mackenzie's 'exploration' in East Africa that his role in expanding British colonial territory is supposedly infused with serious moral purpose. His own view of his actions in Africa is captured in an atypically reflexive speech:

> You'll think me very silly, but I'm afraid I'm rather – patriotic. It's only we who live away from England who really love it. I'm so proud of my country, and I wanted so much to do something for it. Often in Africa I've thought of this dear England, and longed not to die till I had done my work. Behind all the soldiers and the statesmen whose fame is imperishable, there is a long line of men who've built up the Empire piece by piece. Their names are forgotten, and only students know their history, but each one of them gave a province to his country. And I, too, have my place among them. For five years I toiled night and day, and at the end of it was able to hand over to the Commissioners a broad tract of land, rich and fertile.[31]

The play endorses this highly sentimental and stridently imperialist view of the explorer's work. To some extent this speech obscures the bloodshed behind the annexation of this 'rich and fertile' land, and by extension the contemporary realities of territorial annexation in British East Africa.

But that bloodshed is referred to elsewhere in the play. The plot hinges upon an episode in which the 'exploration' party is seeking to pacify hostile tribes, in order to establish British hegemony. A young member of the party, George Allerton, rapes and murders an indigenous woman, then tries to shoot Mackenzie when the latter indicts him for his actions. Escaping for their lives from an attack by local people sparked by the rape and murder, Mackenzie sends Allerton into a dangerous situation, knowing he may well be killed, but intending that his crimes will die with him. Allerton's sister is the woman Mackenzie hopes to marry. On their return to London, another member of the party, who does not know of Allerton's crimes, publicly accuses Mackenzie of sending Allerton to his death. London is thrown into an uproar, in which Mackenzie is blacklisted and condemned, in a fashion that Maugham presumably intended to echo earlier public condemnations of Stanley. Mackenzie refuses to reveal the facts of Allerton's crimes and death, because he does not want Allerton's sister to have to face the truth of her brother's actions. In the end, she forgives Mackenzie without learning the full facts, because she knows he is trustworthy. In a rather maudlin stance that Maugham seems to be suggesting may well have been Stanley's, Mackenzie insists:

> After my death England will forget my faults and my mistakes. I care nothing for the flouts and gibes with which she has repaid all my pain, for I have added another fair jewel to her crown. I don't want rewards. I only want the honour of serving this dear land of ours.[32]

The play thus acknowledges that some Britons, like Allerton, did indeed commit heinous and violent crimes against Africans. But it suggests that they are in the minority, and that the real heroic 'explorers' are the unheralded backbone of the empire. Maugham echoes Conrad in one key, gendered element of the play. Like Kurtz's 'intended' in *Heart of Darkness*, Lucy Allerton represents wilfully oblivious feminine innocence. She is shielded from the truth of her brother's violence, and does not know the details of Mackenzie's work in Africa. She trusts implicitly in his patriotism and heroism. While she is cast in the quintessentially feminine role of staying home, adoring and waiting, in *The Explorer*, unlike, *Heart of Darkness*, she is also the voice of reason and wisdom, taking the position Maugham suggests the public ought to have taken.

'Science', sex and imperial gentlemen

Recent scholarship shows that the sexual exploitation of African women by some ivory traders was no aberration in the broader picture of manly explorers and geographical science in the latter nineteenth and early twentieth centuries. Lisa Sigal has demonstrated that some men in the most prestigious scientific circles in Britain both read and wrote pornography with distinctly imperialist dimensions. The Cannibal Club, as it was known to its members, was formed by the prominent explorer and writer Sir Richard Burton and ran from the 1860s through the 1880s. It included influential British men, many of whom were members of the London Anthropological Society and the Royal Geographical Society. Luminaries such as Algernon Charles Swinburne the writer, Monckton Milnes (Lord Houghton) a Member of Parliament, Sir James Plaisted Wilde (Lord Penzance) a divorce court judge, and General Studholme John Hodgson whose scope of service had included Ceylon and Burma were amongst its members. These prominent and powerful men were united in the Cannibal Club by their interest in sex, and particularly by their predilections for the purportedly scientific study of the sexuality of colonized cultures, and their belief that scientific and literary pursuits could be entwined with sexual indulgence. Mostly not politically radical in socioeconomic terms, this group took an anti-orthodox view of censorship and used their connections to import and distribute pornography. Burton, for example, translated the *Kama Sutra* and had it published in England, making it more pornographic than the Hindu original. Members' work ranged from the flagrantly pornographic to the more scientific, the latter including studies of physiological and cultural aspects of sexuality in other cultures. The unifying theme was the club's stance of scientific objectivity, yet as Sigal argues cogently, their work and activities inscribed and shored up racial and sexual hierarchies. Their assumptions were overtly masculinist, not least their obsession with the phallus. They also evinced a taste for the violent and macabre, such as Burton's 1863 promise to Frederick Hankey that he would bring him back from Dahomey, Africa, a human skin with which to bind his volumes by the Marquis de Sade, specifically a skin stripped from a living African woman.[33] The Cannibal Club, and its overlap with the Royal Geographical Society and the Anthropological Society, show that the sexual abuse by explorers and traders of women in Africa and elsewhere was not temporarily insane behaviour brought on by overwhelming tropical and colonial exigencies, but was consonant with the values of higher reaches of metropolitan imperial culture.

The Royal Geographical Society, founded in 1830, was closely tied to the cult of the African explorer and indeed lent it scientific gravitas. In the 1850s and 1860s the society made the most of popular interest in Africa, particularly quests such as those for the sources of the Nile. It became a sponsor of, and closely associated with, David Livingstone, whom it awarded its gold medal in 1857, but it also gave accolades to other African explorers such as Burton, John Speke and James Grant.[34] The society had a rather more troubled relationship with Henry Morton Stanley, whom it initially treated with scepticism and class-based condescension, but whom it was reluctantly forced to acknowledge through the sheer public success of his, in Francis Galton's sneering term, 'sensational geography'.[35] The Royal Geographical Society was one of several official and powerful imperial organizations that helped to entrench conceptions of heroic masculinity based on 'exploration' and imperial adventuring. One of the prestigious imperial edifices in London was the Royal Colonial Institute founded in 1868. Originally called the Colonial Society before receiving royal endorsement in 1869 (and later royal charter and patronage), the institute aimed to be a rendezvous for colonial men and to promote the importance and the interests of the colonies in Britain itself.[36] To this end, it built a library, arranged the regular presentation of papers on colonial subjects and emphasized serious discussion. From the beginning, members of the institute included political leaders in Britain and from the colonies and dominions. Although the membership was overwhelmingly white, from the 1880s at least it included some non-white men from South Asia, the West Indies and Africa.[37] The Royal Colonial Institute was a forum for the likes of Cecil Rhodes, a venue where the power brokers of empire met, where investors, authors and journalists from around the empire gathered. In short, it became a Tory proimperialist bastion. While commerce and capitalism were central to the institute's concerns, it too endorsed the related importance of 'exploration' and travel to and within the colonies. Its inaugural dinner in March 1869 included notable explorers, such as Captain Charles Sturt and W.C. Wentworth from the Australian colonies.[38] The institute was biased towards the colonies of settlement, particularly Australia, Canada and South Africa, but its library and the papers presented at its regular meetings, and then published, aimed to inform members (and by extension the British imperial public) of matters in diverse parts of the empire.

Hunters and racialized contests of masculinity

A hypermasculine cultural figure, closely linked to that of explorer, was the big game hunter. Big game hunters, who had their heyday in the late nineteenth and early twentieth centuries, were privileged and often powerful EuroAmerican men who went to Africa and India in order to pursue, conquer and possess animals that were considered both dangerous and exotic. By bringing home their trophies, big game hunters established a proprietorial relationship with the colonies and their fauna. At the same time, they asserted their own race-based superiority: the superiority of their skills and weapons, and their virility or masculinity. Ivory, of course, was one of the prizes most sought by hunters, not least because of its commercial value. Britons, other Europeans and Americans' fascination with hunting was linked to the imagined exoticism of tropical colonies, and the conquest of exotic wild animals was ideologically linked to colonial conquest. John MacKenzie has argued that, while hunting has been a human activity since prehistoric times, the big game hunting of the late nineteenth and early twentieth centuries was a historically and culturally specific form rooted in European global supremacy. Accounts left by big game hunters show that shooting animals overlapped, both in their minds and in practice, with shooting indigenous people.[39] Colonial administrators frequently hunted as a recreational pursuit, thus directly connecting hunting with imperial rule. If actual big game hunting was the pastime of the privileged few, its cultural celebration was partly the result of the many published travelogues based on hunting narratives. The Victorian armchair traveller could identify with the supposed qualities of British manliness such as coolness, bravery, restraint and humour that the hunter reputedly embodied.

The manliness culturally associated with big game hunters, despite their dependence on local men to act as their indispensable guides and beaters, is strikingly captured in George Orwell's 1934 novel *Burmese Days*, based on

Orwell's experience in the Imperial Police in Burma in the 1920s. Orwell's alter ego James Flory, a forestry merchant in a remote station of upper Burma, desperately woos a newly arrived conservative Englishwoman against the odds of his disfiguring birthmark and radical politics. His pursuit is doomed to tragedy, but at one point in the plot he comes very close to success. Significantly, it is when he took her hunting that she almost accepts him. Her own thrill at the bloodsport, and his prowess with a shotgun, convince her of his masculinity and induce a powerful erotic charge: 'she felt almost an adoration for Flory now that she had seen how he could shoot ... She was conscious of an extraordinary desire to fling her arms round Flory's neck and kiss him; and in some way it was the killing of the pigeon that made her feel this.'[40] In a perhaps misogynistic portrait of a cold and unfeeling colonizing woman who rejects the protagonist partly because of his critique of colonialism, Orwell suggests that the hunter represented the imperial man at his apotheosis.

Hunting was, however, a central arena for British men's competitive construction of masculinity in relation to the masculinity of colonized men. In geographically diverse colonies, invading British men found themselves in a complicated relationship to the local men, who knew the land and its fauna in ways that the British needed to learn and imitate. Henry Reynolds has detailed the ways in which British men in early Australia, both explorers and settlers, depended upon Aboriginal management of the landscape, pathways, knowledge of waterholes, ambassadorial service and tracking and hunting skills.[41] Imperial men observed native men's hunting skills with a mix of attention, admiration and condescension that evolved over time as the British established trading and settlement in a given area. Elizabeth Vibert has analysed the complex and shifting contests over masculinity between British fur traders and indigenous men in the Plateau region of northwest North America in the early nineteenth century. As British fur trading companies entrenched their commercial interests in the region, they were dependent on the local people for pelts and hides. British male traders waxed eulogistic in their praise for the Plateau Indians who hunted buffalo: the Salish and Kutenai hunters, they reported, were brave, proud, honest, diligent and warlike. The British had a particular investment in praising the Plateau people, whose traditional enemies the Plains Indians, especially the Blackfoot Confederacy, had successfully resisted the traders' earlier incursions. Traders' accounts reveal their satisfaction in having supplied the Plateau hunters with the muskets that gave them the edge over their rivals, and enabled them to extend their buffalo hunting territory. The guns had augmented the hunters' traditional skills and also their claims to manhood, a conceptual linkage that the Indians themselves apparently made.[42] Yet the British traders, in their narratives, cast themselves as the superior men next to whom the Indians could only approximate real manhood. The traders themselves also hunted the wild buffalo, they recounted, in the tradition of British sportsmen who had taken their favourite pastime to the colonies in the form of big game hunting. While the native hunters of the Plateau region showed manly attributes, they were still essentially primitive people who were dependent on the British for the supply of the guns that were vastly superior (the traders claimed) to the bow and arrow. British traders' admiration for Indian hunters, Vibert argues, was a temporary cultural concession: later in the period of settlement, when the British no longer needed the Indians and saw them instead as an impediment to settlement, their hunting skills were no longer so admirable or manly.[43]

Contests over skills with weapons were tied to racialized notions of masculinity. They were also directly tied to issues of power and dominance, as is clear in the 1870s episode in southern Africa that William K. Storey has studied in which Africans were prohibited from using guns in a policy aimed at maintaining white supremacy. For all of the contextual debate over whether Africans truly were skilled with guns, British fears of armed Africans produced a discriminatory policy of disarmament.[44] Conversely, we know from the story of Archibald Meston, the Southern Protector of Aborigines in Queensland from 1898 to 1904 and principal author of the 1897 Queensland Aborigines Protection Act, that some white men felt impelled to prove their own manhood through their skills with native weapons. William Thorpe has described how Meston, who considered himself quite an athlete, held public performances throwing spears and boomerangs to demonstrate that a white man could deploy Aboriginal weapons as well as any Aboriginal man. His 'Wild Australia' shows in the 1890s included physical combat between himself and Aboriginal men armed with nullas and shields. Meston seemingly intended these spectacular contests of racialized masculinities to demonstrate visually what he considered to be white superiority, the superiority of supposedly pure tribal Aborigines over those of mixed race, and hence the necessity for the segregation that was the cornerstone of his policy of 'protection'.[45] As Duncan Waterson has shown, among the most symbolic of Meston's spectacles were those he organized as part of the celebrations of Australia's federation in 1901, including dances, corroborees and mock fights staged in Brisbane by seventy Aboriginal men and one Aboriginal woman from places ranging across Queensland and as far away as Western Australia. Aboriginal participation in Brisbane's federation ceremonies as exemplars of warlike primitivism included Meston's creation of an 'Aboriginal Arch' during the May 1901 visit of the future King George V and Queen Mary. The arch, one of several erected for the ceremonial procession, was covered in greenery and topped by a troupe of Aborigines in war paint wielding spears.[46] It represented Aborigines as serious fighters and yet, at once, highlighted their demise and marginalization in the new Australian state.

'Martial races'

Racialized contests for masculinity went beyond organized spectacles, to include essentialist notions of racial difference. Historian Heather Streets argues that from 1857 onwards, British military officials actively constructed what became the popular idea of 'martial races', that is, the belief that some races were inherently warlike, brave, strong and manly. In particular, the Scottish Highlanders, Punjabi Sikhs and Nepalese Gurkhas were idealized as masculine and warlike 'races' who produced the best soldiers, and therefore became the recruiting targets for imperial forces. The construction of these supposedly ethnic groups masked their actually diverse constituencies. In fact, soldiers in the 'Highlander' regiments included Lowland Scots and even some men from other parts of the

British Isles; Sikhs of course are a religious rather than an ethnic group; and those the British called 'Gurkhas' were from a variety of ethnic groups in Nepal. Martial race ideology constructed and connected these three groups based partly on their comparable feats of bravery, and what were initially coincidences of their fighting together, such as when Sikhs and Highlanders fought together in what the British called 'the relief of Lucknow' in 1857. But the connections between these three reputedly martial groups were consciously developed, to the point that by the late nineteenth century Sikh and Gurkha regiments occasionally dressed in kilts, and more often boasted pipe bands that played tunes such as 'Hielan' Laddie'.[47]

Streets amply demonstrates the historically contingent process underlying this racial ideology. It arose during the 1857–58 uprising of army sepoys against the British Raj in India, and was catapulted into popular imperial culture because of the sensationalist narratives that circulated about those events. The concept of 'martial races' was founded on those British troops who performed well, and the colonized troops who proved their 'loyalty' to the British during the bloody suppression of the uprising. 'Loyalty' was translated into valour, strength and other martial qualities, then 'martial' soon became elided with 'manly' characteristics. The idealized types of 'manly' Sikhs and Gurkhas emerged in tandem with the conception of the effeminate Bengali '*babu*' which Mrinalini Sinha has analysed. As Streets points out, these gendered stereotypes of colonialism were directly linked to imperial politics: 'effeminate *babus*' were middle-class leaders of the nascent nationalist movement whom the British sought to trivialize, while 'manly' Sikhs and Gurkhas were poorer northern men who lacked economic alternatives to enlistment and whom the British valourized.[48] The ideology of 'martial races' was entrenched by latter nineteenth-century developments in both racial 'science' and the global politics of imperial defence. It was also linked to the racial theory of Aryanism: men from the north of India were considered to be most closely linked by descent to the Aryan race, and hence to be nearer to Europeans both physiologically and morally.[49] As Streets shows well, the ascendancy of martial race ideology was a product of multiple confluent factors, including the rise of print media, the efforts of British military leaders to win public support for their campaigns, the rapid growth of 'scientific' racism, and imperial politics. By the turn of the twentieth century, she shows, it had resulted in a skewed makeup of imperial forces: in 1904 57 per cent of the Indian army was drawn from the 'martial races' and by 1914, that figure had risen to 75 per cent.[50] Enlistment patterns were linked to a widespread belief in the ideology itself with attendant popular images of these supposed heroic types, and increased popular support for imperial military campaigns.

Streets shows that even the military leaders who were most responsible for the discourse of martial races understood its constructed nature, even as they relied on contemporary belief in racial 'science'. In her final chapter she assesses the impact of the discourse on the supposed 'martial race' men themselves, analyzing their mostly economic motives for enlisting, but also their own reasons for subscribing to the ideology. She discusses as well the ways in which this popular discourse has served historically to mask the economic and geopolitical circumstances of the regions from which these soldiers were drawn. In sum,

Streets argues convincingly, her study of martial race ideology demonstrates that: 'ideologies of gender played an important role in the development of the logic of imperial defence in the last half of the nineteenth century, and that those ideologies also helped to shape Victorian ideals of masculinity more generally'.[51] Streets's study is an exemplar of the importance of transnational or transcolonial approaches to history, and is significant not least for its analysis of an imperial ideology that crossed racial boundaries even as it constructed a racial ideology. While the roots of Highlanders' image as manly and martial lay in their earlier associations with barbarism, by the latter nineteenth century they had been racially assimilated into Britishness. Despite its links to Aryanism, martial race ideology shows how complex, fluid and contradictory racial ideologies have been, and how conceptions of gender – such as militaristic manliness – have operated as a kind of racial glue.

Conceptions of martial races resonated in various imperial locations. Sydney's celebrations of Australian federation in January 1901 included an evening's entertainment at the Town Hall involving a military display of Highlander, Indian and English troops, and some Aborigines, one of Archibald Meston's spectacles of racialized masculinity. In contrast to the New Zealand Maori, Aborigines have often been denigrated as nonmilitaristic and passive, yet on this occasion they were presented as among the empire's warrior races.[52] The *Sydney Morning Herald* called the evening's program a 'grand assault-at-arms'. Events included a fencing contest among Highlander and other British troops, a 'singlesticks' competition by Indian troops, a swordfighting contest, a bayonet competition, and 'a clever exhibition of club swinging by Corporal McNeil'. The Aborigines performed a corroboree in 'war paint', posed with boomerangs and clubs, and demonstrated a spear fight. The paper described the evening as a 'novel and interesting' event attended by officials, members of the military, and the public; its messages seem to have included imperial unity, Australia's new role as a federated nation and the martial manliness of multiple races of the empire.[53] Notions of Maori as a martial race were linked to British arguments, as Tony Ballantyne has demonstrated, for their Aryanism, that is their at least partial descent from the Aryan races of India, and in turn the conception of the Aryan races of northern India as manly and warlike – a theory of racial descent that Maori themselves rejected.[54] Despite their rejection of Aryanism, at least some Maori embraced the conception of themselves as a martial race, not least during their fighting service for the empire in the First World War.[55]

Militaristic definitions of manhood

Martial race ideology was one dimension in which eugenicist theory and gender were interconstitutive in British imperial culture. Another dimension was the converse worry, especially significant in the Edwardian period in the wake of the Anglo-Boer War, that working-class British men were not sufficiently healthy and virile. It was this pervasive concern about the fitness of British men to perform as imperial troops that underlay the launching in 1908 of the Boy Scout movement. Robert Baden-Powell had become a popular hero during the Anglo-Boer War for his role in the British 'defence' of Mafeking, and then built on his public visibility through his concern over British boyhood. Adapting his earlier work on military manuals, including the techniques of military scouting, in 1908 Baden-Powell published *Scouting for Boys*. The book tapped into British public concern over the fitness of the army, but it also powerfully echoed the gendered messages propagated by Henty and other adventure-story writers. *Scouting for Boys* launched the boy scout movement, which was so hugely popular that by 1910 it could boast more than 100,000 members in Britain alone, figures that doubled in the following decade and then grew further.[56] It became one of the major popular cultural movements of the twentieth century, embracing colonies and dominions of the empire and many other countries. Like boys' adventure stories set in colonial contexts, scouting told boys that the great outdoors, such as the colonial frontier, was the place in which real men were made through exercise, mountaineering and practical survival skills. By equipping themselves actively and purposefully through hiking, camping and orienteering, British boys would become true men (as opposed to effeminate city loafers) and at once contribute to the national and imperial cause.[57] Tammy Proctor has argued that the boy scout movement walked a fine line between emphasizing military skills and preparedness, on the one hand, and at the same time denying a role in military recruitment, a charge often laid against it by concerned parents and other critics.[58] Despite the boy scout movement's denials, it was one cultural source among others that created widespread popular enthusiasm for war, and a belief that real masculinity was directly linked to expeditions, physical challenges, and national and imperial service, including preparedness to risk the ultimate sacrifice. Such a conception of manhood must surely have been in the minds of many of the hundreds of thousands of boys and young men who enlisted during and after August 1914.

I want to suggest that during the height of the Victorian and Edwardian British Empire, militaristic definitions of masculinity became dominant, in a complex interplay of imperial expansionism and jingoism, an increase in printed popular culture particularly adventure stories for boys, the celebration of the hunter and the explorer as heroic icons, and racialized contests over true manhood. As R.W. Connell has suggested in his succinct outline of the historical rise of Western gender ideology, 'masculinities are not only shaped by the process of imperial expansion, they are active in that process and help to shape it'. Connell contends persuasively that masculinity and violence have become intimately interlinked in a global historical process, that of the EuroAmerican conquest of the rest of the world since the fifteenth century.[59] What I have sought to show in this chapter are historical specificities of British imperialism at its zenith, the ways in which it was driven by the articulation of competitive, racialized, imperialist conceptions of masculinity, and at the same time the ways in which it shaped them. For the boys who grew up reading imperial adventure stories or who excitedly followed the exploits of Henry Morton Stanley, the promise of a dominant adventurous manhood that might take them to any one of the rapidly multiplying British colonies and to strike it rich (or at least become comfortably off) could be a dangerous inducement. The call to arms that so many British men across the empire responded to, in wars that included Sudan in the mid-1880s, the Anglo-Boer War 1899–1902 and the Great War, promised escape from feminized domesticity, travel, adventure, and above all manliness. The prices many paid for such cultural rewards were probably more than they would have been willing to give up, had they known. If British and white-settler dominion men enlisted in the First World War because they believed in the empire, or in their own country, or felt that they had to show themselves to be men (or e.g. Australian men or Canadian men), for colonized men enlistment was less a matter of choice. Indians, West Indians, Africans from various colonies, Fijians, and indigenous men from New Zealand, Canada and Australia all served the British Empire during the First World War, and tens of thousands were killed in the process. Over 800,000 Indians served as imperial troops, of whom at least 135,000 fought in France.[60] Over 60,000 Indians were killed fighting for Britain during the war. Colonized men were little celebrated as heroes, nor rewarded by independence after the war as many hoped, but were given more menial, labouring assignments, and treated with discrimination when stationed in Britain itself. Their sacrifices, made all the harsher for the cultural traumas they endured as a result of their military service, were an enormous contribution to the empire that was hardly acknowledged at the time or in the war's aftermath. For most of them, claims to masculinity were not such a recognized prize of war, although here as elsewhere the 'martial races' were singled out for praise. Yet colonized men were also caught up in the imperial and militarist ideology of masculinity that was arguably a major cause of the First World War itself. We know, too, that some colonizing men engaged in racially related violence during the war itself, presumably in the performance of their white masculinity; Suzanne Brugger's book on Australians in Egypt, for example, shows aspects of Anzac behaviour that have not been enshrined in national mythology – acts of assault, arson, looting and rape against Egyptians whom Australian soldiers mocked, derided and considered racially inferior.[61]

★　★　★

Too often, historical explanations of the causes of wars such as the First World War rely on conceptions of nationalism, imperialism or other political ideologies imagined as somehow unsullied by the social or the sexual. Even economic determinist arguments usually ignore cultural imperatives. I hope that this brief survey has revealed the central importance of gender ideology in driving wars, including the Great War. It is critical to recognize militarist masculinity as a major historical force linked to global violence. At the same time, we must not fall into the essentialist trap of believing gender to be biologically based or immutable. Rather, we need to recognize the historical specificities of gender construction. Imperial masculinities that valourized military service, explorers and hunters, were a specific set of ideas forged in the context of the Victorian and Edwardian empire. It is crucial to identify their basis in imperial aggression, expansionist territorial acquisition, racialized contests over true manhood, and, not least, the eroticization of violence. By reading across the work of a generation of scholars of different imperial locations, the pervasiveness and influence of militarist masculinity becomes apparent. It may have been so naturalized and seemingly innocent that boys around the late Victorian world were given

G.A. Henty's stories for Christmas, but its roots and its consequences were not innocent at all.

Notes

1. 'Mr. G.A. Henty', *The Times*, 17 November 1902, p. 10, cols. b–c.

2. Martin Crotty, *Making the Australian Male: Middle-Class Masculinity 1870–1920* (Melbourne: Melbourne University Press, 2001), esp. pp. 135–6.

3. 'Henty, George Alfred (1832–1902)', *Dictionary of National Biography Supplement 1901–1911* edited by Sir Sidney Lee (Oxford University Press; London: Humphrey Milford, 1912), pp. 249–51.

4. *The Times*, 17 November 1902, p. 10.

5. Patrick A. Dunae, 'Boys' Literature and the Idea of Empire, 1870–1914', *Victorian Studies* vol. 24 (Autumn 1980): 110.

6. Joseph Bristow, *Empire Boys: Adventures in a Man's World* (London: HarperCollins Academic, 1991), p. 147.

7. Bristow, *Empire Boys*, pp. 146–7.

8. G.A. Henty, *Jack Archer: A Tale of the Crimea* (first pub. 1884; New York: W.L. Allison Co., ca. 1900), pp. 11–12.

9. Henty, *Jack Archer*, pp. 10–11.

10. Henty, *Jack Archer*, pp. 14–15.

11. Henty, *Jack Archer*, p. 263.

12. G.A. Henty, *With Roberts to Pretoria: A Tale of the South African War* (London: Blackie & Son, 1902), Preface.

13. G.A. Henty, *The Dash for Khartoum: A Tale of the Nile Expedition* (London: Blackie and Son, n.d. (1890s)).

14. On *With Kitchener in the Soudan*, see Bristow, *Empire Boys*, pp. 147–153.

15. Dunae, 'Boys' Literature and the Idea of Empire', pp. 108–9.

16. Kelly Boyd, *Manliness and the Boys' Story Paper in Britain: A Cultural History, 1855–1940* (Houndmills, Basingstoke: Palgrave Macmillan, 2003).

17. 'Henty, George Alfred', *Dictionary of National Biography Supplement*, p. 250.

18. G.A. Henty, *A Final Reckoning: A Tale of Bush Life in Australia* (London: Blackie & Son, n.d. (1890s)), Preface.

19. Richard S. Phillips, 'Spaces of adventure and cultural politics of masculinity: R.M. Ballantyne and *The Young Fur Traders*', *Environment and Planning D: Society and Space* vol. 13 (1995): 594.

20. Phillips, 'Spaces of adventure', pp. 598–605.

21. Richard Phillips, *Mapping Men and Empire: A Geography of Adventure* (London: Routledge, 1997), pp. 76–87.

22. Mary Louise Pratt, *Imperial Eyes: Travel Writing and Transculturation* (London: Routledge, 1992), pp. 201–8.

23. Felix Driver, *Geography Militant: Cultures of Exploration and Empire* (Oxford: Blackwell Publishers, 2001), p. 125.

24. Felix Driver, 'Henry Morton Stanley and His Critics: Geography, Exploration and Empire', *Past and Present* vol. 133 (1991): 141–2. Also on

Stanley's early biography, see Adam Hochschild, *King Leopold's Ghost: A Story of Greed, Terror, and Heroism in Colonial Africa* (Boston: Mariner Books, 1999), pp. 21–6.

25. Driver, *Geography Militant*, pp. 131–8.
26. Hochschild, *King Leopold's Ghost*, pp. 48, 61.
27. Hochschild, *King Leopold's Ghost*, p. 49.
28. Hochschild, *King Leopold's Ghost*, p. 63.
29. Hochschild, *King Leopold's Ghost*, pp. 71–4.
30. Hochschild, *King Leopold's Ghost*, pp. 144–9.
31. W. Somerset Maugham, *The Explorer: A Melodrama in Four Acts* (London: William Heinemann, 1912), p. 141. I thank Kurt Koenigsberger for alerting me to this play.
32. Maugham, *The Explorer*, p. 141.
33. Lisa Z. Sigel, *Governing Pleasures: Pornography and Social Change in England, 1815–1914* (New Brunswick, NJ: Rutgers University Press, 2002), p. 50. This paragraph summarizes much of Sigal's chapter 2 'Sexuality Raw and Cooked: Empirical and Imperial Pornography'.
34. Driver, *Geography Militant*, pp. 78–9.
35. Driver, *Geography Militant*, pp. 127–8.
36. Trevor R. Reese, *The History of the Royal Commonwealth Society 1868–1968* (London: Oxford University Press, 1968), p. 15.
37. Reese, *History of the Royal Commonwealth Society*, p. 23; Henry Miller (ed.), *1868–1968: Royal Commonwealth Society Centenary Souvenir* (London: Royal Commonwealth Society, 1968), p. 37; *The British-Australasian*, 4 July 1912, p. 19.
38. Reese, *History of the Royal Commonwealth Society*, p. 16.
39. John M. Mackenzie, *The Empire of Nature: Hunting, Conservation and British Imperialism* (Manchester: Manchester University Press, 1988), pp. 7, 159–60.
40. George Orwell, *Burmese Days* (San Diego: Harvest Books, 1934), pp. 165, 167.
41. Henry Reynolds, 'Conquering the Interior', *With the White People: The Crucial Role of Aborigines in the Exploration and Development of Australia* (Ringwood, Vic.: Penguin Books, 1990), chapter 1.
42. Elizabeth Vibert, 'Real Men Hunt Buffalo: Masculinity, Race and Class in British Fur Traders' Narratives', in Catherine Hall (ed.), *Cultures of Empire: Colonizers in Britain and the Empire in the Nineteenth and Twentieth Centuries: A Reader* (New York: Routledge, 2000), p. 288.
43. Vibert, 'Real men hunt buffalo', p. 290.
44. William K. Storey, 'Guns, Race, and Skill in Nineteenth-Century Southern Africa', *Technology and Culture* vol. 45, no. 4 (Oct. 2004): 687–711.
45. William Thorpe, 'Archibald Meston and Aboriginal Legislation in Colonial Queensland', *Historical Studies* vol. 21, no. 82 (April 1984): 60–3.
46. D.B. Waterson, 'Above and Behind the Arches: Aboriginals and the 1901 Federation Celebrations', *The New Federalist: The Journal of Australian Federation History* no. 6 (December 2000): 46–8.

47. Heather Streets, *Martial Races: The Military, Race and Masculinity in British Imperial Culture, 1857–1914* (Manchester: Manchester University Press, 2004), pp. 142–3.
48. Streets, *Martial Races,* pp. 162–7.
49. Streets, *Martial Races,* pp. 94–5.
50. Streets, *Martial Races,* p. 100.
51. Streets, *Martial Races,* p. 10.
52. Waterson, 'Above and Behind the Arches', p. 45.
53. 'Assault-at-Arms: The Town Hall Crowded', *The Sydney Morning Herald,* 10 January 1901, p. 5.
54. Ballantyne, *Orientalism and Race: Aryanism in the British Empire* (Houndmills, Basingstoke: Palgrave, 2002), chapter 2 and pp. 167–8.
55. S.R. Worthy, 'A Martial Race? Maori and Pakeha New Zealand Soldiers of the Great War in Imperial Context', unpublished paper presented at the British World Conference, University of Calgary, July 10–12, 2003. Cited here with kind permission of the author.
56. Tammy M. Proctor, *On My Honour: Guides and Scouts in Interwar Britain* (Philadelphia, PA: American Philosophical Society, 2002), p. 16.
57. Allen Warren, 'Popular Manliness: Baden-Powell, Scouting and the Development of Manly Character', in J.A. Mangan and James Walvin (eds), *Manliness and Morality: Middle-Class Masculinity in Britain and America 1800–1940* (Manchester: Manchester University Press, 1987), pp. 201–2.
58. Proctor, *On My Honour,* pp. 14–16.
59. R.W. Connell, *Masculinities* (Berkeley: University of California Press, 1995), pp. 185–6.
60. Philippa Levine, 'Battle Colors: Race, Sex, and Colonial Soldiery in World War I', *Journal of Women's History* vol. 9, no 4 (1998): 105.
61. Suzanne Brugger, *Australians and Egypt 1914–1919* (Carlton, Vic.: Melbourne University Press, 1980), pp. 42–3.

4
Gender and Everyday Life under Colonial Regimes

The power relations of imperialism were negotiated not only through dramatic episodes such as war, but importantly through the quotidian practices and customs of creole and colonial societies. A close focus on a range of aspects of everyday life can help identify the shifting dynamics among British rulers, colonizing settlers and indigenous people, the dynamics that shaped the overarching histories of British colonialism. Gender identities, masculinities and femininities, constituted one axis through which colonial regimes established their legitimacy, and through which colonized subjects accommodated new realities, forged new cultural practices and resisted the subordination of colonialism. For men, the evolving and pervasive passion for sport was an arena in which the politics of colonialism were played out overtly, where the colonized or colonials could hope at least symbolically to defeat their imperial superiors. Workplace relations, such as engineering construction sites and the finely calibrated hierarchies of colonial bureaucracies, were another arena in which racialized notions of masculinity were delineated.

Interracial sexuality was a messy and blurred liminal area in which gender relations were shaped in the most intimate and telling ways – across racial boundaries as well as within and across class divisions. The household and domestic labour comprised a crucial site for racial hierarchies, even after the legal ending of slavery. Colonized women and men obeyed the orders of, and performed menial tasks for, European mistresses and masters, and in so doing were vulnerable to abuse and assault, even as they were privy to their supposed superiors' most intimate lives. British missionaries, teachers and doctors sought to instil European notions and practices of femininity in colonized women, at least at times regardless of the respective practicalities of local versus European womanly behaviour. This chapter looks at the body and the household as crucial sites of gender contestation across the empire, showing just how commonplace and ubiquitous were the daily intersections of gender and colonialism.

Sport

C.L.R. James, an African-Caribbean writer, cultural critic and political theorist born in Trinidad at the beginning of the twentieth century, helps us to understand the intertwined histories of cricket, Britishness and colonialism. An author both of fiction and history, a political activist and interpreter of West Indian history and culture, James chose to structure his 1963 autobiography *Beyond a Boundary* around cricket. Recalling how he watched local cricket matches from a bedroom window as a young child, his lifelong passion for the sport emanates from the pages. He remembers cricketing stars from his neighbourhood, even their individual best shots, and remembers that when his father gave him a bat and ball at age four 'never afterwards was I without them both for long'.[1] His voracious reading included everything he could find on imperial cricketing legends W.G. Grace, of Australia, and Ranjitsinhji, of India. The thrill of cricket so shaped his life that, when he won a place at the secondary school Queen's Royal College in Port of Spain, a battle began between his desire to play and his duty to keep up his schoolwork. No matter how his parents urged him to get home to study, he couldn't resist one more over. The English public-school moral values encoded in cricket were lessons that he and his schoolmates absorbed so thoroughly that 'Eton and Harrow had nothing on us'. In contrast to their recalcitrance in the classroom, on the playing field discipline and good behaviour were serious business.

> We were a motley crew. The children of some white officials and white business men, middle-class blacks and mulattos, Chinese boys, some of whose parents still spoke broken English, Indian boys, some of whose parents could speak no English at all, and some poor black boys who had won exhibitions or whose parents had starved and toiled on plots of agricultural land and were spending their hard-earned money on giving the eldest boy an education. Yet rapidly we learned to obey the umpire's decision without question, however irrational it was. We learned to play with the team, which meant subordinating your personal inclinations, and even interests, to the good of the whole. We kept a stiff upper lip in that we did not complain about ill-fortune. We did not denounce failures, but 'Well tried' or 'Hard luck' came easily to our lips. We were generous to opponents and congratulated them on victories, even when we knew they did not deserve it.[2]

As several critics have pointed out, while James had a sharp political analysis of racism, colonialism and political economy, when it came to cricket his passion dulled his critical edge. Thus, rather than see cricket itself, the game and its moral code, as a vehicle for colonialism, he blames instead the white authorities of the game who presided over its racial hierarchies. As Helen Tiffin argues, James's commitment to cricket as an art form allows him only to see it as a level playing field where the West Indian could demonstrate his own abilities; he does not interrogate the cultural meanings of the game within colonialism, or 'ever really extricate the Caribbean reality from the English ideal'.[3]

The striking volume of scholarly writing on cricket – certainly more than on any other particular sport except perhaps hunting – has compelled us to consider the historical interconnections among British colonialism, the demise of the empire and the evolution of cricket as a global sport dominated by the British Commonwealth nations. Dominic Malcolm notes that not only did an *Imperial* Cricket Conference form in 1909 at much the same time as other sports were forming *international* governing bodies, at the beginning of the twenty-first century cricket continues to be dominated by Britain and its former colonies, including the West Indies, Pakistan, India, Sri Lanka, Australia, South Africa, Zimbabwe and New Zealand.[4] We can study the history of cricket for insight into the contradictory dynamics of decolonization. Although there is a belief in British popular culture that sport has become open to all Britons regardless of colour, Malcolm documents a historical stacking of African-Caribbean players in the role of bowler, considered a less decisive role than that of batsman, a pattern of racial stacking that he argues was shaped by an older pattern of class hierarchies in the sport.[5] C.L.R. James believed that the 1961 West Indian cricket tour of Australia, in which a victorious West Indian team, captained by a black man Frank Worrell, was given an emotional farewell by a huge crowd in the streets of Melbourne, showed that West Indians were finally accepted as equals by white colonials.[6] Other commentators, however, note the historical continuation of colonial and racial tensions. In 1934 great hostility erupted between Australia and Britain over the 'Bodyline' bowling of the visiting English team, while in the mid-1990s Australian complaints about both the bowling and the batting by a visiting Sri Lankan team led to international media recriminations, subsequent to which the Australians cancelled a planned return tour to Sri Lanka.[7] Moreover, as various scholars point out, cricket clubs from the nineteenth century onwards reified divisions within colonies, with their memberships often defined by class, caste, 'race', ethnicity or religion.

Both Simon Gikandi and Arjun Appadurai argue that in the last decades of the twentieth century the decolonization of cricket has gone well beyond the victories over Britain by teams from former colonies: rather, the most crucial evolution has been the changed nature of cricket itself, such that cricketing practices originated by former-colonial teams (such as the fast bowling that became a powerful weapon of West Indian teams in the 1980s) have altered the game even in Britain, and thus, given cricket's iconic place in national culture, the very terms of Britishness.[8] Appadurai shows the ways in which, at the end of the twentieth century, cricket became a sport with a mass following in India, including magazines and media broadcasts in multiple vernacular languages, a corporate economic base, and a site of celebrity rivalled only by Bollywood films, with so much national passion attached that games against Pakistan are sublimations of international hostilities.[9] No longer a vehicle for teaching English 'civilisation' to Indians, cricket has been thoroughly rendered indigenous.

Within this corpus of scholarship on cricket, only a small amount of analytical attention has been paid to the obvious issue of gender. When C.L.R. James was growing up, learning cricket and the public-school sporting ethos in the West Indies of the 1910s, he was steeped in the codes of English masculinity. Aware of class privilege and racial subordination, he seems unaware of his privileges as a bright black West Indian boy, rather than a bright black West Indian girl. The playing-field moral codes that he and his racially mixed schoolmates learnt were shaped by expectations that they would have influential careers, mix in the public world of the British Empire, and operate according to the masculine values of the sporting chance and the stiff upper lip. Their homosocial world, including the imperial boys' adventure stories that he read (not least G.A. Henty), stressed the importance of male social bonding, and among James's most poignant memories are the bonds he formed, albeit temporarily, with white boys, often through cricket. The pride of place that cricket has occupied in imperial culture, even as it has driven and reflected processes of decolonization, has been directly linked to its status as a ubiquitous and definitive pastime of boys and men. The boys around the empire who learned to pick up a cricket bat, to appreciate the crack of the bat on the ball, the values of subtlety and endurance of the game, were all imbibing gendered behavioural codes, in an atmosphere that excluded girls and in which women (or servants) were restricted to making the afternoon tea. Because of the casual and inclusive nature with which neighbourhood cricket is played in many former colonies, the bodily experience of cricket is one with which a huge number of men can identify. As Sevendrini Perera contends, 'along with the embodied practice of cricket, the colonized imbibed a particular style of English masculinity, one that also underwrote assumptions of future self-government and "national" status'.[10] On a daily basis, colonial boys, despite racial subordination, were learning the rudiments of imperial culture and values in a form that would equip them to contend for imperial citizenship. Cricket's overt role of gendering has continued from the lessons of the nineteenth-century school playing field to the present: in 1995 when the Australian team cancelled their return tour to Sri Lanka, the Sri Lankan foreign minister called them 'sissies'.[11] Appadurai points out that, in contrast to men, for Indian women cricket is a sport twice removed, for their roles as spectators – often via television – means they are usually watching men watching other men play.[12]

The white-settler dominion that has not celebrated cricket is Canada, presumably because of its climate. Yet there too sport and masculinity have been intertwined with the history of colonialism. Gillian Poulter contends that sport was a central means through which British Canadians established their cultural identities and practices in the mid-nineteenth century, in the formative political decades following the Durham Report, as Britain sought to assert itself culturally over French Canada, and Canadians sought to achieve Responsible Government. Asserting their cultural hegemony in an overtly gendered fashion, British Canadian men used sport as a demonstration of their physical prowess and imagined cultural superiority. Poulter demonstrates that British Canadian men adapted three indigenous practices and formed their own sporting codes and clubs. In the middle decades of the century snowshoeing, lacrosse (based on an indigenous game called *baggataway*) and tobogganing were all adopted from Native American practices, and carefully turned into sporting pastimes emblematic of Canadian vigour and manly embrace of their cold environment. Snowshoeing and lacrosse particularly became vehicles for Canadian middle-class masculinity, with elaborate customs, uniforms and codes that sought to show the superiority of the Europeans even as they acknowledged the sports' indigenous roots. Lacrosse, for example, was held to demonstrate European men's greater tactical skills, in contrast to the imagined primitive, wildness of Native Americans, who were handicapped in playing against Europeans by the latter's development of their own rules.[13] In Canada too, like hunting, organized sports became a popular site for the elaboration and demonstration of manly behaviour, which itself framed the political contests of colonialism.

Engineering and construction

In the nineteenth and twentieth centuries, European colonies were central sites of global modernity, places where the technology and science often considered hallmarks of the modern were most dramatically staged. The impressively rapid construction of colonial infrastructures in many diverse locations – mapping the land, and the building of cities, ports, bridges, roads, railroads and telegraph lines, in short time spans – seemed to many to exemplify the modern and at once to justify and demonstrate European superordination, even as they obliterated indigenous landscapes. Yet the massive engineering and construction work that produced these feats of industrial technology was a collaboration of British and other European supervisors and workers, and indigenous, convict or indentured lower-level supervisors and labourers. Men, of course, vastly outnumbered women participants in these projects, such that engineering and construction sites were a crucible for the negotiation of colonial masculinities. Race, nationality, class, education, technical, logistic and administrative skills, and physical strength were all in play in shaping the hierarchies of masculinity and authority on construction sites that could involve thousands and go on for years. In the intimate and extended interactions of working on such projects, creole notions of gender were hammered out, even as relationships mediated the categories on which they were based. Engineers, supervisors and labourers on the vast stretches of roads and railroads, the huge bridge-building projects, the telegraph lines, the digging and working of mines, and the building sites in towns and cities, judged each other by varying measures of manliness.

Rudyard Kipling painted an evocative and detailed picture of hierarchies and relationships on a colonial construction site in his 1919 Indian story 'The Bridge-Builders'. Notions of manliness, as well as race, the authority of the colonizer, and class are all central to Kipling's story of the climax of a three-year project to build a bridge over the River Ganges. The bridge is a mile and three-quarters long, a lattice-girder truss bridge standing on twenty-seven brick piers; moreover, the project includes three miles of stone embankment on both sides of the river in each direction. Each pier is twenty-four feet in diameter, and is sunk eighty feet below the riverbed. The bridge has two levels, one a railway-line, and above it a road and footpaths. At each end of the bridge stands a massive brick tower designed also as a gun battery. In short, it is an enormous project that has involved thousands of workers, numbers of whom have died on the job. There are three key protagonists, including Findlayson, the Chief Engineer who believes the bridge will bring him senior promotion within the public works department, and his young engineering assistant Hitchcock, whose career the bridge has supposedly assured. Their most valued subordinate is Peroo, from a coastal town north of Bombay, a lascar with years of experience in the merchant marine, which had taken him as far away as the Australian colonies and London. Having given up the sea for inland construction, Peroo is held in high esteem by his British supervisors because of his technical skills learnt as a sailor. 'For his knowledge of tackle and the handling of heavy weights, Peroo was worth almost any price he might have chosen to put upon his services; but custom decreed the wage of the overhead men, and Peroo was not within many silver pieces of his proper value. ... No piece of iron was so big or so badly placed that Peroo could not devise a tackle to lift it – a loose-ended, sagging arrangement, rigged with a scandalous amount of talking, but perfectly equal to the work in hand. It was Peroo who had saved the girder of Number Seven pier from destruction when the new wire rope jammed in the eye of the crane.'[14]

Through his manly engineering skills, Peroo has earned the trust and respect of his supervisors, in specific contradistinction to nearly all the other workers. Kipling details Findlayson's view of the hierarchy beneath him, a hierarchy in which masculinity, generation and race are all crucial: 'the burden of the work had fallen altogether on Findlayson and his assistant [Hitchcock], the young man whom he had chosen because of his rawness to break to his own needs. There were labour contractors by the half-hundred – fitters and riveters, European, borrowed from the railway workshops, with, perhaps, twenty white and half-caste subordinates to direct, under direction, the bevies of workmen – but none knew better than these two, who trusted each other, how the under-lings were not to be trusted.'[15] In this worksite hierarchy, trust correlates with race, but it is also linked to skill.

The tale's plot consists of a pitched battle between European civilization as represented by engineering technology (the bridge), on the one hand, and nature which is linked to traditional Indian culture, on the other. When 'Mother Gunga' floods two months ahead of the season and threatens the not-yet-complete bridge, the alliance between Findlayson and Peroo to defend the bridge suggests that intelligent (and manly) Indians are capable of turning their backs on tradition and superstition and embracing 'progress'. Interestingly, in their long and taxing vigil, Peroo convinces Findlayson to take some opium to sustain him. The two men then share what is either a mystical experience or a hallucination, in which they eavesdrop on a conversation among the Hindu gods. It is Hanuman who explains to the other assembled deities that the people have seen Western civilization and progress and are turning from the old ways. 'You should have slain at the beginning when the men from across the water had taught our folk nothing. Now my people see their work, and go away thinking. They do not think of the Heavenly Ones altogether. They think of the fire-carriage and the other things that the bridge-builders have done, and when your priests thrust forward hands asking alms, they give a little unwillingly. That is the beginning.'[16] At the end of the story, with the bridge having withstood the flood, Peroo turns against his religion. The astute Indian, Kipling suggests, can see the way of the future, and it consists of European technology. In their manly shared commitment to the bridge, the lower-class Indian and the British engineer had joined forces.

Relations across racial barriers in the colonial service take on a more tragic aspect in Joyce Cary's 1939 novel *Mister Johnson*, based on Cary's experience in Nigeria in the 1910s. In this story too, an engineering project is central, this time the building of a road from the bush town of Fada to connect with the main road running through this remote area of Nigeria. Building the road becomes the shared passion of the two main characters, District Officer Rudbeck, and his mission-educated African clerk Mister Johnson. As Rudbeck predicts, the road greatly enhances trade to and from Fada and boosts movement within and the economy of the local region. The story is essentially that of the impossible position of an African trying to make it in the highly bureaucratic colonial service. Mister Johnson, with his mission education, his good English, and his Western clothes, believes himself to be a gentleman and of superior station to the local Fada people, who are ethnically different from himself. He speaks of England as 'home', wears white suits, patent leather shoes, and other items he associates with an English gentleman, and pretends to know England and English culture well. Ironically, in contrast to the working-class English storekeeper who viciously beats his African mistress, Johnson refuses such behaviour because 'in England ... we do not beat our wives'.[17]

Despite Johnson's pretension and fantasy, it is not these characteristics that distinguish him from his superior Rudbeck, so much as the difference in their racially determined stations. Rudbeck too is a dreamer, happiest when absorbed in his road-building project and therefore able to ignore the more prosaic demands of his job. Cary paints Rudbeck as something of a buffoon, unaware of people and events around him, and whose basic good nature leads him to wonder about colonialism's effects on Africans briefly before putting the subject out of his mind. Together they falsify their accounts in order to use more money for the road than has been allotted, so that they can build it as far as the main road. Johnson, dismissed for his first efforts at cheating the accounts, becomes Rudbeck's main assistant on the road, where his efforts at finding labour – he alone understands how to motivate the local labourers – and raising funds enable its completion. Again, after it is built, he is dismissed for his creative accounting. Each time Rudbeck has chosen to ignore the budgetary falsifying going on under his nose and lets Johnson take the fall. When Johnson, desperate for cash to salvage his self-respect, robs the store, is caught in the act by the storekeeper and murders him, it becomes Rudbeck's responsibility to oversee his execution. Rudbeck's final act towards Johnson is the kindness of, at Johnson's request, shooting him instead of the regulation hanging. Johnson and Rudbeck are tied together not only by the road, but by their whimsical natures, and to some extent by a shared sense of honour. Thus while Rudbeck, in contrast to other more clever and ambitious district officers, seems to be a kind of bumbling and fairly decent English gentleman, the tragically unrealistic Johnson suggests the impossibility for an African of negotiating manly success within the colonial service. Unlike the masculine bonding through technical skill of Findlayson and Peroo in Kipling's story, Rudbeck and Johnson are to some extent both failures as men, neither of them fitted for the demands of the colonial bureaucracy, despite their joint success at building the road.[18]

Politics and the colonial civil service

In India too everyday interactions in the colonial service and the arena of politics were an important context for the construction of masculinities, especially the oppositional categories of the 'sahib' and the 'babu'. The gentlemanly authority of the sahib, as E.M. Collingham has shown, emanated in multiple ways from his body. Collingham argues that after 1853 when the Indian Civil Service was opened to competition by examination, and thus no longer filled by sinecure, British anxieties about the calibre of men in the ICS came to focus on particular bodily qualities. Especially after 1857, when India was brought under direct imperial control and its administration reformed and elaborated, civil servants needed to behave in expected ways because they were seen as representing the Raj. No longer comprised only of the upper classes or men from the top British public schools, civil servants' physical and sporting prowess had to be demonstrated rather than assumed. Only by being muscular, fit and skilled on the playing and hunting fields could the sahib assure others of his self-discipline and his fitness to rule. These benchmarks of masculinity were set in part by the prejudice and habits of the upper classes, who regarded those who entered the ICS through examination as likely to be weak and crude products of the middling and lower orders. To prove themselves, civil servants strove to dress according to the proper colonial code, participated in sports such as polo and tennis, and fostered the late-nineteenth- and early-twentieth-century cult of big game hunting. Big game hunting, previously considered a sport of the aristocracy and gentry, was a venue in which middle-class civil servants acted out their masculinity in the jungle and through the skins they used as rugs and the heads they hung as trophies on their walls. The masculinity of the sahib was displayed in ceremonies such as the durbars which became increasingly theatrical stagings of British power. While civil servants learnt to conduct themselves in an imperious manner befitting their gentlemanly authority and British prestige, their status was also enacted around their body by the numerous servants who attended to their every need at home and on tour, including the servants who bathed and dressed them.[19]

Although there was a finely graded hierarchy within the British ranks of the Raj, such that some men clearly outranked others and by no means were all Englishmen in India considered 'gentlemen', the sahib and English gentleman had a definitional opposite. As Mrinalini Sinha has argued, the 'effeminate Bengali *babu*' was a historically specific product, a racially constructed stereotype that the British articulated in the latter nineteenth century at much the same time that the idea of the sahib gained importance. The category of the Bengali *babu* was comprised of well-educated, middle-class Hindus who formed a politically conscious group, and from whom the nationalist movement emerged in the last decades of the nineteenth century. Especially because of their elite position in indigenous society, their status as professionals and intellectuals, and their oppositional role in colonial politics, the British sought to denigrate this class of Bengali men in specific and detailed gendered ways – although the plasticity of colonial discourse meant that other Indian men could be included in the slur. Colonial discourse in the late nineteenth century represented elite Bengali men as effeminate, cowardly, weak, passive, soft, enervated, stunted, sensual, feeble, sedentary and languid, in short the opposite of both the martial Indian races such as the Sikhs, and of virile British gentlemen. The political ramifications of this historically specific gendered construct included the resonances and resolution of specific legislative issues. An example is the controversy surrounding the Ilbert Bill in 1883–84.

The bill proposed to give certain Indian officials in the administrative service criminal jurisdiction over Europeans living in country towns in India. Intended as a way of controlling European exploitation of Indian labour in rural areas, the bill was greeted with outrage on the part of Anglo-Indians. The protest against the bill was gendered through its purposeful discursive focus on issues surrounding British women: the horrific spectre of an Englishwoman being subjected to the authority of a native magistrate – particularly in cases involving rape or marital issues – was whipped up against the bill. Moreover, debate on the issue of racial equality itself was displaced to a debate surrounding the fitness of Indian officials, especially Bengalis, to carry out these authoritative duties. Thus the alleged effeminacy of elite Bengali men was invoked to support protests against the bill, in an equation of manliness with objectivity and fitness for authority. Opponents of the bill manipulated notions of British manliness against its supporters, accusing them of failing to protect English womanhood, considered a central responsibility of true manhood. Colonially derived notions of masculinity thus directly affected the shaping of colonial policy, and reverberated in debates over gender in the metropole.[20]

Sexuality and prostitution

A key arena, of course, for the construction of masculinities and relations between men was that of sexuality, a complex and fraught part of everyday life in colonial societies. Debate among historians over sexuality as a component of the whole empire has been framed in part by Ronald Hyam. In the 1980s Hyam suggested that it was high time for historians of the British Empire to consider sex seriously because, he argued, it had operated as a driving force. Sexual desires and energy had fuelled imperial expansion, as British men found greater sexual opportunities in the colonies than at home. Britons in the colonies engaged in sex so commonly, and found exotic sexual partners so attractive, that sex became an incentive for colonial service and a consolation for its hardships and deprivations. The high incidence of prostitution in the colonies especially in the late nineteenth and early twentieth centuries was directly linked to the high rates of venereal disease, not least among British military forces. Sexual liberties flourished particularly in plantation societies and on the frontiers of the white settler colonies.[21] While Hyam's recognition of sexuality as an important topic was useful, as many historians have argued, the problem with his approach is that it is written from the perspective of the privileged white male colonizer, and thus sees sex only as a question of engaging in gratification or not. Mark T. Berger has outlined the shortcomings of Hyam's work succinctly, noting that he fails to analyse power relations under colonialism, does not understand the operation of gender, ignores racism, and calls 'sexual opportunity' what often ought to be regarded as sexual exploitation and rape. In particular, Hyam turns a blind eye to the economic and social structures that underlay prostitution in colonial societies.[22]

An important contribution of Hyam's work, despite its analytical weaknesses, was his discussion of male homosexuality in British colonies. Hyam drew attention to the significant incidence of British colonial officials engaging in sex with boys and men (European and indigenous), the homoeroticism of some male relationships in colonial settings, the practice of homosexuality in the Australian convict colonies and other situations where colonialism forced men to congregate without women, and the existence of male brothels in various sites.[23] It was some time after Hyam's controversial work before more nuanced studies of colonial homosexuality emerged, but we are now beginning to apprehend not only its ubiquity but its complex interlinkings with other aspects of British imperial culture. Christopher Lane and Robert Aldrich have both argued that homosexuality was not simply a matter of pleasure or gratification, but was also linked to colonial failures and fantasies, expansionist impulses, cultural and national disunity, repression and alienation.[24] Aldrich proffers compelling cameos of famous imperial heroes, such as Cecil Rhodes and Lawrence of Arabia. Rhodes's penchant for attractive young male assistants, and in particular his highly romantic multi-year relationship with Neville Pickering, secretary of his De Beers Company, renders the ambitious imperialist as a complicated and sometimes sentimental man.[25] T.E. Lawrence, who had repressed his sexuality in England, found the Arabian deserts a sensual environment in which his appreciation for physicality and his own emotions developed, even though he remained repressed his whole life, to the extent that late in life he engaged in masochistic flagellation in order to achieve ejaculation. Aldrich reveals how Lawrence's political goals in Arabia were inextricably intertwined with his personal emotions, specifically his love affair with a young Arab man, Selim Ahmed also known as Dahoum, whom Lawrence met in 1911 when the latter was fourteen. The relationship between the two developed on journeys in the Middle East and to Britain, but during the First World War while Lawrence was posted to Cairo, Dahoum died at the Carchemish archaeological site where Lawrence had worked. Aldrich argues convincingly that the romantic and erotic poem, with which Lawrence dedicated his magnum opus *The Seven Pillars of Wisdom* to Dahoum, shows the extent to which Lawrence's efforts to free the Arabs from Ottoman control were driven by his own personal passion, and were for him marked by failure because of his lost love.[26]

If we are beginning to understand the extent of homoerotic and homosexual inclinations among significant numbers of the imperial pantheon, we are still learning how extensive homosexual relations were among the less well known, and to what extent they shaped imperial culture. We know from Matt Houlbrook's intriguing and culturally rich work on the subculture of homosexuality among guardsmen in twentieth-century London that, at the heart of the empire, homosexuality was linked to military men whose brigades served overseas. Houlbrook's research in court records, newspapers and other printed sources reveals how the figure of the large and hypermasculine guardsman became an icon of gay culture. In multiple parts of London guardsmen engaged in a widespread practice as 'rent boys' selling sex to gay men often richer and more privileged than they. This pervasive sexual culture practised by the guardsmen included long-term relationships, and the sexualities that coalesced here were multivalent. Challenging some of the categories of previous gay history, Houlbrook shows that guardsmen who rented their bodies for extra cash often claimed to enjoy the sex itself despite their own basic heterosexuality. Some were very mercenary, beat their clients violently and robbed them, or used blackmail to end longer affairs and maximize their take. Because the figure of the imagined heroic and handsome guardsman was widely considered an icon of public and tourist London, the homosexual culture for which they were also known was a subversive element in popular culture, one that undercut mainstream notions of national and imperial masculinities.[27] This rich recent work on male homosexuality and its imperial meanings exposes just how much we have yet to learn about homosexuality among women under British colonialism, beyond the enormous anxiety registered by officials about the lesbianism practised by convict women in early colonial Australia.

It has been famously alleged, by historians as well as other commentators, that British women were the undoing of the Empire because their arrival in particular colonies in significant numbers ended a golden age of interracial sex, and heralded instead exclusive racial hierarchies and social and sexual barriers that then led to anti-colonial resentment. Feminist historians of the empire have resoundingly refuted this simple story, pointing out that it obscures changes within colonial societies that occurred anyway, and arguing that it is a sexist attribution of blame that ignores European women's real contributions to the colonial enterprise.[28] One problem with the myth of the interracial sexual golden age is that it implies that European men's early colonial cohabitation with women was some kind of idyllic and stable situation, free of racial tensions and resentments, and a good arrangement for the women. Evidence suggests otherwise. George Orwell drew a searing portrait of the relationship between a colonial merchant and his indigenous mistress in his 1934 novel *Burmese Days*, based on his years in the imperial police force in Burma. Flory, an English timber merchant and longterm resident of the small northern outpost Kyauktada, has a stable but tense relationship with his local mistress Ma Hla May, whom he bought from her parents for three hundred rupees. He instructs her in particular intimate habits, and has regular sex with her despite his own misgivings about the morality of the relationship and lack of real feelings for her. Her position in his household is ambiguous because she shares power with Flory's manservant Ko S'la, who resents her deeply, and whose younger brother is her real lover. Despite this latter relationship, Ma Hla May enjoys her status as Flory's mistress, the clothes and jewellery he buys her, and tells her parents and village that she is a white man's wife. As soon as an attractive young and single Englishwoman, Elizabeth, arrives in Kyauktada, Flory instantly and unceremoniously dismisses Ma Hla May. Although having an indigenous mistress was standard practice for a bachelor in that part of the Raj, he rightly fears that Elizabeth will be put off by such an arrangement. Flory barely manages to overcome Elizabeth's misgivings on this and other counts, and is near winning her hand, when Ma Hla May presents herself in church in front of the entire British community and denounces Flory for throwing her out and reducing her to starvation. In consequence, Elizabeth rejects him, after which Flory shoots himself. Colonial concubinage, Orwell suggests, failed to make European men happy and was an economic and social arrangement of practicality for indigenous women. If the arrival of the Englishwoman disrupted the situation, it was because Flory had always wanted a relationship far more satisfying than the one he had with his mistress, who herself had never loved him.[29]

Sexual relationships across racial barriers in the white-settler colonies of the empire need to be seen on a spectrum running from marriage, through concubinage, to prostitution and ultimately rape. Arguably, the spectrum should be viewed as a loop, with evidence that women's experiences ran in both directions. For indigenous women, relationships with colonizing men have been fraught and precarious, commonly involving abuse and exploitation, but also survival, children, and occasionally, the possibility of emotional support. First Nations women in mid- to late-nineteenth-century British Columbia widely entered into concubinage and marriage with the European men who arrived to participate in the fur trade, the gold rush and other mining and commercial ventures as this new colony rapidly developed. As Adele Perry has argued, these were not simply interracial relationships, they were deeply gendered, with the vast majority of the Europeans being men, and most of the indigenous people in the mushrooming urban areas, particularly the capital Victoria, being women. The cultural perceptions that grew around these relationships, in Ottawa and London as well as British Columbia itself, constituted a highly gendered discourse in which British and other white men succumbed to the temptations and vice associated with shameless and lustful indigenous women. First Nations women were seen as primitive, close to nature, dirty, licentious and difficult to control, in quite specific ways the definitional opposites of respectable white women. While indigenous women were thought to be the sources of evil and temptation in these backwoods of the world, white men were held to be seduced and degraded by the women, not the other way around. For First Nations women, stereotypes of sexualization and depravity meant that they were particular targets of missionary evangelism as well as official control. But these essentialist conceptions were used to justify abandonment by their white 'husbands', and worse, domestic violence, and rape. They also underlay worries about the potential of the colony itself and specifically the capabilities and potential of mixed-race children.[30]

Much of the worry surrounding interracial sexual relationships in the Canadian Pacific colony was over prostitution. In this rapidly changing, turbulent frontier society where there were very few European women, indigenous women traded sex for money and goods in a variety of exchanges. In some places, solicitation was open and direct. Somewhat less direct were the dance halls where miners drank and cavorted with indigenous women, places that missionaries and others condemned in strong terms. On a longer-term basis, European men sometimes used material goods as inducements for concubinage, a bartering that moralists decried but that was not totally dissimilar to traditional indigenous arranged marriages that included the payment of goods to the woman's family. Missionaries and others who condemned material inducements to concubinage denied First Nations women's agency and ability to make choices for their own lives. If interracial unions did not always last very long, some did, even in defiance of attempts by missionaries, government officials, and First Nations men to make women return to their communities and reserves. Jean Barman argues that there was a patriarchal alliance between these three disparate sets of men, that aimed to control indigenous women's sexuality and lives by forcing them to abandon interracial unions in favour of sanctioned and Christianized marriages with indigenous men. The existence of this alliance suggests that colonialism drove a gendered wedge between indigenous women and men, in which women's economic options became defined through sexuality, in a moral discourse with which colonized and colonizing men sought to contain them.[31]

Ann McGrath's pioneering work on Australian Aborigines in the pastoral and mining areas of the Northern Territory in the early to mid-twentieth century reveals the pervasiveness and complexities of cross-racial sex and relationships. McGrath shows how difficult it is to separate concubinage from prostitution, and prostitution from rape. Aboriginal groups and families used European men's demands for access to their women as a survival strategy; women were bartered for money, food and goods. Such negotiations could be for one sex act, or they could be for living arrangements of weeks, months or even longer. Scholars have debated whether Aboriginal women had any agency in this process, or whether they were exploited by their men. As McGrath demonstrates, this is not easy to decide, because there is contradictory evidence, including some evidence that women found sexual gratification, economic survival and perhaps even emotional satisfaction in these arrangements. Respectable European society regarded such relationships as morally degenerate and men who engaged in them as social outcasts, yet their very pervasiveness fed the taboo. Aboriginal women suffered from the moral and eugenicist lines drawn against interracial relationships, because they were unable to attain social respectability and their illicit status aggravated men's emotional and physical abuse. It was, as McGrath shows, also difficult for the men, not least those who established a long-term family but had to accept their social isolation. This creole society soon developed its peculiar hierarchies, including the ambiguous status of 'half-castes'; 'half-caste' men had some of the same sexual prerogatives as European men. It was a violent culture, in which prostitution easily blended with rape.[32] And, as we now know, it became part of the context for the Stolen Generations, the removal of children from Aboriginal mothers in order to be raised and thus 'assimilated' in white society.

In most of Australia, especially in the north from the mid-nineteenth century onwards, ethnic diversity went beyond black and white, as Chinese, Afghan and Japanese men sought economic opportunities, and Pacific Islanders were kidnapped as labourers for the sugar industry. Interracial relationships included this broad diversity, from Aboriginal women working as prostitutes for Japanese pearlers in Broome, to European women marrying Chinese men in eastern Australia. Rae Frances, in her concise history of prostitution in Australia, points towards the changing intersections of race, class and sexuality, particularly changing attitudes towards non-Anglo-Saxon prostitutes. In colonial Queensland, authorities welcomed Japanese prostitutes because they supposedly averted the racial horrors of nonwhite men being sexually serviced by white women. And in Western Australia, Japanese, French and Italian prostitutes also helped preserve the fiction of a pure white nation secure from racial contamination. In the twentieth century, however, attitudes shifted, and authorities deployed the dictation test barrier of the Immigration Restriction Act to keep out prostitutes, men linked to the sex trade, and others considered sexually dubious such as those suspected of homosexuality.[33]

Philippa Levine's large-scale study of prostitution and the regulation of venereal disease in four British colonies helps to place Australia within the broader empire. Levine compares Queensland with the Straits Settlements (Singapore, Penang and Malacca), Hong Kong, and British India, in the latter-nineteenth and early-twentieth centuries. She shows that the regulation of prostitution was a central technology of imperial rule, linking domestic Britain with its colonies in a rapid global wave of legislation and regulation from the 1860s to the 1880s. Medicalized Orientalist notions of sexuality and hygiene shaped structures of public order, as well as hierarchies of gender and race. Victoria and Tasmania also had Contagious Diseases ordinances, but Levine has chosen to focus on Queensland in her comparative analysis. Racial assumptions overlapped between Queensland, a settler colony with responsible government by 1859, and the three crown colonies in Asia. The ethnicities of women working in the Queensland sex trade included European, Aboriginal, Islander, Japanese and Chinese; some, of course, were of mixed heritage. The data collected by colonial officials, and used to determine policy regarding prostitutes and lock hospitals, created racial categories and imposed them on women's bodies and lives. But in critical ways Queensland was different from the Asian colonies. Aboriginal women prostitutes were excluded from the purview of the Contagious Diseases act, falling instead under the authority of the protector. The Queensland Contagious Diseases Act was more like the domestic British legislation in its supposed aim of redeeming prostitutes, yet it sought to protect the colonial civilian population from the threat of disease prostitutes were seen to represent.

In the crown colonies as in the English port areas under contagious diseases (CD) surveillance, soldiers and sailors, their health and efficiency, were the primary objects of regulatory measures, although it was women who were controlled.[34] In the composite colony of the Straits Settlements, women in the sex trade were mostly migrants from poor areas of China and Japan, servicing a population of men who outnumbered them by around ten to one. The men were a largely migrant population too, drawn from China, India and elsewhere to work in the tin mines, agriculture and the ports of the Straits. In the late-nineteenth century, Singapore in particular became a very valuable port for the British, strategically located as it was at the hub of Asian shipping lanes. Its development was tied to the growth of rubber, tin and other plantation commodities on the Malay peninsula.[35] The demand for labour in Singapore included the rapid construction of buildings, roads and railroads, and the expansion of warehouses and commercial institutions linked to the busy port. Jim Warren has made the good point that the peasant Japanese and Chinese women who migrated to Singapore and became prostitutes should be seen as migrant labourers, just like the peasant men who became 'coolies', rather than as 'fallen women'. Part of the accelerating modernity that transformed colonial Southeast and East Asia, they too comprised the social fabric of Singapore's dense working-class neighbourhoods. Oral history research has shown that some Japanese women survived their hard times in Singapore and returned to rural Japan later in life. While women and men both worked hard, and suffered from the venereal disease that became epidemic among Singapore's Chinese community at the end of the century, women in the sex trade suffered from the exploitation of brothel keepers as well as from the system of medical inspection and treatment.[36]

In the context of British colonialism in Africa, Luise White has shown that the twentieth-century evolution of prostitution in Nairobi was a shifting product of women and men's negotiations amidst economic change produced by colonial capitalism, migrant labour and urbanization, all aspects of colonial modernity. From the 1890s, British colonization disrupted East African marriage systems and an economy based on cattle-owning and agriculture. In the early-twentieth century, within the new context of migrant labour, women turned to prostitution as a survival strategy, and as a means of capital accumulation that would enable them to buy property; thus they became Nairobi's first year-round residents. Evolving in response to imperial wars, colonial state policies, and economic change, prostitution expanded and took on different forms. White argues convincingly that women who engaged in prostitution served to reproduce the labour force by sustaining male workers in ways that the colonial state could not. At the same time, they made money both through prostitution and as landlords, made choices about family and households, and established areas of social autonomy beyond the limits of colonial control.[37]

Concubinage and prostitution were ubiquitous aspects of colonialism, itself a core part of global modernity. Colonialism drove the movement of huge numbers of people – not only armed forces and colonial officials, but large populations of labourers, including slaves, convicts and indentured labourers. As groups of workers moved under coercion, or followed economic opportunities, often there were far more men than women. Women moved too, because they were forced off their lands, because of economic hardship, or in response to the growth of concentrations of male labourers; or, they intermixed with the new arrivals. Prostitution on a large scale was an integral part of colonial migrations, economic activity and social dislocation. The racialized and gendered hierarchies that colonial prostitution and concubinage produced circulated globally, back to European metropoles, and on to various creole cultures. Sexual relations between women and men in the colonies shaped gendered notions according to which women were sexualized and objectified, and indigenous and non-European women in particular were considered available for privileged men, notions that continue in the global sex trade. At the same time, on a daily basis, women who lived in colonial societies could and did find economic, practical and even emotional advantages to liaisons they forged amidst turbulence and change. It is important to recognize both colonized women's subordination, and their strategies and accommodations.

Missionaries and women's bodies

In ways that go well beyond prostitution and concubinage, women's bodies and domestic spaces were the focus of contestation and debate under colonialism. British missionary organizations were founded around 1800 and grew exponentially over the course of the nineteenth century. Throughout the century, mission organizations were dominated by men, but from the 1820s women missionaries began working with girls and women in India, for example, and the

Society for Promoting Female Education in China, India and the East was launched in 1834. British women missionaries claimed that their great advantage was their ability to enter the secluded women's areas of Indian households, the *zenanas*. One group was titled the Church of England Zenana Missionary Society. In the decades either side of the turn of the twentieth century, the plethora of missionary societies were substantial employers of educated British women. British missionaries in India became obsessed with cultural practices surrounding women's bodies and social status, from *sati* (the immolation of Hindu widows on their husbands' funeral pyres) to child marriage and the status of widows. In 1829–30 the British government in India outlawed the practise of *sati*, effectively beginning its drastic reduction, although it did not disappear. As Lata Mani has argued, the debates surrounding *sati* were so laden and fraught that the widows' suffering and their deaths were marginalized by the voices and interests of multiple groups with their own political and cultural agendas. *Sati* had been justified by a patriarchal Hinduism that claimed scriptural sanction for a largely upper-class Hindu practice. The debate over its prohibition drew in colonial officials, missionaries and the indigenous male elite in India; and church groups, government officials and the public in Britain. One particularly vexed area within this debate was that of questions about authenticity, tradition and the impulse for reform within Hindu religion and culture, a volatile mix that presaged continuing debates surrounding modernity, nationalism and colonial rule, often linked to women's place and domesticity.[38] The voices that joined the clamorous debate over Hindu women's burning bodies were mostly male, but Clare Midgley has shown that evangelically minded British women took up the cause through petitions and fund raising, placing it as an issue alongside that of the abolition of slavery, and making it one of the first campaigns that linked their own political activism with issues regarding colonized women.[39]

British people in India, as elsewhere in Asia and the Middle East, were fascinated by the gendering of space through the practice of mostly affluent women's seclusion in zenanas (or seraglios in the Middle East), and the practice of purdah. In their annual reports and newsletters, the Society for Promoting Female Education made explicit their view that Zenana women were 'literally "captives" ', held in comfortable 'prison-houses'. Even though the women of higher caste and class who lived in seclusion did not suffer the physical hardships of poor women, in this view their lot was that of mind-numbing removal from the world, with only trivia and petty jealousies to occupy them. Women missionaries cast themselves in masculine terms as the chivalrous saviours of these unfortunate captives, able as they were to 'penetrate into the recesses of their dwellings' to bring them the news of salvation that could help them throw off their barbarous shackles. The zenana was a favourite subject of cross-cultural wonderment and indictment in British women's missionary publications, but they also expounded on what they considered the pitiable condition of Hindu widows, especially young widows dependent upon their mothers-in-law.[40] British army officers' wives too saw themselves as emissaries of civilization to benighted women trapped in their homes. For example, in 1936 Mrs. L.A. Underhill, based in Peshawar, reported to the Empire Social Services' Group of the Royal Empire Society in London that the wives of NCOs and sepoys 'were more than delighted to be visited in their homes in the married lines of the regiment and others outside my husband's regiment asked for visits! These women are, generally speaking, still in strict purdah, yet longing for knowledge of the world without. I started purdah parties held at different bungalows which were very popular and Indian officers used to beg for invitations for their wives'.[41] Whatever simple cross-cultural curiosity existed on both sides of such interactions, it could hardly have competed with the overwhelming assumption by most British women of their cultural superiority and message of enlightenment.

The complicated negotiations that constituted colonialism, and the historical changes it impelled, are well illustrated by the crisis of the 1920s–1930s over female genital excision in the British East African colonies. Continuing through the 1950s women's bodies and the rites surrounding them were a subject of contestation among British colonial officials in Africa, the Colonial Office in London, missionaries and indigenous people, especially the Kikuyu who led the Kenyan anti-colonial nationalist movement. The crisis began particularly in the central highlands of Kenya, in the mid-1920s when missionaries and colonial officials produced a policy of restricting female genital excision to a limited clitoridectomy, as opposed to the traditional procedure of excising the clitoris, the labia minora and labia majora, and infibulation leaving only a small opening. The controversy blew up in 1929 when missionaries sought to enforce this new rule by excommunicating church members who refused to adhere to it. Indigenous Christians who sought to balance their old and new cultural practices reacted vigorously. At the same time, the Colonial Office was confronted by questions raised in Parliament by two women MPs, the Duchess of Atholl and Eleanor Rathbone. British colonialism in Kenya had been wreaking drastic changes for decades, with aggressive settler occupation of the most desirable lands, the resultant dislocation and containment of indigenous people, forced labour by indigenous people in the service of the settlers, and colonial control of indigenous people's farming practices. The mission settlements of various Protestant churches with their educational and health services had disrupted traditional cultural practices, and attracted an emergent group of indigenous Christians. It was an explosive context in which the violent rites surrounding girls' passage into adult womanhood were represented as pagan and barbarous by missionaries and some officials and observers, but in good part because of this condemnation became imbued with nascent nationalist symbolism and thus integral to the evolving political struggle between colonial rulers and Kenyan activists. The crisis over female genital excision reflected the multiple agendas colliding under British colonial rule in East Africa, and how central sexuality and gender were to this highly political struggle.[42]

Domesticity and households

Commonly, European missionaries sought to impose contemporary European notions of gendered respectability on their colonized subjects. Around the globe in the nineteenth century, missionaries urged indigenous people to abandon traditional communal ways of life in favour of domestic arrangements modelled on idealized European workers' cottages. In British Columbia, for example, missionaries sought to shift First Nations people into humble nuclear-family dwellings, in which Christian patriarchal heads of households would be the breadwinners while women would perform reproductive labour. Their desire to impose what they considered the righteous model for family living was spurred in part by their horror at the communal houses on that part of the Pacific coast, the 'big houses' shared by multiple families. Missionaries' imaginations had been excited by visions of sexual promiscuity which, they thought, must have flourished in an arrangement where a large open building was divided between families only by partitions.[43]

In New Zealand, Kathryn Rountree shows, early missionaries in the 1820s and 1830s focussed on Maori women's bodies as a crucial site for their work of conversion. Maori women's bodies, Rountree suggests, were at greater variance with British notions of feminine respectability than Maori men's bodies were with ideas of masculinity. Maori women struck the first British women settlers as free, unkempt, unclothed, violent, mobile and disorderly. Convincing Maori women to groom, dress and comport themselves in a more respectable manner became a yardstick by which British missionaries measured their own evangelical success. Marianne Williams, a missionary wife in the employ of the Church Missionary Society, recorded in her journal her quotidian battles with Maori women over their bodies. Convincing Maori women to wash themselves, cut their hair, wear dresses and to become sexually virtuous and monogamous was at the heart of her conversion strategies, as well as her goal to impose methods of British domesticity.[44]

Colonizers' households were a dominant, if not the primary, contact zone of colonialism. The officials, missionaries, traders, army personnel and settlers who set up house in colonies around the world turned to indigenous people, indentured labourers or imported slaves to be their servants and run their houses. Mistresses and masters dealt with servants constantly in myriad ways. The quotidian interactions and power relations of domestic service were a site of intensive cultural learning in both directions, and gave colonizers ample opportunity to observe, instruct, criticize and ridicule. A popular literary genre of the nineteenth and early twentieth centuries were colonial household advice manuals, which were written purportedly to instruct those about to depart the metropole for the colonial frontier, but were also sold as a form of travel literature.

One writer of such books was Mary Anne Barker, later Lady Broome, whose upbringing and marriages took her to Jamaica, India, South Africa, Mauritius and New Zealand and thus allowed her to write with authority on 'colonial servants'. Her books included *A Year's Housekeeping in South Africa* (1877) and *Colonial Memories* (1904). That Broome saw domestic service as a means of civilizing heathens is made clear from the story of a Zulu nursemaid Maria, who spans both these books. In her 1877 book, Maria is introduced as 'a Kafir girl, who is a real comfort and help'. Broome usually refers to Maria in the text as 'Malia' to make fun of Zulu people's difficulty with pronouncing 'r's. This first description of Maria notes that she 'is a short, fat, good-humoured-looking damsel of fifteen years of age, but looks thirty. Regarded as a servant, there is still much to be desired, in spite of the careful and excellent training she has enjoyed in the household of the Bishop of Natal.' Despite Maria's propensity to break dishes, Broome continues, she speaks three languages, is eager to learn, and is musically talented. In particular, Broome notes, Maria is keen to read religious texts and goes to church every other Sunday 'dressed in the smartest of bright pink cotton frocks, made very full and very short, a clean white apron, and a sky-blue kerchief, arranged on her head in a becoming turban'.[45] Broome continued the story of Maria in her 1904 book, describing how she was so taken by her qualities as a servant and her interest in bible-reading, that when Broome and her husband left Maritzburg to return to England they took Maria with them. In London 'she adapted herself marvellously and unhesitatingly to the conditions of a civilisation far beyond what she had ever dreamed of', taking to life in London 'as if she had never known anything else'. Still, when an English friend was going out to Natal to live, Broome arranged for Maria to go with her as her servant, in order to return to her own family. Maria had been such a hit with Broome's London friends that as a farewell gift they bestowed on her 'two large boxes of good clothes'. Yet to Broome's enormous disappointment, soon after returning to Natal, Maria married an African man and adopted a traditional way of life. To Broome, Maria's return 'to the savage life she had not known since her infancy' was 'an amazing instance of the strength of race-instinct'. Broome seemed to take it as a personal failure, that after all of her careful instruction, Maria's 'Christianity had fallen away from her, and she had practically returned, on the first opportunity, to the depth of that savagery from which she had been taken before she could even remember it'.[46]

Yet Broome's catalogue on colonial servants includes praise for Africans, commenting that when she first went to Natal she made the mistake of taking three English servants with her, who rapidly proved unsatisfactory, but that she was able to replace them with Zulu servants 'in whom I was really very fortunate'. Servants she later had in Mauritius were 'the best I have ever come across out of England. ... The cooks were excellent, so were the butlers'. Indeed, her most extensive complaints are reserved for the English and Irish servants whom she employed in New Zealand in the 1860s. Class and ethnic difference, compounded by the geographical isolation of colonial life, made these English 'factory girls' and poor Irish women her most severe trial. Complaining that because of their scarcity they commanded 'enormous wages', she berates 'the absolute and profound ignorance of these damsels'. The cook 'knew nothing whatever of any sort of cooking and the housemaid, had never seen a broom'. Despite her own ignorance of running a household (having always relied on servants), she found herself having to teach the English migrant women how to sew, wash and clean. Worst of all, they did not know their place, and were impertinent enough that one dared ask to borrow her riding-habit as a pattern to give the tailor, so that she could go to the races on horseback.[47]

Relations between colonial domestic servants and their employers, while structured by race and ethnicity as well as economic power and colonizing authority, varied a good deal. Not least, in colonies ranging from South Africa to Papua domestic servants could be dominantly 'houseboys' and therefore affected by different expectations of gender from women servants, while also the subject of concern about feared sexual assault of white women. Embodied experiences of humiliation and subordination for colonial servants therefore were contingent on gender, time, place and colonial cultures. For Glenyse Ward, an Aboriginal servant to an Anglo farming family in southern Western Australia in the mid-twentieth century, the oppression of domestic service included its loneliness and isolation, the harshness with which she was dealt and specific physical humiliations. Taken away from her mother and brought up in a Catholic mission, at sixteen she was assigned out to work without a choice. Her first lesson in humiliation was delivered as soon as she arrived at the Bigelows' house and was made to drink tea out of a tin mug, while her employers used china cups and saucers. Next, she is shown her bedroom: an awful dirty room in a garage. In response to her protests she was told that as a 'dark servant' she had no right to complain. The work demanded of her was very long and arduous, but it is the physical humiliations that constitute her most poignant memories. After the first time her employer Mrs. Bigelow drives her into town for an afternoon's shopping, the minute they return to the house Glenyse is instructed to wash down the car seat on which she had been sitting with disinfectant. In such intensely symbolic, physical ways her status as 'a dark servant' was enacted.[48] In mid-twentieth century Australia, the household and the body continued to be sites of colonialism. Although colonized men were servants too, for colonized women household labour was a common experience of the subordination of colonialism, the menial and grinding work expected of them, and typically the lack of economic alternatives.

*   *   *

The daily practices and relationships of colonialism were gendered in ways that were often embodied. Colonized men's work on construction sites, in the military, on plantations or in the colonial service mostly carried with it expectations of physical labour or technical skills thought appropriate to men. Their relationships with masters and supervisors were mediated through notions of work and manliness, and racialized socio-economic hierarchies that limited their choices. For colonized women, prostitution, concubinage and domestic service were dominant occupations in colonial regimes, along with agricultural work and trading. Bodily dimensions to their labour often intersected with colonial constructions of domesticity and households that were structured around the comfort and routines of the colonizers. For women it meant patterns of work related to food preparation, cleaning, washing, childcare and sexual service. If colonialism depended upon the superior military force and economic and political power of the colonizers, its social and cultural meanings, its points of negotiation and resistance, perhaps occurred mostly at the level of the quotidian, through intimate interactions and daily practices. Colonized people often faced the daily realities of colonialism in atomized situations, but the commonalities of their experiences could produce fertile ground for resistance and, ultimately, anti-colonial movements.

Notes

1. C.L.R. James, *Beyond a Boundary* (London: Hutchinson & Co. Ltd., 1963), p. 19.

2. James, *Beyond a Boundary*, p. 34.
3. Helen Tiffin, 'Cricket, Literature and the Politics of De-colonisation: The Case of C.L.R. James', in Hilary McD. Beckles and Brian Stoddart (eds), *Liberation Cricket: West Indies Cricket Culture* (Manchester: Manchester University Press, 1995), p. 363.
4. Dominic Malcolm, ' "It's not Cricket": Colonial Legacies and Contemporary Inequalities', *Journal of Historical Sociology* vol. 14, no. 3 (Sept. 2001): 254.
5. Malcolm, ' "It's not Cricket" ', p. 272.
6. Simon Gikandi, *Maps of Englishness: Writing Identity in the Culture of Colonialism* (New York: Columbia University Press, 1996), p. 10.
7. Suvendrini Perera, ' "Cricket, with a Plot": Nationalism, Cricket and Diasporic Identities', *Journal of Australian Studies* no. 65 and *Australian Cultural History* no. 19 Special Joint Issue (2000): 19.
8. Gikandi, *Maps of Englishness*, pp. 11–13; Arjun Appadurai, *Modernity at Large: Cultural Dimenions of Globalization* (Minneapolis: University of Minnesota Press, 1996), p. 107.
9. Appadurai, *Modernity at Large*, pp. 97–113.
10. Perera, ' "Cricket, with a Plot" ', p. 18.
11. Quoted in Perera, ' "Cricket, with a Plot" ', p. 17.
12. Appadurai, *Modernity at Large*, p. 111.
13. Gillian Poulter, 'Giving Canadians "Our English Character": The British Contribution to Colonial Identity', unpublished paper presented at the British World Conference, University of Calgary, July 10–12, 2003. Cited here with kind permission of the author.
14. Rudyard Kipling, 'The Bridge-Builders', in his *The Day's Work* (Garden City, NY: Doubleday, Page & Co., 1919), p. 8.
15. Kipling, 'The Bridge-Builders', p. 6.
16. Kipling, 'The Bridge-Builders', p. 40.
17. Joyce Cary, *Mister Johnson* (originally published 1939; New York: New Directions Books, 1989), p. 65.
18. Cary, *Mister Johnson, passim.*
19. E. M. Collingham, *Imperial Bodies: The Physical Experience of the Raj, c. 1800–1947* (Cambridge: Polity Press, 2001), pp. 117–41.
20. Mrinalini Sinha, *Colonial Masculinity: The 'Manly Englishman' and the 'Effeminate Bengali' in the Late Nineteenth Century* (Manchester: Manchester University Press, 1995), Introduction and chapter 1.
21. Ronald Hyam, 'Empire and Sexual Opportunity', *Journal of Imperial and Commonwealth History* vol. 14 (Jan. 1986): 34–89.
22. Mark T. Berger, 'Imperialism and Sexual Exploitation: A Response to Ronald Hyam's "Empire and Sexual Opportunity" ', *Journal of Imperial and Commonwealth History* vol. 17 (Oct. 1988): 83–9.
23. Hyam, 'Empire and Sexual Opportunity', pp. 34–8, 41, 46, 53, 57–9, 68, 72.
24. Christopher Lane, *The Ruling Passion: British Colonial Allegory and the Paradox of Homosexual Desire* (Durham: Duke University Press, 1995), pp. 2–4.
25. Robert Aldrich, *Colonialism and Homosexuality* (London: Routledge, 2003), pp. 91–3.
26. Aldrich, *Colonialism and Homosexuality*, pp. 71–9.

27. Matt Houlbrook, 'Soldier Heroes and Rent Boys: Homosex, Masculinities, and Britishness in the Brigade of Guards, circa 1900–1960', *Journal of British Studies* vol. 42 (July 2003): 351–88.

28. For a discussion of this see Margaret Strobel, *European Women and the Second British Empire* (Bloomington: Indiana University Press, 1991), pp. 1–15.

29. George Orwell, *Burmese Days* (San Diego: Harvest Books, first pub. 1934).

30. Adele Perry, ' "The Prevailing Vice": Mixed-Race Relationships', *On the Edge of Empire: Gender, Race, and the Making of British Columbia, 1849–1871* (Toronto: University of Toronto Press, 2001), chapter 2.

31. Jean Barman, 'Taming Aboriginal Sexuality: Gender, Power, and Race in British Columbia, 1850–1900', *BC Studies* no. 115/116 (Autumn/Winter 1997/1998): 237–66.

32. This paragraph is based on Ann McGrath, 'Black Velvet', *'Born in the Cattle': Aborigines in Cattle Country* (Sydney: Allen & Unwin, 1987), chapter 4.

33. Rae Frances, 'Sex Workers or Citizens? Prostitution and the Shaping of "Settler" Society in Australia', *International Review of Social History* vol. 44 (1999) Supplement 7: 101–22.

34. Philippa Levine, *Prostitution, Race & Politics: Policing Venereal Disease in the British Empire* (New York: Routledge, 2003).

35. Levine, *Prostitution, Race & Politics*.

36. Jim Warren, 'Retrieving Prostitutes' Live Source Materials and an Approach for Writing the History of the Ah Ku and Karayuki-San of Singapore', *Itinerario* vol. 14, no. 1 (1990): 96–122; James Francis Warren, 'Prostitution and the Politics of Venereal Disease: Singapore, 1870–98', *Journal of Southeast Asian Studies* vol. XXI, no. 2 (Sept. 1990): 360–83.

37. Luise White, *The Comforts of Home: Prostitution in Colonial Nairobi* (Chicago: University of Chicago Press, 1990).

38. Lata Mani, *Contentious Traditions: The Debate on Sati in Colonial India* (Berkeley: University of California Press, 1998).

39. Clare Midgley, 'Female Emancipation in an Imperial Frame: English Women and the Campaign Against Sati (Widow-Burning) in India, 1813–30', *Women's History Review* vol. 9, no. 1 (2000): 95–121.

40. Adam Matthew Publications microfilm collection of the Church Missionary Society Archive, Section II, Missions to Women, Part 3, Reel 33 *The Indian Female Evangelist* vol. 1, no. 1, Jan. 1872, pp. 43–7; vol. 1, no. 2, April 1872, pp. 89–94; vol. 1, no. 4, Oct. 1872, pp. 182–7; vol. 2, no. 14, April 1875, pp. 241–8; vol. 3, no. 23, July 1877, pp. 292–7; Reel 34 *The Indian Female Evangelist* vol. 4, no. 27, July 1878, pp. 110–17; vol. 4, no. 32, Oct. 1879, pp. 353–56.

41. 'Women's Work for Women in India', *United Empire* [magazine of the Royal Empire Society] no. 27 (Feb. 1936): 95.

42. On this episode see Susan Pedersen, 'National Bodies, Unspeakable Acts: The Sexual Politics of Colonial Policy-Making', *Journal of Modern History* vol. 63, no. 4 (Dec. 1991): 647–80.

43. Barman, 'Taming Aboriginal Sexuality', pp. 258–9.

44. Kathryn Rountree, 'Re-making the Maori Female Body: Marianne Williams's Mission in the Bay of Islands', *The Journal of Pacific History* vol. 35, no. 1 (June 2000): 49–66.
45. Mary Anne Barker, Lady Broome, *A Year's Housekeeping in South Africa* (1877) from Adam Matthew Publications Colonial Discourses microfilm Series 1, Part 1, Reel 18, pp. 161–4.
46. Mary Anne Barker, Lady Broome, *Colonial Memories* (1904), from Adam Matthew Publications Colonial Discourses microfilm Series 1, Reel 22, pp. 211–14.
47. Barker, *Colonial Memories*, pp. 208–14; Barker, *Letter VI*, 1891, Reel 22, p. 44.
48. Glenyse Ward, *Wandering Girl* (Broome, WA: Magabala Books, 1987), pp. 12–41.

5
Women and Gender in Anti-Colonial and Nationalist Movements

Over the course of the twentieth century there was a fundamental shift in British and other Western women's relationship to the armed forces. At the beginning of the century, women were quintessential non-combatants; by the century's end they were integrally involved in the armed services. Women's incremental involvement in war was linked to their quest for economic and political citizenship. The total wars of the twentieth century made the gendering of citizenship more negotiable. The massive recruitment of civilians for the total effort of the First World War, which erupted at a time when feminist movements were stronger than they had ever been, opened up war participation especially in Britain but other combatant nations too. Russia went even further than other combatant nations, using women for combat, especially in the dramatically named 'Battalion of Death'. In the First World War, the heroic and mythical figure of the British soldier remained resolutely male, yet the introduction of women's paramilitary organizations (the Women's Army Auxiliary Corps, the Women's Royal Naval Service, and the Women's Royal Air Force) in the war's final years meant that women went well beyond the role of the nurse, and breached the masculine domain of soldiering. During the Second World War, without controversy, Britain conscripted women into paramilitary organizations and munitions work. This incorporation of women into the armed forces occurred before and after the staggered enfranchisement of British women in 1918 and 1928.[1]

The story of British and other Western women's participation in the world wars is by now well-trodden scholarly ground. What are much less familiar and yet in some ways parallel are the stories of women's involvement in anti-colonial and nationalist struggles within the twentieth-century British Empire. Like British women's participation in the armed forces and the world wars, these stories too revolve around gendered definitions of citizenship and gendered struggles for inclusion in the nation-state. For Britain, women in the military meant reconceptualizing the nation as a more inclusive entity. In colonial contexts, women's participation in nationalist movements raised questions of the form the nation-in-the-making would take, who would and would not be citizens. In both arenas, issues of legal status and entitlements were at stake.

As colonies fought to throw off their imperial rulers in the early to middle decades of the twentieth century, in many instances women's active participation in such struggles was connected to indigenous movements for women's rights and improved political and social status. Taking a broad look at the history of women's participation in late-nineteenth and twentieth-century anti-colonial nationalist struggles will help to chart the connected ways in which women's movements and nationalisms have been imbricated in global modernity. Of course, it must immediately be said that militarism and feminism have not been natural or easy allies, and violence is hardly a feminist goal. Indeed, historically, feminism has been more associated with pacifism than militarism. As will become clear from my examples, women's actions in nationalist struggles have ranged from non-violent civil disobedience to terrorism and membership in armed forces.

This chapter focuses particularly on four different sites of evolving nationalisms, from around the empire and mostly in the twentieth century, in order to explore these issues: India, Kenya, Ireland and Canada. These four episodes (along with a few others mentioned briefly, including South Africa and Palestine) represent a variety of nationalist struggles, and their histories reveal a spectrum of women's contributions to twentieth-century anti-colonial movements. The role of war varies considerably among them, but together they reveal women's engagement in multiple forms of struggle and conflict. The nation-states, where they emerged, showed that women were better rewarded in some instances than others for their involvement, yet in each case women participated in some way in the evolving constructions of the nation. Even in what is perhaps the most muted of these nationalist movements, that of Canada, which was constitutionally already a nation while still attached to Britain, women sought their inclusion in national mythology. After the survey of women's involvement in these disparate nationalist struggles, the chapter conclusion returns to some overarching issues.

The Indian nationalist struggle

A flourishing body of recent scholarship has increasingly pointed to the interconnected growth of the women's movement in early twentieth-century India and the nationalist struggle for independence from Britain. Nationalist agitation was the political milieu within which Indian feminism developed, while feminists soon put the issue of gender and citizenship on the nationalist agenda. Scholars have outlined connections between late-nineteenth and early twentieth-century women social reformers and the emerging nationalist movement in India; women's growing involvement in campaigns to boycott British products and for self-rule; the development of independent women's political organizations in the context of the nationalist movement and individual Indian women's dedication to the anti-colonial struggle. Issues of Indian women's status were a favoured topic of British colonial reformers in the nineteenth century, a subject framed to evoke notions of the backwardness of Indian culture and the necessity for colonial intervention. Women's bodies became the site of a debate joined by British administrators and missionaries, and leading Indian social reformers, who for most of the nineteenth century were dominantly male.

British and Indian men discussed women's bodies and lives in relation to the practices of *sati* (the immolation of widows on their husbands' funeral pyres) and child marriage; and issues of the infanticide of female children, the status and rights of widows (such as the right to remarriage), and education for women. By the late nineteenth century, Indian women reformers and advocates included Pandita Ramabai who was active in the cause of women's education, including that of child widows; and Swarnakumari Debi, who founded a women's organization dedicated to helping widows and orphans, and was one of the first women to become prominent in the Indian National Congress.

In the early twentieth century, in the milieu of political activism catalyzed by the nationalist movement, women founded their own political organizations in the beliefs that women's status would not be improved until India was free of colonial rule, and that women must add their own voices to the nationalist clamour. Women launched magazines aimed at women readers. Their writings covered a host of topics, challenging fundamental assumptions about gendered social arrangements. For example, in 1937 the writer Nazar Sajjad Hyder questioned the practice of purdah, calling it a 'social and national waste': '[Men] fear that, when she who has been a prisoner for ages leaves her prison, then the desire to see the world will certainly stir in her ... . A noble inheritance, blue blood, the restrictions of tradition are but mere excuses for this. ... [M]en fear that if the women are given freedom, they will also become like them. Therefore, [men conclude] it is wise to keep the women confined.'[2]

One of the most significant of the women's organizations was the Women's Indian Association founded in 1917 by a group of feminists including Dorothy Jinarajadasa, who would also become active in international feminist circles, and the British theosophist feminist Annie Besant. Besant had moved to India in 1893, and by 1914 had become active in the Indian National Congress. In 1916 she was a founder of the Home Rule League which she saw as based on the Irish Home Rule Movement. Interned in 1917 for her nationalist activism, Besant's reward on her release was her election as the first woman president of the Indian National Congress. Along with Indian feminist Sarojini Naidu, she used the 1917 Calcutta Congress platform to focus on the role of women in the nationalist movement, asserting: 'The strength of the Home Rule movement was rendered tenfold greater by the adhesion to it of a large number of women who brought to its help the uncalculating heroism, the endurance, the self-sacrifice, of the feminine nature. Our League's best recruits and recruiters are among the women of India.'[3] Another significant women's organization, the All India Women's Conference, was founded by an Irish suffragette, Margaret Cousins who had arrived in India in 1915 and was active in Indian nationalist and feminist circles. In 1927 the Conference convened for the first time to discuss women's education. Subsequent annual conferences, which drew women from diverse constituencies, expanded their agendas to include topics such as child marriage, women's inheritance laws, conditions for women workers, maternity benefits and women's suffrage.[4]

After the British Government conceded in 1917 the possibility of moves towards Indian self-rule, feminists in the nationalist movement made sure that the issue of votes for women was on the table – despite Secretary of State for

India, Edwin Montagu's dismissal of the issue when it was first put to him in 1917, Indian feminists were not so easily dissuaded. The Women's Indian Association held public meetings on votes for women, and feminists lobbied the nationalist organizations including the Home Rule League, the Indian National Congress and the Muslim Congress, which all passed resolutions supporting the franchise for women. In 1919 Sarojini Naidu, Annie Besant and others presented evidence before a Joint Committee of the British Parliament in favour of women's right to vote. The British Parliament decided to leave the matter to the Indian provincial legislatures. The result was that between 1920 and 1930, state by state, Indian women were granted the right to vote for provincial legislatures on the same terms as men and even to stand for election. The proportion of women thus enfranchised was small, but women kept up a campaign to expand their political rights. Mrinalini Sinha has shown that, following the 1927 publication of Katherine Mayo's polemic against Indian self-government *Mother India*, Indian liberal feminists' organized responses shaped the nationalist campaign itself by positioning the modern Indian woman as the model of Indian citizenship and modernity.[5] In 1931 the Indian National Congress adopted a resolution against sex discrimination and supporting universal adult suffrage. In 1935 the British Parliament passed the Government of India Act which enfranchised women over 21 who owned property, were literate or were wives or widows of men who owned property; some seats in Congress were reserved for women. While this act enfranchised five times as many men as women, in the first elections held under it, in 1937, 80 women were elected, which made India the third country in the world in its number of women legislators, behind the United States and the Soviet Union. But it was not until independence in 1947 that women obtained full constitutional political equality.[6]

The strong support of the Indian National Congress for women's suffrage from the First World War onwards was due in part to the respect women had earned in the campaign for self-rule and in the *swadeshi* movement, the boycott of imported goods and campaign to support home production. When the British Indian Government partitioned Bengal in 1905, a powerful Bengali nationalist movement was launched. Women energetically joined the movement, refused to buy British textiles, symbolically smashed foreign-made goods and actively supported the expansion of local production of textiles and clothing. Nationalist rhetoric emphasized political dimensions to women's roles as wives and mothers. From 1920, in the wake of the First World War, the 1919 Rowlatt Acts which extended wartime restrictions on civil rights, and the Amritsar Massacre in April 1919 when around 400 unarmed protesters were shot dead, Gandhi escalated his civil disobedience movement. Again women boycotted foreign goods and promoted the production and sale of *khadi*, homemade cloth. This time in Bombay and Calcutta they also organized the continuous picketing of liquor shops (which were an important source of revenue for the British Indian government), and shops selling foreign clothing. Although Gandhi did not include women in his first salt march in 1930 (aimed at disrupting the British monopoly on the manufacture and sale of salt), Sarojini Naidu and other feminist leaders insisted that women participate. The salt protest both marked the high level of women's involvement in the nationalist campaign by 1930, and was an action easily available to women young and old, of all classes and regions. Large numbers of women manufactured small quantities of salt from pitchers of sea water, and stood on street corners selling small packets of it.[7] Even though he had initially excluded women from his salt march because he saw it as a publicly political protest, Gandhi viewed women as exemplary members of his *satyagraha* campaigns, his non-violent non-cooperation campaigns based on self-discipline and individual commitment to simple values.

Gandhi's notion that women were eminently suited to being *satyagrahis* (participants in these campaigns) was linked to his essentialist views of women's nature and roles. Gandhi often and publicly espoused a belief in the equality of the sexes. He claimed that 'woman is the companion of man, gifted with equal mental capacities', and considered himself 'uncompromising in the matter of women's rights'.[8] Yet his views of women's qualities and abilities, and their roles, were based on a vision of complementarity and difference. Gandhi saw women as noble, self-sacrificing, able to endure suffering, self-controlled and loyal. Although he supported women's right to divorce and spoke against sexual double standards, he believed that chastity was good for both men and women. Women should be educated, but in order to enable them better to run the domestic realm and to raise and educate their children. Historian Kumari Jayawardena has argued that, in contrast to Jawaharlal Nehru who supported women's rights to education in all subjects and to economic independence, Gandhi did not recognize women's economic equality or access to public careers as an issue.[9]

Significantly, the Indian nationalist movement generated powerful contradictory understandings of femininity, which can perhaps be linked to the simultaneous and contradictory invocation of different female Hindu deities. On the one hand there was Sita, the Hindu deity whom Gandhi preferred, the mythical, loyal and self-sacrificing wife of Rama. But from the late nineteenth century Hindu nationalists had also increasingly celebrated Durga, the demon-slaying mother, and Kali, the punitive and destructive mother. Notions and invocations of 'Mother India', then, carried implications of a feminized use of violence against the colonial oppressor.[10] Thus while Gandhi saw the masses of Indian women who participated in civil disobedience movements as exemplifying non-violent ideals of self-sacrificing femininity based on Hindu tradition, other nationalists embraced violent action on the part of women. Tanika Sarkar has argued that, on the one hand, the nationalist movement, because of its roots in religion and tradition, sought to limit the gender transgression of women's involvement in nationalist acts even when violent.[11] Yet, Sarkar has further argued that even the non-violent participation of masses of women in the nationalist movement, as well as women's publicly political actions, demonstrations, arrests and imprisonment made 'a mockery of the language of traditionalism.'[12]

The story of the Indian nationalist movement includes numerous women who undertook violent and terrorist actions. For example, in December 1931 two 16- and 17-year-old school girls, Shanti Ghose and Suniti Choudhury, walked into the office of a British magistrate on the pretext of obtaining his permission for a swimming competition, and shot him dead. Apparently their motivation lay in a pattern of sexual abuse of Bengali girls by British magistrates. Then in September 1932, a 21-year-old teacher Preetilata Wadedar, whose father had lost his job for complaining about the behaviour of a British officer, led a raid on the Pahartali Railway Officers' Club in Chittagong in eastern Bengal. Wadedar led a group of fifteen young men in their attack on the club on a Saturday night when it was crowded with British officers and their wives. In the shooting one woman was killed and others were wounded. The young men raiders escaped, but Wadedar took potassium cyanide and her body, in men's clothing, was found outside the club. She had earlier told a friend that only when she was ready to take her own life in the nationalist cause, would she be willing to kill someone else.[13]

The point at which the gendered story of Indian nationalist violence intersects most with that of Western women's participation in the two world wars is the formation of the Rani of Jhansi Women's Regiment. During the Second World War radical Congress leader Subhas Chandra Bose formed the Indian National Army to fight the British for India's freedom. In October 1943 a women's regiment of the Indian National Army was formed, and named for the royal woman warrior who had led a military campaign during India's 'First War of Independence', often called the 'Indian Mutiny', of 1857–58. The Rani of Jhansi regiment was formed in Singapore under the leadership of Dr. Lakshmi Swaminathan, mostly of young women, and at its greatest extent consisted of a thousand women based in three camps in Singapore, Bangkok and Rangoon. The regiment consisted of two divisions, one trained primarily for fighting, and the other for nursing. All of the women in the regiment wore soldiers' uniforms including jodhpurs, and many cut their hair short. Although at least some were keen to fight, they did not see active service; by the time they were sent into Burma in 1945, the Indian National Army was in retreat.[14] The regiment, nevertheless, was a powerful counterpoint to the Gandhian nationalist equation between femininity and non-violence.

Women's participation in the Indian nationalist movement spanned the gamut from non-violence to inclusion in the armed forces, and thus challenges any essentialist notions of women's political behaviour. Moreover, this brief outline demonstrates the thorough impact of feminists on the evolving Indian nationalist movement, the role of nationalism as a catalyst to Indian feminism, and the importance of women to this anti-colonial struggle.

Kenya and Mau Mau

The tensions surrounding women's central role in Indian nationalism are connected to continuing contradictions in post-independence India: the constitutional promise of equality that has not been fully delivered upon, and the continuation of discrimination, yet at the same time the existence of a vigorous and effective feminist movement. Similarly contradictory legacies have obtained in Kenya, where women's substantial role in the nationalist movement of the 1950s must be seen as a precursor to the post-independence political presence of women in Kenya, but a presence that women have had to struggle to assert. The Mau Mau movement of radical nationalism ostensibly lost its bloody and bitter struggle against British settlers and the British colonial administration in Kenya, but indubitably it was a catalyst in the winning of independence by

1963. As historian Luise White has shown, the Mau Mau – also known as the land and freedom movement – engaged in a central struggle over gender definitions, both masculinities and femininities. The Kikuyu were the ethnic group most involved in Mau Mau. For young, urban Kikuyu men, Mau Mau was in part a generational conflict about their access to land, and thus their ability to fulfill traditional notions of proper Kikuyu adult masculinity.[15] The heart of the Mau Mau struggle occurred in guerrilla fighting based in the forests of the central province of Kenya from 1952 to 1956. Gender relations were a principal concern of the forest guerrillas, even a marker between the two factions of the literate and higher-status fighters versus the illiterate labourers who claimed that the other faction were too Westernized. The more literate group of forest fighters emphasized cohabitation and marriage, and women were held to have more power, indeed to reach a point of equal power, in this faction's councils. In the culturally more traditional, less literate faction, women fought alongside men, but women and men lived in separate groups.[16]

Recent scholarship and testimony about women in Mau Mau reveals just how central they were to the movement. Although they constituted a minority of the forest guerrillas, women were crucial to the support structures that the guerrillas depended upon, the provision of food, ammunition and information. Under the severe restrictions that the colonial authorities placed especially upon the Kikuyu during the years of the rebellion, women had more freedom of movement than men and thus were vital actors in the dangerous and secretive work of supplying the guerrillas.[17] Women were active participants in the administration of the oaths that Mau Mau depended upon to instil loyalty. Cora Ann Presley has suggested that some nationalist families adopted a strategy whereby the men in the family pretended to be loyalist while their women were active in the nationalist struggle, a theory supported by evidence that it was only when the colonial government began jailing women in greater numbers and targetting them for reeducation and social services that the movement was contained.[18]

Mau Mau activist Wambui Waiyaki Otieno presents compelling evidence in her memoirs that women were crucial to Mau Mau. For the important work of gathering intelligence in the planning stages of an attack, she asserts simply, 'scouts had to be women'. Women were less suspected when they travelled or loitered in public places, they could easily disguise themselves through the use of wigs and makeup and by adopting the voluminous clothing of Muslim women, and of course they could flirt if necessary. At one stage in her career in the movement, Otieno led a group whose assignment was to acquire weapons and ammunition. She organized a contingent of women who seduced British soldiers in bars, had access to military barracks in the guise of prostitutes, and successfully smuggled out guns and ammunition.[19]

From a prominent Kikuyu family but raised as a Christian, Otieno became active in the nationalist movement on her own accord as a teenager. In 1954 at age 18 she ran away from her village home, to Nairobi, where she dedicated herself fulltime to Mau Mau. After Mau Mau was suppressed, she became active in the Nairobi People's Convention Party and the Kenya African National Union, led desegregation protests and was subjected to tight police restriction and observation. In 1960 she was arrested and placed with her children in a detention centre, where she was violently raped by the British officer who interrogated her. Her memoirs make clear her pride in her commitment and work for the movement, in the risks she took and even in the deaths for which she was indirectly responsible through her work as a scout. During the Mau Mau struggle, she records, her nickname was 'Msaja' meaning 'man or mister' because 'I was known to be as strong and as brave as a man.'[20] She continued her political work after independence, and, significantly, became active in national women's organizations and international feminism. She was one of the organizers of the 1985 United Nations women's conference held in Nairobi, an undertaking that, she reported, she and other Kenyan feminists hoped would enable Kenyan women to meet women from all over the world. Moreover, they saw it as a chance for 'the developed world to see for themselves the problems facing women in developing countries.'[21]

Clearly, the motivations and determination that led Otieno to be a nationalist activist in the 1950s and 1960s were directly linked to her political work on behalf of women in the 1970s and 1980s. Otieno believed that she faced sex discrimination when she ran for political office in the late 1960s and early 1970s, and that 'women freedom fighters' – she and other Mau Mau women – were neglected after independence by the Kenyatta government and not appropriately recognized and rewarded for their efforts.[22] Yet her own national prominence, the ambassadorial roles that the Kenyan government has asked her to undertake, and the very fact of the 1985 UN and NGO women's conference being held in Kenya all speak to a visibility of women in post-independence Kenyan politics that is the legacy of their critical role in the nationalist movement. Moreover, Wambui Otieno is still a nationally provocative feminist figure. The latest controversy swirling around her concerns women's right to marry younger men. In 2003 at age 67, Otieno married a 28-year-old man, and sparked a national debate on the traditional double standard regarding age gaps in marriage. Otieno used the debate to raise other women's issues, such as the rights of widows, polygamy and female genital mutilation.[23]

Women's involvement in Kenyan nationalism was not the only instance in Africa. Also in the 1950s, women played a crucial role in the Tanganyikan nationalist movement, linking their struggle to improve their own status to the nationalist cause. At the end of 1955, for example, a year of important growth for the Tanganyikan African National Union (TANU), women constituted a majority of its membership.[24] Bibi Titi Mohamed, the leading woman activist in TANU, urged other Tanganyikan women to join the Union by arguing that the nationalist cause needed women's power: 'I told you [women] that we want independence. And we can't get independence if you don't want to join the party. We have given birth to all these men. Women are the power in this world. We are the ones who give birth to the world!'[25] And in the 1970s and 1980s a women's council became an important part of SWAPO (South West Africa People's Organisation), fighting for more rights for women as an integral part of the struggle for independence for Namibia.[26] Women's inclusion in the Kenyan and Tanganyikan anti-colonial struggles shows that the Indian nationalist movement was not unique in spurring and being shaped by women's political activism. In these instances too, evidence suggests that nationalisms and women's movements to improve their own status evolved in tandem.

Maternal images and nationalisms

Rosalind O'Hanlon has argued that iconic images of women as mothers were central to various nationalist and anti-colonial movements. Such images were available to competing political constituencies in the turbulent milieux of the late stages of colonialism. Contests over these nationalist images of women often continued beyond the end of formal colonialism. Maternalist images were deployed by conservative and religious movements, creating challenges for feminists seeking to pursue more liberal and secular agendas.[27] At the same time, as Margaret Jolly contends, women themselves have participated in the construction of nationalist images of the mother, images that have borne some relation to the daily reality of women's lives as mothers. Moreover, nationalist images of the mother have not been a fixed or homogeneous category: they have been variously inflected (such as the several Hindu deities connected to 'Mother India'), have shifted over time, have correlated with women's economic and social power as mothers and have diverged on ethnic and class lines.[28]

One instance of the centrality of maternal images to nationalism points also towards the great variability of twentieth-century nationalist movements, a variability evident just within the continent of Africa. Afrikaner nationalism developed in South Africa in response to British victory in the South African War of 1899–1902. Forcibly included in the British-dominated Union of South Africa, Afrikaners developed a political and cultural nationalist movement, a highly gendered movement pivotted on the iconic image of the volksmoeder (mother of the nation). The Afrikaner mother was represented as the locus of the suffering of the volk and as the vessel that would ensure the continuity of racial purity.[29] As the Afrikaner nationalist movement built itself up politically and articulated its racist agenda in the 1930s and 1940s, Afrikaner women were reminded of the importance of their domestic roles versus the temptations offered by newly available industrial work, and presented with warnings against the horrors of mixed marriages.[30] Yet Afrikaner women were active contributors to the building of this nationalist ideology and movement, particularly in the years before white South African women were granted the vote in 1930.[31] Thus they participated in the construction of a nationalism that valourized the mother and sought to conflate women with the domestic, a powerfully gendered nationalism that limited their political participation once they had the vote. White women served in the South African armed forces temporarily during the Second World War but were demobilized at war's end. Then, in a move that reflects the malleability of racialized gender ideology, in the 1970s when the South African Government faced growing militancy against its Apartheid regime and escalated hostilities against neighboring states, suddenly white women were actively recruited into the South African Defence Force. But far-right Afrikaner nationalist women disapproved of white women joining what they condemned as 'an integrated army'.[32]

There are interesting points of comparison between the Afrikaner nationalist movement and the anti-colonial nationalist movement in Ireland that also had longer historical roots but became militant in the late nineteenth and early twentieth centuries. Both movements sought to draw international attention to what they represented as struggles against British colonialism. The Irish nationalist movement also valourized the suffering mother, and the integral role of the wife and mother in cultural if not racial nationalism. Just as the 1930 suffrage for white women in South Africa did not herald the inclusion of Afrikaner women into politics but rather preceded their further political marginalization, so the granting of adult suffrage under the 1922 constitution of the Irish Free State was followed by the subordination of Irish women. Yet the gendered differences between the two movements are at least as significant as their similarities.

Anti-colonial nationalism in Ireland

At moments in the Irish nationalist movement, feminists sought to leverage its emancipatory potential to raise the political, economic and social status of women. Various scholars have pointed to the critical role of women in the Land League, and the anti-feminist backlash that ensued and marked the nationalist movement. Beginning in 1879, the Land League sought to promote nationalism by organizing rent strikes and drawing attention to the extortionate system of land tenure that impoverished many tenant farmers. When the Land League was threatened by the imprisonment of its male leaders, a Ladies' Land League was formed, led by Anna Parnell, sister of the Irish parliamentary leader Charles Stewart Parnell. The Ladies' Land League was highly organized and effective; indeed, so effective that it was crushed by the male nationalist leadership when, released from prison in 1882, they sought a constitutional compromise with the British Government. Margaret Ward has suggested that this was a defining moment for the gender hierarchy within Irish nationalism. The feminists of the Ladies' Land League had threatened the male dominance of the movement; their subsequent forced disbandment signalled the subordinate role women would be allotted in the Irish nation.[33]

Feminist nationalists continued to participate in politics, forming the cultural nationalist group Daughters of Erin, starting their own journal, and helping to found Sinn Fein in 1905. With the rise of the militarist phase of Irish nationalism from 1913, women's subordination was again articulated: only one of the new groups, the Irish Citizen Army, admitted women equally. Although women supported nationalist fighters during the years of civil war, and made some gains in local government following their partial enfranchisement in 1918, from 1922 the Irish Free State worked to restrict women's public presence and legal rights.[34] Women's access to employment was legally restricted, their service on juries reduced, and the 1937 constitution undercut the equality that had been built into the 1922 constitution.[35] While at the turn of the century Irish nationalism had taken as its female archetype *Cathleen Ni Houlihan*, from the W.B. Yeats play in which the prominent feminist nationalist Maud Gonne represented Ireland, by the 1930s male Irish leaders vaunted instead the self-sacrificing mother who had stayed home but given her sons to the cause.[36] If the Irish feminist movement had been weakened by a split over the primacy of nationalism versus suffrage, as well as the divide between nationalists and loyalists, women's subordination in the Irish Free State was presaged by masculinist insistence on their subordination during the nationalist struggle. The Irish story underscores the fact that women's dedicated participation did not guarantee their full inclusion in citizenship once the nation came into being.

Palestine

The inchoate nature of the feminist agenda of women who participated in some nationalist struggles is illustrated by evidence from yet another locus of the British Empire, the Mandate in Palestine. During the British Mandate period, and especially from 1929 to 1947, Palestinian Arab women participated actively in the nationalist movement to resist Zionist land appropriation in Palestine, the British colonial regime that facilitated it, and the consequent massive disruption to their society and culture. We know of Palestinian Arab women's nationalist efforts thanks to the extraordinary research efforts and oral history interviews of Ellen L. Fleischmann, who has pieced together this history from what she calls shards and fragments. In the absence of a national archive or other research infrastructure, Fleischmann has assembled her evidence into an important account of women's visible and critical activism. The women's nationalist movement had its roots in women's charitable organizations and was led by elite urban women, some of whom were married to nationalist male leaders. These women organized the First Arab Women's Congress in 1929, formed the Arab Women's Association, presented their own nationalist resolutions to the British High Commissioner, staged public demonstrations and received extensive coverage in the contemporary Arabic press. They also undertook practical work such as giving financial and other material assistance to the families of men imprisoned and executed, as well as protesting executions.

Nationalist women's activism extended beyond elite women's organizations. It included peasant and village women's public protests, and active and practical support of clandestine rebel fighters (not unlike the women who sustained Mau Mau in Kenya). Village women engaged in violence, stoning and assaulting British police, and numbers of women were killed in skirmishes with British troops. As Fleischmann points out, women's nationalist activism of the 1920s to 1940s constitutes important and previously obscure historical context for Palestinian women's involvement in the Intifada of the 1980s and beyond. Much of women's nationalist activism from the 1920s to the 1940s transgressed dominant gender prescriptions, yet there was great variation (including by class and religion) among the women in regard to cultural practices such as dress, veiling and public behaviour. Fleischmann carefully argues that, although Palestinian women activists' agenda was explicitly nationalist and only implicitly feminist, they insistently built their own separate movement, they conducted their own protests as well as joining with men, and their goals included the advancement of Arab women as well as women's participation in the urgent nationalist struggle. In these ways, Fleischmann contends, the epithet 'feminist' is justified.[37] Moreover, it was no coincidence that the Palestinian women's nationalist movement arose soon after the emergence of the women's movement in Egypt, also forged in the context of anti-British nationalism, and with overtly feminist elements.[38]

Canada

As the examples I have already presented show, nationalism in the twentieth century was a polymorphous entity, even within the British Empire. To understand how polymorphous it was, we need to include in this brief survey one of the nationalisms of the white-settler dominions of the empire. Although Canada had become a self-governing dominion in 1867, as for both Australia and New Zealand, the Great War was a formative moment for Canadian national mythology. Historian Jonathan F. Vance argues compellingly that it was upon the myth of the Canadian Expeditionary Force (CEF) soldier, his noble sacrifice and heroic imperial contribution, that Canadian nationalism became firmly established. Prior to the war, the Canadian constitution unified the country but an emotional patriotic spirit was not yet fully developed. During the war, Canadian pride swelled at the spectacle of the CEF sailing across the North Atlantic and fighting valiantly on the Western Front. The soldier came to stand for Canada by representing the national virtues of purity, health and vigour forged in the untamed Canadian woods, mountains and plains, and the bracing northern climate. This idealized masculine figure represented the Canadian past through connections that were drawn between the First World War and earlier wars in Canadian history. He also represented the future in his unsullied youth and optimism, and in the strong bond believed to exist between the soldier and his mother, who herself stood for continuity and stability. In this version of Canadian national mythology, which became entrenched through popular iteration and celebration in the postwar years, the Canadian soldier was superior to the British soldier in his wilderness-forged health and cleanliness, as well as in his voluntarism compared to the conscripted British troops. Canadians held their soldier, too, to have made a more significant contribution to the outcome of the war than his American counterpart who arrived so late on the scene.[39]

The crucial role of the war in the forging of Canadian national mythology paralleled similar processes in Australia and New Zealand, where there was no need to compete with American war mythology, but the comparison with British troops developed a bitter edge. Australian and New Zealand mythology incorporated a searing belief that British commanding officers had sacrificed Antipodean troops on the bloody beaches and hillsides of the Gallipoli peninsula in 1915. These war-based mythologies inflected relations between the dominions and Britain in the 1920s and 1930s, when the dominions' desire for greater autonomy was realized in the 1926 Balfour Declaration and the 1931 Statute of Westminster. Further, in all three dominions Indigenous peoples contributed soldiers to the war, and hoped that the postwar period might bring greater national recognition and legal rights, but these hopes were disappointed.

Thus in these white-settler dominions, the First World War became a vehicle for the ascendancy of masculinist national mythologies, national legends and understandings that valourized the noble contributions and sacrifices of soldiers, and marginalized women's contributions to the nation. Yet the primacy of these legends of male heroism occurred in a context in which new national iconographies were being written and rewritten. Gender definitions were contested in the flux of nationalist stories. Colin Coates and Cecilia Morgan have documented and analysed the significance for Canadian nationalisms (both French and British Canadian) of two celebrated and transgressive national heroines, Madeleine de Vercheres and Laura Secord. Although Vercheres defended her family property and fort in 1692, and Secord walked nineteen miles with news of a planned American attack on British troops in 1813, national celebration of these women's brave and indeed masculine actions was at its height from the 1890s to the 1920s. They were inscribed in national Canadian history through local historical societies, amateur historical publications, monuments, children's books, novels, plays, films and advertisements. Women amateur historians took the lead in their creation and recreation as figures in the national pantheon, underscoring the gendered significance of their inclusion. Moreover, men historians were prominent in challenges to their authenticity and significance in the 1920s and 1930s. If their waning visibility was in some way a result of the new primacy of the First World War soldier and veteran, their prominence in those decades of building national identity reflects an admittedly partial inclusion of women in the Canadian nation. Vercheres of course was a symbol of French Canadian nationalism in particular, while Secord represented at once the importance of Canadian national identity and loyalty to the British Empire.[40] But both became vehicles for Canadian aspirations to distinguish itself at once from its imperial metropole and its southern neighbour.

At the same time, the proimperialist Canadian women's organization the Imperial Order Daughters of the Empire (IODE), founded in 1900, evolved in a trajectory that also reveals women's engagement with the shaping of Canadian national identity. The IODE's programme, ranging from erecting memorials for the Canadian war dead in the South African War and the two world wars, to awarding educational bursaries for the children of those who died in war, to producing patriotic educational materials, to the awarding of postgraduate scholarships. Historian Katie Pickles shows that these conservative, privileged, imperialist women gradually contributed to the shaping of Canadian national identity through the memorials they erected, their propaganda and the choice of subjects and universities for which their postgraduate scholarships could be used. In these subtle ways, even such a conservative women's organization, through the maternal work of child nurture and educational provision, came to promote Canadian universities as equal to established metropolitan ones, and helped to determine Canadian research and policy priorities. The IODE emphasized the support of women students in an understated feminist impulse. Empire loyalty blended into dominion self-assertion, which in turn developed as Canadian nationalism, partly through the work of elite Anglo-Celtic Canadian women.[41]

*   *   *

Connections between gender and nationalism are no surprise, although it is salutary to remember that, as Anne McClintock puts it: 'All nationalisms are gendered, all are invented and all are dangerous.'[42] This mini-survey of twentieth-century nationalist struggles within the British Empire also reveals the multiple valences of racial hierarchies in anti-colonial nationalist movements. Nationalist movements in India, Kenya and Ireland can all be construed as struggles by indigenous colonized peoples to throw out their British imperial oppressors, despite the fact that Irish people, at least in this period and context, were constructed as white. And of course this simple analysis obscures the fact that both Indians and Irish were divided by religious and regional differences, while Kenyans were riven by ethnic identities and loyalties. Afrikaner nationalism depended upon a racist agenda as much as on sexual divisions, asserting the superiority of Afrikaners to indigenous Africans at the same moment as asserting their differences from British South Africans and ambitions for political ascendancy. Palestinian nationalism susbscribed to the recently constructed Pan-Arab movement, asserting notions of Arab ethnicity, unity and territorial rights, at the same time as rejecting British colonial rule and the claims of Zionists. And Canadian national identity was built through an amalgam of the subordination of Indigenous peoples, reconciliation between French and British Canadians, demonstrations of imperial loyalty, and desires for greater dominion autonomy from the metropole – that is, a mix of racial hierarchy, ethnic difference and white-settler imperial identity.

It is important to reiterate that engagement in violent conflicts per se has not typically been a feminist goal, nor has militarism historically been an ally of feminism. But we need to see the connections between women's participation in nationalist struggles both violent and non-violent, and their political inclusion in nation-states, even when partial, circumscribed or reluctant. If participating in anti-colonial and nationalist movements has not guaranteed women full equality in the resulting nations, it has provided them with political legitimacy and recognition from which they could work towards greater political inclusion and, at times, more legal and social rights.

In an outline of the whole twentieth-century history of feminist internationalism, a major feature would be the dramatic growth of non-Western women's participation and achievement of leadership positions. As Leila Rupp has demonstrated, around the turn of the twentieth century large EuroAmerican-dominated international women's organizations coalesced, and developed resilient structural bonds that would even survive the test of world war.[43] The critical work of scholars like Chandra Talpade Mohanty, Antoinette Burton, Vron Ware and others has forced us to examine the power dynamics based on race, religion and culture that were integral to these large Western women's organizations.[44] First-wave feminist internationalism was complicit with European and American imperialism, often justified itself through notions of the superiority of Christianity and Western civilization, and frequently sought to speak for – and to build its own authority *by* speaking for – colonized women and women in non-Western nations.

Several historians have investigated feminist internationalism of the interwar period, and found both continuity and change in relation to earlier decades.[45] New regional and transnational groups including in Asia, the Middle East, the Pacific and Latin America, challenged the hegemony of the large EuroAmerican feminist organizations and showed the role of nationalism in spurring women's participation in local, regional and international feminist movements. Non-Western women increasingly participated in interwar internationalism, even as Western women continued to dominate the organizations and conferences. If at one level it seems perhaps paradoxical that *nationalism* spurred women's involvement in feminist *internationalism*, we need to pay more attention to the crucial if problematic role of nationalisms in building women's movements in the twentieth century. This becomes most apparent if we take a broad, global perspective, and consider especially the evolution of women's movements in countries beyond Europe and America. Such a perspective helps us to identify the roles of political and military conflict, struggles against colonialism and imperial rule, and the processes of nation- and state-building in the growth of women's movements, and at once the centrality of women's contributions to these conflicts, struggles and processes. A broad, transnational view helps us to see the twentieth century as riven by great conflicts, at the same time that it witnessed the tremendous growth of feminisms and significant changes in women's status in multiple parts of the globe. These two phenonema were, albeit unevenly and variously, linked, as women in European and other colonies and in non-Western nations developed their own movements in the context of specific and local struggles, often anti-colonial and nationalist struggles. The disintegration of the British Empire has not usually been linked by historians to issues of gender, but it ought to be. While the history of decolonization is often narrated as though decisions in Whitehall were what mattered, this survey shows nationalist movements in colonies and conflicts within colonial cultures – specifically, conflicts tied to women's struggles to improve their status – to have driven historical change.

Notes

1. On this subject, see Angela Woollacott, *On Their Lives Depend: Munitions Workers in the Great War* (Berkeley: University of California Press, 1994); and 'Women Munition Makers, War, and Citizenship', in Lois Ann Lorentzen and Jennifer Turpin (eds), *The Women & War Reader* (New York: New York University Press, 1998), pp. 126–31. See also Nicolette F. Gullace, *'The Blood of Our Sons': Men, Women, and the Renegotiation of British Citizenship During the Great War* (New York: Palgrave Macmillan, 2002).

2. Nazar Sajjad Hyder, 'Purdah', in Susie Tharu and K. Lalita (eds), *Women Writing in India: 600B.C. to the Present* Vol. I (London: Pandora Press, 1991), p. 393.

3. Excerpt from Besant's presidential address to the Indian National Congress, quoted in Radha Kumar, *The History of Doing: An Illustrated Account of Movements for Women's Rights and Feminism in India, 1800–1990* (London: Verso, 1993), p. 55.

4. Kumar, *The History of Doing*, p. 68.

5. Mrinalini Sinha, 'Refashioning Mother India: Feminism and Nationalism in Late-Colonial India', *Feminist Studies* vol. 26, no. 3 (Fall 2000): 623–44.

6. Rozina Visram, *Women in India and Pakistan: The Struggle for Independence from British Rule* (Cambridge: Cambridge University Press, 1992), pp. 31–9, 50.
7. Kumar, *The History of Doing*, pp. 74–8.
8. Kumari Jayawardena, *Feminism and Nationalism in the Third World* (London: Zed Books, 1986), pp. 95–6.
9. Jayawardena, *Feminism and Nationalism in the Third World*, pp. 95–9. On Gandhi's views on women see also Kumar, *The History of Doing*, pp. 82–5.
10. Kumar, *The History of Doing*, pp. 44–9. Indira Chowdhury argues that the compounded image of 'Mother India' or 'Bharat Mata' developed by nineteenth-century nationalists incorporated aspects of 'Mother' Queen Victoria. Chowdhury, 'Motherhood, Heroism and Identity', *The Frail Hero and Virile History: Gender and the Politics of Culture in Colonial Bengal* (Delhi: Oxford University Press, 1998), chapter 4.
11. Tanika Sarkar, 'Bengali Women in Politics – The 1920s and 1930s', in Kumkum Sangari and Sudesh Vaid (eds), *Women and Culture* (Bombay: SNDT Women's University, Research Centre for Women's Studies, Working Paper No. 1, 1994), pp. 121–4.
12. Tanika Sarkar, *Hindu Wife, Hindu Nation: Community, Religion, and Cultural Nationalism* (Bloomington: Indiana University Press, 2001), p. 267.
13. Kumar, *The History of Doing*, pp. 85–7; Visram, *Women in India and Pakistan*, p. 41.
14. Visram, *Women in India and Pakistan*, pp. 46–7.
15. Rosalind O'Hanlon, 'Gender in the British Empire', in Judith Brown and Wm. Roger Louis (eds), *The Oxford History of the British Empire* Vol. IV *The Twentieth Century* (Oxford: Oxford University Press, 1999), pp. 390–1.
16. Luise White, 'Separating the Men from the Boys: Constructions of Gender, Sexuality, and Terrorism in Central Kenya, 1939–1959', *International Journal of African Historical Studies* vol. 23, no. 1 (1990): 10–15.
17. Tabitha Kanogo, 'Kikuyu Women and the Politics of Protest: Mau Mau', in Sharon Macdonald, Pat Holden and Shirley Ardener (eds), *Images of Women in Peace and War: Cross-Cultural and Historical Perspectives* (Madison: University of Wisconsin Press, 1988), pp. 89–93.
18. Cora Ann Presley, *Kikuyu Women, the Mau Mau Rebellion, and Social Change in Kenya* (Boulder, CO: Westview Press, 1992), pp. 168–9.
19. Wambui Waiyaki Otieno, *Mau Mau's Daughter: A Life History*, edited by Cora Ann Presley (Boulder, CO: Lynne Rienner Publishers, 1998), pp. 38–43.
20. Otieno, *Mau Mau's Daughter*, p. 92.
21. Otieno, *Mau Mau's Daughter*, p. 117.
22. Otieno, *Mau Mau's Daughter*, pp. 103–7.
23. Marc Lacey, 'A Kenyan Iconoclast and Her Unusual Husband', *The New York Times*, 27 September 2003, p. A4.
24. Geiger, 'Women in Nationalist Struggle: TANU Activists in Dar ES Salaam', *International Journal of African Historical Studies* vol. 20, no. 1 (1987): 2.

25. Quoted by Susan Geiger, 'Women in Nationalist Struggle: TANU Activists in Dar Es Salaam', *International Journal of African Historical Studies* vol. 20, no. 1 (1987): 20.
26. Tessa Cleaver and Marion Wallace, *Namibia: Women in War* (London: Zed Books, 1990), pp. 80–7.
27. O'Hanlon, 'Gender in the British Empire', pp. 386–8.
28. Margaret Jolly, 'Motherlands? Some Notes on Women and Nationalism in India and Africa', *The Australian Journal of Anthropology* 1994 vol. 5, nos. 1 and 2: 57–8.
29. Jolly, 'Motherlands?', 53–5. Anne McClintock has analysed the symbolism of this movement in *Imperial Leather: Race, Gender and Sexuality in the Colonial Contest* (London: Routledge, 1995), pp. 369–79.
30. Jonathan Hyslop, 'White Working-Class Women and the Invention of Apartheid: "Purified" Afrikaner Nationalist Agitation for Legislation Against "Mixed" Marriages, 1934–9', *Journal of African History* vol. 36 (1995): 57–81.
31. Louise Vincent, 'The Power Behind the Scenes: The Afrikaner Nationalist Women's Parties, 1915 to 1931', *South African Historical Journal* vol. 40 (May 1999): 51–73.
32. Elaine Unterhalter, 'Women Soldiers and White Unity in Apartheid South Africa', in Macdonald, Holden and Ardener (eds), *Images of Women in Peace and War*, p. 119.
33. Margaret Ward, 'The Ladies' Land League and the Irish Land War 1881/82: Defining the Relationship Between Women and Nation', in Ida Blom, Karen Hagemann, and Catherine Hall (eds), *Gendered Nations: Nationalisms and Gender Order in the Long Nineteenth Century* (Oxford: Berg, 2000), p. 243.
34. Margaret Ward, 'National Liberation Movements and the Question of Women's Liberation: The Irish Experience', in Clare Midgley (ed.), *Gender and Imperialism* (Manchester: Manchester University Press, 1998), pp. 104–22.
35. Maryann Gialanella Valiulis, 'Power, Gender, and Identity in the Irish Free State', *Journal of Women's History* Double vol. 6, no. 4 and vol. 7, no. 1 (Winter/Spring 1995): 117–36.
36. Tamara L. Hunt, 'Wild Irish Women: Gender, Politics, and Colonialism in the Nineteenth Century', in Hunt and Micheline R. Lessard (eds), *Women and the Colonial Gaze* (New York: New York University Press, 2002), p. 60; Valiulis, 'Power, Gender, and Identity,' pp. 117–18.
37. Ellen L. Fleischmann, *The Nation and Its 'New Women': The Palestinian Women's Movement, 1920–1948* (Berkeley: University of California Press, 2003), especially chapters 1, 5 and 6.
38. On the Egyptian women's movement, see Kumari Jayawardena, 'Reformism and Women's Rights in Egypt', in her *Feminism and Nationalism in the Third World* (London: Zed Books, 1986); and Beth Baron, *The Women's Awakening in Egypt: Culture, Society, and the Press* (New Haven, CT: Yale University Press, 1994).

39. Jonathan F. Vance, *Death So Noble: Memory, Meaning, and the First World War* (Vancouver: University of British Columbia Press, 1997), especially chapters 5–8.

40. Colin Coates and Cecilia Morgan, *Heroines and History: Madeleines de Vercheres and Laura Secord* (Toronto: University of Toronto Press, 2002), esp. pp. 10–11.

41. Katie Pickles, *Female Imperialism and National Identity: Imperial Order Daughters of the Empire* (Manchester: Manchester University Press, 2002), esp. ch. 6 ' "Other than stones and mortar": war memorials, memory and imperial knowledge'.

42. McClintock, *Imperial Leather*, p. 352.

43. Leila J. Rupp, *Worlds of Women: The Making of an International Women's Movement* (Princeton, NJ: Princeton University Press, 1997).

44. Chandra Talpade Mohanty, 'Under Western Eyes', in Chandra Talpade Mohanty, Ann Russo, and Lourdes Torres (eds), *Third World Women and the Politics of Feminism* (Bloomington: Indiana University Press, 1991); Antoinette Burton, *Burdens of History: British Feminists, Indian Women, and Imperial Culture 1865–1915* (Chapel Hill: University of North Carolina Press, 1994); Vron Ware, *Beyond the Pale: White Women, Racism, and History* (London: Verso, 1992).

45. See, for example, Mrinalini Sinha, 'Reading *Mother India*: Empire, Nation, and the Female Voice', *Journal of Women's History* vol. 6, no. 2 (Summer 1994): 6–44; Fiona Paisley, 'Citizens of Their World: Australian Feminism and Indigenous Rights in the International Context, 1920s and 1930s', *Feminist Review* no. 58 (1998): 66–84; and Mrinalini Sinha, Donna J. Guy and Angela Woollacott (eds), *Feminisms and Internationalism* (Oxford: Blackwell, 1999), including my essay on the British Commonwealth League and the Pan-Pacific Women's Association.

6
Gender and Empire in the Metropole

Colonialism and its gendered dimensions have been shaping influences on the British Isles since the sixteenth century; post-Second World War migration from South Asia and the West Indies only made them impossible to overlook. From the late-sixteenth century, the empire was a focus of high politics. By the late-nineteenth century, parliament and Whitehall were consumed by the administration and challenges of the empire. But the imbrication of the empire was far more subtle and pervasive than just government. As a school of work has demonstrated, imperialism saturated modern British society, cultural representations, trade and economy, and colonial hierarchies shaped domestic British class, race and gender relations.[1] English country houses were built from the profits of colonial trade and plantations, English fiction was stocked with characters who washed up on British shores from the colonies or quickly disappeared to them, and British shops and advertising were filled with goods from the empire and gendered images of them. While English schoolboys were being trained for the responsibilities of empire on the playing fields of Eton, British housewives were urged to consider the empire when shopping for their families, and the propaganda of migration societies and schemes sought to lure men to the colonies with promises of wide, open spaces and the chance to be a better breadwinner, while women were encouraged to migrate through improved prospects for matrimony.

British history is currently fired by debate over the issue of the impact of empire and colonialism within Britain itself. Scholars and political commentators who resist the idea of imperial impact on Britain denounce 'the new imperial history' and postcolonial scholarship for raising questions they consider either irrelevant or obvious. Biographer David Gilmour recently scolded 'a young American historian' for suggesting that the generations-long history of connections between Britain and India should be a subject for current political analysis. 'Rather patronising advice', Gilmour dismissed this suggestion, 'for a nation which has been analysing and debating it at least since *A Passage to India* and *Burmese Days*.'[2] Various historians have sought to minimize the import of the historical construction of race, and to dismiss the significance of Orientalism, the entrenched cultural edifice of representations of 'the East' and Asia as exotic, sensual and inferior to European 'civilization'. In a recent review essay, historian John Darwin elides the concept of the impact of empire on Britain with that of

British public opinion of the empire, arguing that the British public was always indifferent to the empire. Claiming this view as conventional and trustworthy historical wisdom, he suggests that the new imperial historians 'like geese, have rushed in a flock to the other end of the field'.[3] Dismissing the historical importance of the empire, and especially its impact on Britain itself, conserves the notion of an unsullied British national identity, and serves to deny ethnic or cultural hybridity. At the beginning of the twenty-first century, when the more famous contemporary British writers include Salman Rushdie, Hanif Kureishi and Zadie Smith, such arguments against the historical impact of the empire on Britain have clear political implications for who and what counts as really British. As Antoinette Burton has argued, historical work on the British Isles as one site of the empire

> strikes at the heart of Britain's long ideological attachment to the narratives of the Island Story, of splendid isolation, and of European exceptionalism. It materializes the traffic of colonial goods, ideas and people across metropolitan borders and indeed throws into question the very Victorian distinctions between Home and Away that defined the imagined geography of empire in the nineteenth century.[4]

This chapter is founded on the premise that empire and colonialism permeated British culture, and seeks to demonstrate several ways in which that permeation took gendered forms. I will look at the ways in which spectacles and displays of colonized subjects had constitutive gendering effects, as well as how individual colonial subjects who sojourned in Britain transmitted and reacted to gendered ideas and practices. Institutions, societies and leagues representing the empire proliferated in late-nineteenth and early-twentieth century Britain, especially in the metropole; many of these were shaped by and shaped notions of gender. One way in which the colonies shaped life in Britain were the possibilities emigration was imagined to represent – even the emigration of an escaped convict, according to Charles Dickens in *Great Expectations*, could be the *deus ex machina* through which a 'gentleman' received his necessary income and therefore his status. Finally, the chapter will consider gendered aspects of material culture and standard of living in Britain, as shaped by the empire. In all of these ways, people, ideas and products moved between and among Britain and its colonies, a ceaseless traffic over centuries that shaped British imperial culture in its many scattered locations, not least Britain itself. This chapter, then, will argue for the significance of identifying the interconstitution of the empire and 'home', and the ways in which gender figured therein.

Imperial spectacles and displays

Racialized images of both masculinity and femininity were produced by the material spectacles of empire, in both museums and exhibitions, so popular in Britain and elsewhere at either side of the turn of the twentieth century. Annie E. Coombes has argued that in the 1890s and 1900s British public fascination with Africa was fed by the ethnographic collections and exhibitions that mushroomed in local and national museums, a public cultural face of the emergent 'scientific' disciplines of anthropology, ethnography and eugenics. Representations of African bodies jostled with material cultural artefacts and displays of African fauna, as British imperial annexation of African colonies spread, and colonial officials, hunters and others brought back to Britain the trophies of colonial ownership. Photographs of Africans featuring naked or nearly-naked women authorized voyeurism as an educational pursuit, and allusions to and discussions of African polygamy suggested African degeneration and cultural inferiority. Thus some of the most respected cultural institutions, serious museums at the heart of middle-class enthusiasm for edification, worked to shape popular notions of African men as primitive hunters and fighters, and African women as sexual objects devalued and mistreated by their men.[5] Racialized gendered notions of Africans constituted Britons' sense of their own gendered and racialized selves by purportedly representing the nether end of the scale of civilization, and implying the superiority of British culture and practices.

While museums and large exhibitions proliferated in the late nineteenth century, the metropolitan display of indigenous people originated in previous centuries, part of the Old World interest in the New World dating from the fifteenth century, renewed in the eighteenth century by the Enlightenment's drive for exploration and 'discovery'. Both before and during the rise of the museum and imperial expositions, indigenous people were put on display in circuses, fairs, 'cabinets of curiosity' and other popular venues. Numbers of colonial indigenous people were lured to Europe and North America in the nineteenth century, where they were treated as spectacular specimens and sideshow freaks, what Roslyn Poignant has called 'professional savages'. Some were tempted by promises of wealth. Curiosity about the reputedly superior metropole must have been one factor in their willingness to go, but the recruiting agents who worked for organizers of exhibitions, museums and circuses often resorted to ruse. In 1810 the Khoisan woman from South Africa, who would be invoked in dominant discourses about gender and sexuality for the rest of the nineteenth century, apparently believed that she would make money by agreeing to go to England. Saartjie Baartman was convinced by Hendrick Cezar, her master's brother, and an Englishman Alexander Dunlop, to accompany them to England on the promise of a share of the takings from her own exhibition. After four years of constant display in London and the English provinces, Baartman was taken to Paris, where she was exhibited and studied, and where she died in December 1815. Disparagingly known as the 'Hottentot Venus' [Hottentot was a pejorative term for Khoisan people], Baartman was typically displayed on a combination stage and cage, very much as though she were an animal. One contemporary account recorded that she was

> surrounded by many persons, some females! One pinched her, another walked around her; one gentleman poked her with his cane, and one lady employed her parasol to ascertain that all was, as she called it, '*nattral*'. This inhumane baiting, the poor creature bore with sullen indifference, except upon some great provocation, when she seemed inclined to resent brutality, which even a Hottentot can understand. On these occasions it required all authority to subdue her resentment.[6]

Rosemary Wiss has documented the November 1810 case brought before the King's Bench by the abolitionist African Association, in an attempt to free Baartman from her exhibitors, and to allow her to return to South Africa. The case failed, the Attorney-General concluding that Baartman was on display through her own will and consent.[7]

Baartman's spectacular appeal to Europeans, which remained consistent throughout the years she was on display, lay in the fact that her buttocks were considered large and protuberant, and in the curiosity and speculation about her genitals. She came to represent popular European belief in the excessive and deviant genitalia of black women, which was linked to their imagined primitive and uncontrolled sexuality. In Paris in 1815, while Baartman was still alive she agreed to stand for a full-length nude painting by the anatomical scientist Georges Cuvier. After her death in December, Cuvier obtained permission to study and dissect her body: he made plaster and wax casts, especially of her genitalia. He then dissected and preserved her body parts, which were put on display at the Musee de l'Homme, where they remained on display throughout the nineteenth and twentieth centuries.[8] The great interest, both scientific and popular, in her body parts was spurred by the belief that African women's genitalia were quite different in shape from European women's, larger and differently formed. These imagined physiological differences were held as fundamental proof of difference between the races, and of Africans' separate path of evolution, as well as their proximity to apes. As both Rosemary Wiss and Sander Gilman have argued, it was highly significant that black women's buttocks and genitalia were considered the ultimate proof of racial difference. Ideas about black female bodies stood for more general assumptions about femininity and all women's sexuality: black women represented the extreme form of all women's sensuality and primitiveness, their subsumption by sexuality, in opposition to men's rationality. Gilman shows how throughout the nineteenth century Saartjie Baartman's genitals and body continued to represent the supposed deviancy and degeneracy of black female sexuality, and by extension all female sexuality. Baartman was cited in medico-scientific discourses that linked the clitoris with sexual excess, and female sexuality with corruption, disease and prostitution; by 1905 an Italian 'scientist' claimed that Italian prostitutes had buttocks the same shape as those of the female 'Hottentot'.[9] Even, or perhaps especially, discourses on gender and sexuality that claimed to be 'scientific' could easily slide from purportedly demonstrating racial difference, to asserting cross-racial similarity in the name of sexual difference. It was only in 2003 that Saartjie Baartman's remains were returned by the Musee de l'Homme, flown back to Cape Town, and honoured with a memorial service and burial. Hopes were expressed at the memorial service that Baartman's spirit could now rest properly.[10] Her story, especially the fact of her body parts being on display for nearly two hundred years, and her iconic status in nineteenth-century 'scientific' discourse on female sexuality and racial difference, are powerful evidence of colonialism's role in shaping European ideas and culture, especially ideas about sexuality and gender. If Saartjie Baartman was an extreme instance of the display of the female body, European gender ideologies that invoked her similarly objectified European women as embodiments of sexuality.

While indigenous women were objects of sexual curiosity and 'scientific' theory, indigenous men became yardsticks and mirrors for masculine physical and technological prowess, especially hunting and fighting abilities. Roslyn Poignant has, through exhaustive research in many countries, traced the story of two small groups of Aboriginal people from North Queensland who were persuaded by R.A. Cunningham, a recruiter for the circus impresario P.T. Barnum, to travel internationally with him as itinerant performers, the first group from 1883 to 1888, and the second group from 1892 to 1898. These intrepid Aboriginal people, most of whom died along the way, traversed the United States and continental Europe, and performed in London among many other capital cities and towns, part of the widespread travelling industry of colonized peoples. Their performances, or displays, focused on their bodies, scars and decorations, but a constant theme was their construction and throwing of boomerangs. The boomerang came to stand for their primitive hunting skills and technology, but perhaps as well it held an obvious spectacular appeal and was easily carried and displayed. In 1887 Billy, one of the Aboriginal troupe, both for the Royal Anthropological Institute and at a performance at the Royal Pavilion in Brighton, improvised by making boomerangs out of pieces of cardboard, then demonstrating his ability to make them return.[11] Yet it was not the first time Aboriginal men had displayed Aboriginal weapons in Britain.

In 1868 the first Australian cricket team ever to visit England toured London and several of the provinces; it was composed entirely of Aboriginal men. Erased from Australian public memory for most of the twentieth century, this cricket team not only performed quite well, winning half of their matches, but aroused a great deal of interest in Britain. On 26 May 1868, *The Times* asserted: 'No truer test of the interest taken by the public in the performance of this team from the antipodes can be afforded than that of 7,000 persons congregated at the Oval yesterday, when the first match of a series projected to be played in the three kingdoms came off.'[12] Over the following months, *The Times* continued to report on the Aboriginal cricket team's tour, publishing detailed accounts of the matches and scores. Some of these reports listed the Aboriginal players by name, noting the different colours of the sashes worn by the black players, apparently in order for English spectators to distinguish them individually. The paper also reported the additional entertainment the Aboriginal men provided: demonstrations of their traditional weapons, or what *The Times* called 'an exhibition of native Australian sports'. At the match at Bootle, Liverpool in September 1868, such an exhibition resulted in one of the onlookers receiving 'a severe wound across the brow' from a boomerang that had been caught by the wind.[13] Reports of the Aboriginal team, most of whom were from western Victoria, pointed out that they were 'perfectly civilized', because they spoke English and had 'been brought up in the bush to agricultural pursuits under European settlers'.[14] One commentator made explicit the question of gender, noting that 'it was observed that in all of them there was a manly and dignified bearing'.[15] Able both to play cricket and thus demonstrate quintessential latter nineteenth-century British manliness, and to show their equally masculine prowess with their own weapons, the Aboriginal cricketers of 1868 are a good example of how ideas of gender were shaped at once between metropole and colonies. The team's matches and exhibitions suggest an equivalence, or at least a comparability, between the two sorts of manly performance. Part of a widespread wave of enthusiasm for cricket among Aborigines in the latter decades of the century, much this same team had also performed to great excitement in Australia. In the Australian colonial context, the team's matches were racially driven contests of masculine prowess. In the English context, there was an added layer of investment and interest on the part of the team's Anglo-Australian managers. In both places, issues of race and gender were shaped by the politics of colonialism.

Colonial subjects in Britain

Especially in the modern period, colonial subjects travelled around the British Isles, and stayed for what could be extended periods; some settled in Britain for the rest of their lives. Notions of gender shaped the circumstances from which colonial subjects of diverse ethnicities travelled to the metropole, as well as their motivations for going, and then mediated their movements within it.[16]

The indigenous people discussed above in the context of spectacle and display had their own reasons for agreeing to travel to Europe, and for being willing to perform and to be observed. Saartjie Baartman, the Aboriginal cricketers and boomerang-throwers all had their own conceptions of their performances, and must have had their own thoughts about the Britons they met and metropolitan society and culture. They were knowing participants in the construction of gendered and racialized images, even as they were exploited, suffered physically and were at times derided. Particular stories of colonial subjects who travelled to the heart of empire allow us to see how indigenous and colonized peoples from various imperial locations criticized, appropriated and challenged racist stereotypes and representations. Cecilia Morgan shows the complex interplay of imperial cultural elements at work during the turn-of-the-century English sojourns of two Canadian Aboriginals, both Mohawks from Ontario. Pauline Johnson was the daughter of a Mohawk chief and an English immigrant, who was educated in both the cultures she inherited. As a young woman in the 1880s she began writing poetry and performing in Canada, consciously presenting herself as a representative of both cultures. In England too, during her sojourns there in 1894 and 1906, she would perform at times in a fringed buckskin dress and moccasins, presenting herself as an Indian poetess and ambassador of Mohawk culture. At other moments, sometimes during the same performance, she would appear in elegant and fashionable evening dress, presenting herself as educated and cosmopolitan, at home in both cultures. As Morgan argues, Johnson was an independent, modern woman, making a theatrical career for herself from her ability to travel and to publish, as well as contemporary fascination with ethnic difference and indigenous peoples. Her movement in and out of her role as Indian poetess at once deployed and undercut notions of ethnic identity that were presented in overtly gendered ways. Hence, she managed both to celebrate her Mohawk cultural heritage, and to challenge stereotypes of the degraded North American Indian 'squaw', partly by arguing that Iroquois women wielded more political power in their society than British women.

At much the same time John Ojijatekha Brant-Sero, also a Mohawk from Ontario, spent time in England: he visited there in 1891, then seemingly lived in England from 1900 until his death in London in 1914. In 1900 Brant-Sero travelled to South Africa to volunteer for the British army in the South African war, but was refused enlistment on the grounds of race. In Ontario in the 1890s Brant-Sero was considered an authority on Mohawk history and culture, worked for an archaeologist, and served on the board of the Ontario Historical Society. In London, he presented a paper to the British Association for the Advancement of Science, and was briefly a Fellow of the Anthropological Institute. Like Johnson, his stock in trade were public presentations on Mohawk culture. Brant-Sero challenged gendered hierarchical notions of British soldiers versus Indian warriors, particularly in a 1901 letter to *The Times* in which he related his rejection by the British army in South Africa, and lectured readers on the historical military alliance between Six Nations Indians and the British in North America. Also like Johnson, Brant-Sero consciously juxtaposed 'native' and 'white' gendered stereotypes. While on the one hand he argued for his (and presumably other Aboriginals') contributions to the empire, his performance of Native masculinity – such as in a male beauty contestant at Folkestone in 1908 for which he wore 'native' dress and headdress – seemed to challenge 'white' masculine physicality. Both Johnson and Brant-Sero deployed gendered ethnic stereotypes to their own professional advantage, even as they seemed to move between worlds and cultures, in careers that reveal the complex and contradictory elements of turn-of-the-century imperial culture.[17]

The presence of South Asians in Britain goes back to the eighteenth century if not earlier; from around a century prior to the large-scale migration of the post-Second World War period, significant numbers of Indians and Singhalese passed through or resided in Britain. Coming from various parts of the Indian subcontinent as well as a wide range of classes, Indians in Britain from the mid-nineteenth century included ayahs (nannies) and lascars (sailors), as well as members of the elite and royal classes. We know from the growing body of scholarship on South Asians in Britain that by the late nineteenth century not only were labouring Indians part of the emergent mixed-race communities in British ports, such as in Liverpool, Newcastle, Swansea and the London docklands, privileged Indians, mostly men, lived in Britain in order to study and gain professional qualifications. Statistics show that from 1885 hundreds of Indians, including Hindus, Muslims and Parsis, were students in Britain.[18] Others came as reformers, lobbyists and tourists. The London sojourns of two different South Asian men reveal some of the complexity of gender negotiation across axes of 'race' and imperial rule within the metropole itself. Behramji Malabari, a Bombay Parsi who spent several months in London in 1890 and published an account of his observations, was there as a reformer and advocate of Indian women. In her analysis of his travel account, Antoinette Burton shows how Malabari's London encounters were framed by Victorian cultural understandings of gender, and his gendered responses. Having engaged in political contests over masculinity and social reform with Hindu men in India – challenging men who resisted reform legislation to raise the age of consent for women as 'unmanly' – in Britain, Malabari's position was convoluted in gender terms.

Casting himself as a chivalrous defender, protector and advocate of Indian women, Malabari found his own masculinity under threat as he negotiated London's public thoroughfares. Accosted in the street by both working-class boys and middle-class women, drawn to him by his clothing, headwear and appearance, Malabari sought to assert his masculinity by refusing to be cowed, or having his freedom of movement – a key characteristic of the urban rambler he sought to be – impeded. As Burton notes, Malabari further established his masculinity – under threat in the metropole as a colonized Indian man – through his narration of encounters with working-class British women. By implying that he was solicited by unrespectable women on the bus, and evincing a patriarchal interest in the romantic life of his landlady's domestic servant, Malabari asserted himself as a man by representing his power and authority over women.[19] In the very different world of 1920s London, by which time both sexual politics and political tensions between Britain and India had shifted, the young student of philosophy and aspiring writer Mulk Raj Anand, from Peshawar, asserted his claims to masculinity in quite different ways. Openly engaging in sexual and romantic relationships with English women, Anand publicly challenged racialized restrictions on colonized men's access to white women. Equally boldly, if also carefully, Anand sought to challenge the imperialist and racist assumptions, and ignorance of Indian culture, that he encountered in the Bloomsbury intelligentsia. Amid the politics of late British colonialism in India, for Anand conversational forays that asserted Indian national culture helped to constitute his masculine self-respect and countered the emasculation of his colonized status.[20]

Institutes, clubs, societies and leagues: Colonialism in the West End

Men from the white-settler colonies had fewer challenges to their masculinity with which to deal in Britain, and were not confronted with racism. One report on the lavish coronation festivities in London in 1902 compared 'the Easterns' and 'the Colonials' attending the high-level official celebrations, asserting that 'the Colonials' were not as colourful as 'the Easterns' albeit being 'picturesque in their way; but it is a different way; and, after all, they are ourselves'.[21] Yet their status as colonials, and their distance from the seat of metropolitan political power, presented challenges to white-settler men that they actively sought to overcome through vigorous institution building in the metropole. Among the prestigious West End men's clubs, from the 1880s to the mid-twentieth century, clubs that fostered connections with the colonies flourished. In 1885 the Imperial and American Club was opened for 'non-residents in this country temporarily home [sic] from the United States and Colonies'.[22] As late as 1937 the Australia Club was launched, its connections to imperial power apparent from the fact that its inaugural dinner was held at the Savoy Hotel with Winston Churchill as speaker.[23] The plethora of clubs with imperial connections included the London Colonial Club, the Imperial Colonies Club, the Dominions Club, the Australasian Club, the South African Club, the Canada Club, and the West India Club, to mention just a sampling.[24] The Overseas Club, which began in

1914 and later became the Overseas League, boasted a membership of 26,000 by 1922, a significant proportion of whom lived in the dominions. The founder of the Overseas Club, Major Evelyn Wrench, claimed that he had been inspired by Cecil Rhodes's vision of British interests spreading round the world. The club's Member's Creed, linked to Rhodes's imperial aspirations and asserting an explicit if unexamined connection between the empire and patriarchy, ran: 'Believing the British Empire to stand for justice, pardon, order and good government, we pledge ourselves, as citizens of the British government, we pledge ourselves, as citizens of the British Commonwealth of Nations, to maintain the heritage handed down to us by our fathers.'[25] Not least among these edifices of colonial power in the West End was the Royal Colonial Institute, founded in 1868, and which by the Edwardian period boasted salubrious premises on Northumberland Avenue, where members could mix and network, as well as hear papers read on matters of imperial import. Membership was restricted to men until 1909 when a subordinate category of associate membership was created for women, with limited privileges. While some nonwhite men from the colonies numbered among the Institute's members, they were dominantly elite men from Britain and the white-settler dominions, intent on building trading relations and expanding the empire's territorial and political conquests.[26] The Institute and the plethora of clubs and other West End sites of imperial networking were a crucial arena for the construction of white colonial manhood, right at the heart of the empire.

White colonial women also used gender ideology in order to establish a particular base of authority for themselves in the metropole, and a concept of feminine imperial loyalty. For some women, such an ideology explicitly merged feminism with proimperialism. Mary Gaunt, a successful travel and fiction writer born and brought up in the colony of Victoria, combined her feminism and proimperialism into a construction of the white colonial woman. Living in London from 1901 to the early 1920s, Gaunt was regarded in the metropole as an authority on both West Africa and Jamaica, the two colonial sites where she spent most time (other than Australia) and about which she wrote at length; for example, in 1912 Gaunt was invited to lecture to the British West African Association.[27] If her numerous novels (often with colonial settings) were aimed at a popular audience, her travel writing was serious, but both sold well. *Alone in West Africa*, an account of her travels there in 1908 and 1910 went into four editions, while her 1910 novel set between Britain and West Africa *The Uncounted Cost*, controversial because of its gender politics, had large sales and garnered much attention. Her books were widely and favourably reviewed.[28] Throughout her lifetime her writing was inflected by her sense of herself as a white colonial woman, specifically an Australian woman. One Australian journalist commented in 1912 in a nationalistic character sketch: 'Mary Gaunt left Victoria for London more than ten years ago, but she is still a thorough Australian, energetic, enterprising, with a keen, quick sense of humour.'[29] Gaunt drew upon her early life in Australia in all her nonfiction writing, and invoked her status as a white colonial to comment evenhandedly on the British colonies she toured and on metropolitan Britain, often being quite critical of the metropole.

Throughout her writings, Gaunt constructs an image of the white colonial woman – both herself and other women – as practical, intelligent, secular, brave, enterprising, hardy and likeable, frequently in specific contradistinction to Englishwomen, or at least, what Gaunt represents as the typical or fashionable Englishwoman. Gaunt used the English press as a platform to expound her nationalistic Australian views. In April 1912 she published in *The Daily Chronicle* a polemic against the flawed 'sheltered life' of English girls, which resulted, in her view, in their being 'curiously dependent and self-conscious'. In specific contrast the young Australian woman was 'a creature of resource' whose 'wholesome' education had turned her into an ideal companion for the enterprising man. The inadequate upbringing of English girls had, according to Gaunt, serious imperial implications. The empire depended upon a 'spirit of adventure' that was imperilled if 'half of the nation is not sure of itself'. Invoking her own observations, Gaunt indicted most of the Englishwomen she had met in West Africa as overly fearful: 'They were afraid, heaven only knows what they were not afraid of, from black men and chills to driver ants and crawly things.' And their fears meant that they were 'an intolerable burden to their husbands'.[30] Australian women, Gaunt had explained earlier, were far more capable because the Australian climate and social mores both promoted independence, and the relative lack of domestic help meant even middle-class Australian women learnt practical skills.[31] This message – that Australian and other white colonial women are more suited to and better workers in the imperial enterprise than Englishwomen – recurs throughout Gaunt's travel and fiction writing.[32] Exploiting her success as a travel and fiction writer, Gaunt used her visibility in England to assert what may have been seen as a challenge to metropolitan definitions of femininity – or could have been dismissed as colonial impudence.

Mary Gaunt was unusual in both her career and her prominence as a colonial woman travel and fiction writer based in London, and was notable for the strength of her feminist, imperialist views. But she was far from alone as a white colonial woman seeking to demonstrate and articulate imperial loyalty. White-settler colonial women's imperial loyalty manifested itself in multiple ways in both Britain and the dominions. Historian Katie Pickles has studied women's empire loyalty organizations of the early to mid-twentieth century, including the Canadian-based Imperial Order Daughters of the Empire (IODE), and the Victoria League. Indeed, as Pickles has shown, the two organizations were initially in competition, the IODE having begun in Montreal in 1900 just prior to the 1901 formation of the Victoria League. The metropolitan-based League soon asserted its claim to centrality and therefore preeminence, and the IODE fell into line according to the imperial hierarchies they sought to shore up. The Victoria League was created to commemorate the late queen through an imperial organization that enabled women to establish connections and networks between metropole and colonies, to voice their imperial loyalty, and thus to promote a feminine version of white-settler dominion political support.[33] Moreover, by the early twentieth century some bastions of white-settler masculine politics in London spawned women's auxiliaries. By the 1920s, for example, the Royal Colonial Institute (soon to become the Royal Commonwealth Society) began a regular feature on 'Women and the Empire' in its *United Empire* journal. Comprising a magazine-style coverage of brief notices presumed of interest to 'colonial' and 'Commonwealth' as well as metropolitan women, the journal's women's pages reported activities of the royal family, news of organizations like the International Federation of University Women, and pioneering women's achievements. In January 1927, for example, it noted that Miss Kathleen Hoahing, born in British Guiana, was the first Chinese woman to pass the solicitors' final examination, and was to become the first woman solicitor to practice in China.[34] Such reports worked to meld liberal feminism with imperial politics, and to suggest that nonwhite women could avail themselves of progressive opportunities through the empire.

If women's empire loyalist organizations like the Victoria League consciously sought to incorporate women into the imperial networks centred in London, so too did some feminist organizations. Perhaps the most prominent of these was the British Commonwealth League (BCL), founded in London in 1925. More progressive than the Victoria League in its gender politics, albeit a mixed organization in terms of imperial support – ranging from promotion of imperial unity under the structure of the British Commonwealth, to critiques of colonial administrations and their treatment of women – the BCL sought to draw international attention to women's issues across the empire through their annual conferences held in London. With conferences on themes such as the 'Social and Industrial position of Women other than British Race, governed under the British Flag' (1927), and 'Marriage from the Imperial Standpoint' including 'The Civil Rights of Married Women' and 'Inter-racial Unions' (1932), the BCL sought to promote women's issues across a range of colonies and dominions. Arguably always an organization in which British and white colonial women had the upper hand, nevertheless elite colonized women from, for example, India, Ceylon and Hong Kong used BCL conferences as an international platform from which to speak.[35] While women's empire loyalty organizations inserted women into conservative discourses and activities, and articulated an often maternalist, feminine version of imperialism, feminist organizations like the BCL made sure that women's issues circulated within imperial politics, newspapers and magazines from the early to mid-twentieth century. Some feminists and suffragists had similarly inserted women's issues into imperial politics and culture in the late nineteenth and early twentieth centuries, if partly to claim an imperial dimension to their own maternalist authority. Feminism in the metropole thus included colonial and some colonized women, as well as colonial and colonized women's issues, as part of a circulation that shaped British feminism in multiple imperial sites.

Emigration

A central enterprise of imperialist women's philanthropic and organizing efforts in the late nineteenth and early twentieth centuries was women's emigration, which was seen particularly as a possible salvation for single and unemployed women. Emigration to the white-settler colonies was a primary link between Britain and its empire in the nineteenth and twentieth centuries. As convict transportation gave way to Wakefieldian notions of planned colonies of settlement, and gold rushes in various colonial sites across the second half of the nineteenth century impelled men to travel enormous distances to take their chances at a lucky strike, the colonies came to represent possibilities of redemption and prosperity. The representations of emigration which circulated in Britain in popular culture, and through the propaganda of voluntary emigration societies and government-assisted migration schemes, conveyed a contradictory mix of gendered messages. While there were more males in total emigrating to the white-settler colonies, schemes and emigration evangelists produced their own gendered images of both migrant men and women. In 1850 Caroline Chisholm, advocate for single women emigrants to Australia, expounded in Britain the case for more loans for passages for respectable poor families and single women to escape the clutches of the British workhouse and to create a livelihood from the 'vast resources' that Australia offered. Her arguments for supported and reformed emigration became part of the mid-century imperial imaginary of empire. Chisholm linked emigration to the martial spirit that 'made our soldiers and sailors triumphant all over the world', at the same time that she claimed it would help fathers of working-class families become respectable manly breadwinners, and help poor single women to remain virtuous and find prospective husbands. Setting aside any claims of Australia's Aboriginal inhabitants, Chisholm contended that the English poor deserved to take advantage of 'vast and fair regions unoccupied by man, nature alone being mistress thereof'.[36] Thus notions of gendered respectability for English men and women were directly linked to imperial racial hierarchies and underwrote colonial migration schemes and Britain's claims to territorial conquest.

Migration schemes for single women began as early as the 1830s, and by the 1860s empire feminists began to push what they saw as colonial opportunities not just for poorer women but for 'distressed gentlewomen' too.[37] A linked genealogical chain of feminist societies that aimed to foster women's migration to the white-settler colonies was launched in 1862 with the foundation of the Female Middle Class Emigration Society. Subsequent variant organizations included the Women's Emigration Society (1880–84), the British Women's Emigration Association (1884–1919), the South African Colonization Society (1902–19), and from 1920 the Society for the Oversea Settlement of British Women. But these feminist organizations were far from alone in the work of organizing women's emigration. In the case of making possible 'Sunny Ontario for British Girls' in the first decades of the twentieth century, besides the Ontario and British government's involvement, there were also the Salvation Army, the Women's Domestic Guild of Canada and the Canadian Domestic Guild for Irish domestics. Between 1900 and 1930 more than 170,000 British women migrated to Canada with the declared intention of becoming domestic servants.[38] Organized efforts to send single British women to the Transvaal, South Africa, in the first decade of the twentieth century had the blessing of imperial luminaries such as Joseph Chamberlain, Cecil Rhodes and Alfred Milner, because it was hoped that the settlement of white women in the colony would help stabilize it during its postwar reconstruction, and also boost the proportion of white domestic servants in relation to black servants, including black 'houseboys'.[39] Lisa Chilton has recently analysed the complex views of

Edwardian female imperialists who sought to promote the migration to the dominions of women from 'above the working class'. She shows that, along with their class and racial prejudices, and for all of their imperialism, the women surrounding the journal *The Imperial Colonist* in the first decade of the century sought to counter assumptions of the empire as a masculine-dominated frontier. These well-placed women 'conceived of the empire as a space in which cultured femininity was a dominant force, and they saw themselves as the empire's grand matriarchs, working from the centre to ensure that the right class of women would be in place to domesticate the periphery appropriately'.[40] Similarly, historian Julia Bush has studied the efforts of female imperialists towards promoting women's emigration in the Edwardian period and revealed some complexity, such as their applauding women's efforts to expand the Empire and assert themselves as independent beings at the same time. Ultimately, however, she suggests that female supporters of women's emigration believed that racial duty, and women's responsibilities and roles as mothers, were paramount to the empire's interests.[41]

Despite the efforts of middle-class women's emigration societies, colonial governments and employers foiled their attempts to diversify potential occupations for women in the colonies with unrelenting demands for domestic servants. Jan Gothard has argued that in the nineteenth century the significant programmes of Australian colonial governments to assist the migration of single women were driven above all else by the demand for domestic servants.[42] By the First World War, one of the plethora of women's philanthropic organizations working in the field of emigration was the Young Women's Christian Association (YWCA), which expanded enormously during the war. An internal YWCA report on its emigration work at the end of the war complained bitterly about the obstructive and limited attitudes of dominion governments. Representatives of the YWCA's Emigration Department noted that there was 'at present a large preponderance of women at home, and a prospect of a still larger preponderance after the war, whilst there is a preponderance of men in the Dominions'. But, they argued, the dominion governments were doing themselves harm by creating only a 'limited number of openings for women in the Dominions'.

> The Dominions will in the long run suffer – in fact, they are already suffering – from the policy which their Governments have adopted of limiting the facilities which they offer for female emigration to domestic servants. They really need women who will be the mothers of future generations of colonists; and if they want to obtain women of another class than servants, they must offer facilities and attractions for other work. Instead of doing that, they actually hinder them from coming; for women (other than domestic servants) have to pay their own passages, which uses up their resources; and Canada for instance will not allow them to land unless they possess a certain sum of money.[43]

Thus in the face of determined efforts of imperialist feminists to broaden women's opportunities in the colonies, and thus to diversify the gendered images of emigration for women with more masculine notions of independence and financial autonomy, domestic service dominated women's migration. Migration for women, then, reinforced Victorian conceptions of respectable femininity as domesticated, either performing labour within the households of others, or – for the more fortunate – becoming mistress of one's own household.

Notions of femininity forged through migration also centred on images of hardship and the physical strenuousness of pioneering conditions. Even for the minority of single women migrants who evaded domestic service and took up some other feminized occupation such as teaching, governessing or nursing, colonial conditions were notorious as being difficult and demanding. In 1914 one nurse who had migrated to New Zealand reported back to the British Women's Emigration Association on the demands on nurses to perform domestic labour as well:

> I think it is a very difficult thing to get the right sort of woman for the country life here. To begin with, she must be very well trained and have absolute confidence in herself, for there is often no doctor for 30 or 50 miles. The doctors like to have a well-educated woman to work with, of course, and the patients want someone who will do all the work they have been doing before their illness, for only about one out of 50 has help of any sort, therefore she must be able to wash, cook and clean, look after the children and at the same time often be up a good deal in the night … in fact, she must be a woman who can put up with a great deal, and there are not many well trained women who will do it, I am afraid.[44]

Even for women whose paid work was of a higher professional status than domestic service, the sparse and demanding conditions in the colonies made it nearly impossible to escape domestic labour, which was even harder to perform than in the metropole because of the circumstances. Images in Britain of colonial possibilities for women continually revolved around the household, the domestic and the maternal. Women migrants, even those with hopes of financial and social independence, were reminded that they should expect to do some domestic labour. Lurking behind the representations of work for women in the colonies was often the expectation that they would marry, form their own households and help to expand the settler population through giving birth. For all of the efforts of empire feminists to cast the dominions as places where single women could own a piece of land or find an independent living, circumscribed notions of femininity as domesticated and maternal overwhelmed such representations, and served to reinforce conservative definitions of womanhood in the metropole.

The circulation of material and imperial culture

The culture of empire circulated through Britain in a whole gamut of forms, from popular novels, travel writing and cookbooks, to consumer goods associated with colonial exoticism, to the accoutrements of households that defined social status with gendered and racialized inflections. Chapter 3 considered the pervasive cultural assumptions generated by boys' imperial adventure stories, and how they were linked to metropolitan support for colonial territorial annexation and imperial wars. A feminized genre of popular literature that reached its peak in the twentieth century was the romance novel, which, as Hsu-Ming Teo has argued, often had imperial settings and resonances. In contrast to English schoolgirls' magazines of the early twentieth century, which depicted India as a place for selfless female endeavour such as teaching and medical work, women's romance fiction saw marriage and domesticity as the focal point of women's lives. Single women could have exotic adventures in the Raj, but once a woman reached her mature married status her duty was to support her husband in his imperial work, in good part by sustaining a happy household. A wife's imperial duty was the indirect and subordinate service of supporting her man and enabling his career. Yet in contrast to the Indian women characters in these novels, who tended to be sensuous, passionate and vengeful, Anglo-Indian women were calm and rational. Most Raj romance novels of the early twentieth century fanned the disapprobation of miscegenation, even those which had supposedly sympathetic Indian or Eurasian protagonists. Yet no doubt the excitement of interracial love and sexuality was part of the genre's appeal in the last stages of British colonialism in India. An overarching message of these novels, Teo argues, is that romance itself is a western, indeed English, sensibility, for Indians are represented as 'incapable of developing conjugal affection'.[45] Raj romance novels of the interwar period proffered a mix of gendered messages to their substantial British female readership. At a time when disabled war veterans haunted English society, India was a place where a man could still become an imperial hero. For women, the last days of the Raj offered opportunities for travel and work that would appeal to the adventurous modern woman, but its cultural role was finally conservative in that desire, romance and marriage constituted the ultimate imperial feminine goal. Complicating these mixed messages for British women still further was the basic cultural formulation of the Raj romance: in these novels, romantic and sexual desire were for white people, particularly white women.[46] On the one hand, then, romance and marriage were British women's mission in life even in the post-suffrage interwar period; on the other hand, significantly, their sexual desire and agency were now valourized in mass imperial culture. Arguably, for white women, the cultural recognition – indeed, valourization – of women's sexual desire and subjectivity was a major feminist breakthrough.

The gendered messages contained within imperial culture circulated through the British Isles in a variety of media. Besides romance fiction, in the twentieth century film, television and radio broadcast music, dramas and advertisements with colonial settings or imperial stories. Early films conveyed gendered messages about the imperial civilizing mission, and television dramas well into the last decades of the century purveyed nostalgia for the empire. In the early to middle decades of the century, the empire broadcasting service of BBC radio sustained the cultural metaphor of a global British family. Prior to broadcast media, in the nineteenth century, probably the most effective and certainly the most spectacular vehicle for representations of empire were the great exhibitions.

A body of scholarship has demonstrated the significance of the official and commercial exhibitions that were staged around the world from the mid-nineteenth to the mid-twentieth centuries. Both the products and the vehicles of imperialism and globalization, the exhibitions boosted travel and tourism, and celebrated and displayed industrialization. They vaunted the wealth and imagined cultural superiority of the industrialized nations over the colonies and underdeveloped countries that fed their economies. While 'native' peoples from European colonies across the globe were put on display as spectacles of the primitive at these exhibitions, like the indigenous people discussed earlier, viewers from industrialized nations and white-settler dominions took pride in the displays that celebrated their own modernity in the form of economic and technological progress. In large part, these global exhibitions were festivals of commerce and consumerism, displays of the products that constituted the wealth of imperial and industrial powers such as Britain, France and the United States.

Historian John M. MacKenzie has demonstrated the trajectory of displays at British imperial and colonial exhibitions. While the Great Exhibition of 1851 is often cited as the empire put on display as a triumph of mid-nineteenth century British power, later exhibitions increasingly showcased products and materials from the colonies and dominions. At the Crystal Palace in 1851, goods from beyond Britain were intermingled in such a way that imperial origins were not always clear (and, indeed, the United States made a significant showing). By the 1862 London Exhibition, colonial representation had increased such that there were 7000 exhibits from India, 500 from Victoria, 400 from New South Wales and others from colonies including Bermuda and Borneo. The Colonial and Indian Exhibition of 1886 went further than the 1862 exhibition in its determined display of the resources and economic production of all the colonies and dominions. But it was the 1924–25 British Empire Exhibition at Wembley, staged just as the empire passed its zenith in size and when imperial control and economic strength seemed increasingly uncertain, that went furthest in representing imperial power and wealth. Structures that extended across 220 acres represented dominions and colonies with architecture and art purportedly representing indigenous styles and landscapes. Chinese workers demonstrated their crafts in the Hong Kong exhibit, while Yoruba and Hausa artisans, among others, displayed skills and wares from West Africa. Again the emphasis was on economic resources, production and wealth, with postcards, posters and other images adding to the message of imperial bounty.[47]

If the spectacular exhibitions were the most dramatic means in which the material culture of empire appeared in the metropole, there were many other ways in which goods with commercial value circulated, and represented ideas of gender and race. Nupur Chaudhuri has argued that memsahibs returning to Britain from India became significant carriers of imperial goods and culture. British memsahibs did much to promote the accessibility and popularity of Indian shawls, especially from Kashmir, which became desired objects in Britain and spawned an industry of European-manufactured replicas. While actual Kashmiri shawls were quite expensive in Britain, memsahibs created their own market by privately advertising shawls, other textiles, dresses, jewellery and decorative objects that they brought back from India and sold relatively cheaply by private advertisement for cash or exchange. Memsahibs thus were active agents in the circulation of imperial goods, and the creation of domestic cultural associations among luxury, femininity and Orientalism. At the same time, Chaudhuri notes, the memsahibs who refused publicly to eat curry and rice while they were in India – in an enactment of British cultural superiority – popularized recipes for curry and rice in nineteenth-century Britain, bringing the exotic and Oriental right into the hearth of the British home and the heart of domesticity.[48]

British industry and advertising, at the same time, put domestic space at the nexus between commerce, industry and empire. As Anne McClintock has shown by explicating a plethora of Victorian advertisements, especially in the late nineteenth century images of the empire were used to sell a host of products from toothpaste to laundry bleach. Pictorial images that proliferated in urban metropolitan streetscapes associated the empire with civilization, whiteness, cleanliness and women's work – even as women's work was rendered invisible and without economic value. Commodity culture brought empire into the most domestic and intimate spaces, linking the domestic and thus the feminine to explicitly racist notions. Especially in advertisements for that dramatically expanding, quintessentially Victorian commodity, soap, images such as a black child turning white in the bath represented British industry and commerce as the very vehicle of racial progress.[49] It was a particularly vivid episode in what would become a long history of commercial advertising using exotic, racialized (and often sexualized) images of the empire to sell any number of products.[50]

The gendered imbrication of race and class

Perhaps the most pervasive, yet nebulous, way that gendered and racialized concepts linked to colonialism shaped metropolitan British society was through a social structure in which class status has had specific gendered and racial markers. Frederick Cooper and Ann Laura Stoler, as quoted in the Introduction, have posited the complex interconstitution of race and class between European metropoles and colonies in the modern period. While racial hierarchies in colonies often drew upon class structures historically linked to European societies, the 'language of class itself in Europe drew on a range of images and metaphors that were racialized to the core'.[51] European class hierarchies were shaped through racist assumptions of white superiority, and a racialization of the lower orders, an imbrication of class and race strongly influenced by European colonial regimes. Standards of living became culturally indexed to hierarchies of both race and class. Within this interconstituted social structure, particular occupations and ranks of social order have been inflected as much by gender as by race. Indeed, at times specific racialized and gendered configurations have resonated in metropolitan culture. One such instance, analysed by Anne McClintock, was the mid-nineteenth-century British fascination with and consternation over women workers in coal mines. As bourgeois gender codes came to emphasize physical delicacy and frailty as definitive of feminine respectability, women who performed hard physical labour became masculinized and increasingly seen as culturally aberrant. Victorian bourgeois horror at women working down coal mines, which resulted in 1842 in their being prohibited from working down mines and confined to jobs at the top of the mine shaft, cast colliery women as racially other. Depictions of women coal miners showed them as very masculine, in heavy, loose male workers' clothing and large boots. But such depictions focused too on their blackness. Colliery women's black faces were, of course, the result of coal dust; but representations of these women went further, attributing to them racialized facial features such as low foreheads and flattened physiognomies.[52] If these labouring women's transgression of Victorian social codes included their hard physical labour – and thus their masculinization – their imagined racial otherness was linked too to their supposed sexual unrespectability. Amid the debates that resulted in women's banishment from labour down mines, the idea that these women were immoral and sexually promiscuous was a core anxiety. Out of place in Victorian social order because of their masculinized occupations, the social threat they were seen to pose was cast in both gendered and racialized terms.

Another vector of colonialism influencing perceptions of class status in Britain was through the return home of colonial service and military officials and their families. Both on furlough and during retirement, colonial officials, such as Anglo-Indians who had lived in India for decades, brought back to Britain their expectations and social attitudes forged in the context of colonialism and its social and racial hierarchies. Over the course of the nineteenth century the Indian Civil Service, and the British military in India had both grown substantially, so that the numbers of such officials as well as merchants returning to Britain by the latter decades of the nineteenth century and first decades of the twentieth century were substantial. One of the most marked differences middle-class women and men encountered when they first arrived in India was the far larger number of domestic servants per household. At a time when middle-class households in Britain employed perhaps three to six servants, Britons of such backgrounds arriving in India would find themselves with closer to twenty household servants. For example, in 1839 Emma Walter, living in a cantonment of Bombay Presidency, recorded in her journal that the nineteen servants they employed were no more than was necessary for such a household in India.[53] While domestic service was increasingly a feminized occupation in Britain, in India most domestic servants were men. Anglo-Indian mistresses thus found themselves running households with male servants whom they considered racially inferior and religiously uncivilized, and whose work practices were very different from those of British servants. In British households, except for the top echelons of society, servants worked long days and performed multiple duties. In India, in contrast, servants' jobs were more specialized, and when their tasks were complete or not required servants would rest. For example, some servants were employed specifically to pull the fans called 'punkahs'.

For Anglo-Indians returning home to Britain after decades of colonial life, the cultural shock they encountered specifically included the drop in social status of having considerably fewer servants. Mistresses accustomed to doing almost no household work in India suddenly found themselves confronted by the need to do at least some of their own housework. Elizabeth Buettner, in her subtle analysis of Anglo-Indian families and their contributions to imperial culture, argues that the culture shock of the return to Britain was distinctly gendered. Both husbands and wives of Anglo-Indian families returning 'home' suffered from the drop in their racialized status, in which simply being 'white' no longer entailed a myriad of social privileges. Both women and men also suffered from the drop in family income of scaling down to a pension at the same time as encountering the much higher cost of living in Britain. But the meanings of these adjustments were significantly different depending on sex. For Anglo-Indian men, retirement to Britain usually meant sudden idleness at the end of a career, and a casting about for ways in which to spend the time abruptly hanging heavily on their hands. For women, however, the reverse was true in ways that directly affected their social status. Women used to large numbers of servants suddenly found themselves with few, or even no servants at all. Women unused to household budgeting would be forced to learn economy, at the same time that they would have to learn new domestic skills and perform manual labour. The gendered drop in social status that this transition entailed is captured in a family memoir by M.M. Kaye, whose father retired in the 1920s and the family returned to England. Kaye's mother endured the social embarrassment of suddenly having to do the housework herself, an embarrassment at its most poignant when some neighbours visited her unexpectedly and, caught in an apron and headscarf with grime on her face, she pretended to be her own servant.[54] In convoluted ways, the gendered linkages between racial privilege, social respectability and leisure contributed to perceptions of class status in the metropole.

With the escalation of immigration of colonized and formerly colonized subjects to Britain during and after the Second World War, intersections between race, gender, work and social status acquired new nuances. In a period of social conservatism when women were under renewed pressure to stay at home in order to be seen as socially respectable, or at best to work only part-time, definitions of femininity were newly racialized. Immigrant women, including those from Eastern Europe, were expected to subordinate their family lives to their employment. While 'white' British women culturally and socially were encouraged to be wives and mothers above all else, immigrant women confronted choices and realities that impeded their marital relations and their abilities to be mothers. Migrant women were recruited into jobs, such as particular kinds of nursing and live-in domestic service, that required them to live at their place of employment, thus denying or obstructing their own familial lives. Similarly, women recruited from the Caribbean were employed on terms that encouraged them to leave their children behind. In 1963 a survey of Jamaican women who had migrated to Britain found that 63 per cent were mothers, but most of these had left children in Jamaica, usually to be cared for by grandparents.[55] Motherhood had become a racialized status, one in which 'white' British women were seen as natural and appropriate mothers, while black and immigrant women were identified primarily rather as workers.

The power and poignancy of this social pressure to be workers rather than mothers is captured in Buchi Emecheta's 1974 novel *Second-Class Citizen*. Based on her own experience as an Ibo woman from Nigeria who moved to London in the 1960s with her student husband, Emecheta's novel portrays the quotidian harshness and humiliations of life for 'coloured' people in 1960s Britain. Emecheta describes in detail the system in which Nigerian women sent their children out to 'white' foster-mothers in order to be able to be fulltime workers. In a complex structuring of class, race and gender, poor 'white' women sold their maternal labour, thus preserving their own gendered respectability and enabling Nigerian women to become workers at the expense of their motherhood. 'As soon as a Nigerian housewife in England realised that she was expecting a child, instead of shopping for prams, and knitting little bootees, she would advertise for a foster-mother. No one cared whether a woman was suitable or not, no one wanted to know whether the house was clean or not; all they wanted to be sure of was that the foster-mother was white. The concept of "whiteness" could cover a multitude of sins.'[56] Emecheta's protagonist, Adah, who learns growing up in Nigeria that she is a 'second-class citizen' because she is female, then learns in England that there she is a 'second-class citizen' because she is black, refuses to send her children out to a foster-mother. She thus brings upon herself and her husband social ostracism within their immediate community of other Nigerians. Her refusal to send her children away is interpreted as arrogance, as a refusal of her status as black in England, and therefore as somehow being better than her neighbours. 'Everybody talked and speculated. The trouble was that Adah was like a peacock, who kept wanting to win all the time. Only first-class citizens lived with their children, not the blacks.'[57]

Compared to the extended-family system in Lagos, in which Adah's status as a well-paid library assistant had been facilitated by the childcare and domestic labour supplied by her husband's female relatives, in London Adah confronts poverty, enormous difficulties in balancing her work and childcare, and a very differently gendered relationship with her husband. Francis, Adah's husband, exercises what he sees as the privileges of masculinity in Britain, such as not working any harder than he must, refusing domestic work and childcare, and being sexually unfaithful. While much of his behaviour is consonant with expectations of masculinity in Lagos, the lack of constraints of an extended family means that he has few curbs on his self-indulgence. Moreover, he resents Adah's rejection of her second-class status, and her autonomy. 'Francis looked at her, as if with new eyes. Somebody had warned him that the greatest mistake an African could make was to bring an educated girl to London and let her mix with middle-class English women. They soon knew their rights.'[58] Part of the misery of the marriage, which Adah finally leaves when she is pregnant with their fifth child, is because of the confusion the couple shares about gendered expectations and marital roles. Still influenced by Ibo customs, they abide by notions based on the husband as the patriarchal authority in the family despite the fact that Adah is and always has been the main breadwinner. It takes much misery and suffering before Adah feels strongly that Francis has abandoned his manly duties, and she is therefore entitled to leave him. In this heart-wrenching story that evinces the gendered confusion of colonial migrants in the metropole, the protagonist Adah manages to support herself and her children through work as a library assistant, a more dignified and less menial form of work than the cleaning that Emecheta herself apparently did to support her children in her first years in London. In that crucial respect, Emecheta's actual lot was more typical of African-Caribbean women in mid-twentieth-century England than her character Adah's. Nursing, cleaning, employment in the post office and transport systems, and lower-paid jobs in other service industries were the most accessible areas of employment for nonwhite women from the colonies.

Jobs for men have similarly been shaped by interconstitutive factors of race and class, tied to colonialism. In 1988 David Lodge published his book *Nice Work*, an intertextual novel designed purposely as a 1980s updated interpretation of Elizabeth Gaskell's 1854 novel *North and South*. Gaskell was concerned to explicate northern industrialism to a largely southern readership, introducing the workings of Manchester cotton mills, the free trade capitalism that underlay them, and the industrial class structure that was their corollary. A central thread of Gaskell's plot was southern humanitarian intervention in midlands industrialism, such that a textile mill owner was forced to recognize the humanity of his workers. The recognition of the working class as human, and not an internal other to be despised and exploited, was one of Gaskell's main aims. While class difference and working-class otherness had been a social issue of the 1850s, for the 1980s Birmingham of Lodge's *Nice Work*, issues of racial difference and otherness had merged with those of class. Integral to the 1980s industrial landscape was the presence of South Asian and African-Caribbean workers, who suffered particularly from contemporary unemployment and had to accept the most menial levels of factory work. When Lodge's southern female protagonist Robyn Penrose is given a tour of Pringle's engineering works, she can't help but notice that white workers predominate in the skilled work and less unpleasant atmosphere of the factory's machine shop. The foundry was a different matter: a far harsher and noisier work environment, where many of the workers were Asian and Caribbean. To Robyn, a literary scholar, 'it resembled nothing so much as a medieval painting of hell – though it was hard to say whether the workers looked more like devils or the damned. ... She surveyed the scene, feeling more than ever like Dante in the Inferno. All was noise, smoke, fumes, and flame'. Further on, a huge cauldron of molten metal was 'like a small pinnacle in Pandemonium, dark and hot, and the two squatting Sikhs who rolled their white eyeballs and flashed their teeth in her direction, poking with steel rods at the molten metal for no discernible purpose, looked just like demons on an old fresco'.[59] Nineteenth-century writers had also likened factories and industrial work to hell, but in the 1980s such imagery carried racialized messages about those who lived in modern British hell. While some women were also employed in heavy industrial work in the latter twentieth century, in contrast to the 'white' working-class women of the mid-nineteenth century collieries, now it was black men who came to represent, and to be compelled to perform, harsh physical industrial labour. Menial service work that involved interpersonal caring, like nursing, had come to be racialized and gendered feminine, while the heaviest and most dangerous industrial labour was now racialized and gendered masculine. Both forms of gendered labour worked to position white workers as fitted for higher status jobs that require more education and responsibility, in a reconfigured, newly gendered and racialized class structure. Racialized assumptions about labour that had their roots in slavery and the plantations of the seventeenth to early-nineteenth centuries still operated in late twentieth-century Britain.

* * *

This chapter has presented only a selection of the manifold forms in which imperial culture has shaped the British Isles in recent centuries. In ways both overt and subtle, economic, political and social aspects of the empire have circulated through the metropole, which all along has been one of the interconnected sites of the empire. Ideas and practices of gender and sexuality have taken shape in the colonies and the metropole at the same time in interlinked fashion. Racially contingent understandings of feminine respectability have affected the daily lives of colonizing and colonized women in multiple parts of the empire, linked as they have been to notions of sexual availability and display. White racial privilege has prescribed an avoidance of physical labour for women, as long as there were others to perform it; conversely, the loss of social status for women returning to Britain from the colonies was directly signalled by the necessity to perform more of their own household labour. Racialized notions of masculinity have been indexed by physical strength and contests over technical skills, in scenarios ranging from the 'primitive' hunters put on display at Victorian sideshows and exhibitions, to the industrial labour force of the latter twentieth century. From the spectacles of imperial display, to mass cultural forms of popular literature and the broadcast media, to West End clubs and imperialist leagues and societies, and the very social fabric itself, notions of manliness and womanliness have been freighted with imperial meanings.

Notes

1. For example, John M. MacKenzie, *Propaganda and Empire: The Manipulation of British Public Opinion, 1880–1960* (Manchester: Manchester University Press, 1984); Edward W. Said, *Culture and Imperialism* (New York: Knopf, 1993); Anne McClintock, *Imperial Leather: Race, Gender and Sexuality in the Colonial Contest* (New York: Routledge, 1995).
2. David Gilmour, 'Calcutta in the Cotswolds', *London Review of Books*, 3 March 2005, p. 15.
3. John Darwin, 'Bored by the Raj', *Times Literary Supplement*, 18 February 2005, p. 5.
4. Antoinette Burton, 'Who Needs the Nation? Interrogating "British" History', *Journal of Historical Sociology* vol. 10, no. 3 (September 1997): 231.
5. Annie E. Coombes, *Reinventing Africa: Museums, Material Culture and Popular Imagination in Late Victorian and Edwardian England* (New Haven, CT: Yale University Press, 1994).
6. Account written in 1839 by Mrs. Charles Matthews, quoted by Rosemary Wiss, 'Lipreading: Remembering Saartjie Baartman', *The Australian Journal of Anthropology* vol. 5, nos. 1 and 2 (1994): 15.
7. Wiss, 'Lipreading', pp. 16–19.
8. Wiss, 'Lipreading', pp. 26–31.
9. Sander Gilman, *Difference and Pathology: Stereotypes of Sexuality, Race, and Madness* (Ithaca, NY: Cornell University Press, 1985), pp. 88–101.
10. Rachel L. Swarns, 'Mocked in Europe of Old, African Is Embraced at Home at Last', *The New York Times*, 4 May 2003, p. A3.
11. Roslyn Poignant, *Professional Savages: Captive Lives and Western Spectacle* (Sydney: University of New South Wales Press, 2004), esp. pp. 185–6.
12. 'Eleven Aboriginal Black Australians v. Eleven Gentlemen of Surrey Club', *The Times*, 26 May 1868, p. 5.

13. *The Times*, 14 September 1868, p. 5.

14. 'Eleven Aboriginal Black Australians v. Eleven Gentlemen of Surrey Club', *The Times*, 26 May 1868, p. 5.

15. Quoted in John Mulvaney and Rex Harcourt, *Cricket Walkabout: The Australian Aborigines in England* (South Melbourne, Vic.: Macmillan, 1988), p. 74.

16. Antoinette Burton, *At the Heart of the Empire: Indians and the Colonial Encounter in Late-Victorian Britain* (Berkeley: University of California Press, 1998); Angela Woollacott, *To Try Her Fortune in London: Australian Women, Colonialism, and Modernity* (New York: Oxford University Press, 2001).

17. Cecilia Morgan, ' "A Wigwam to Westminster": Performing Mohawk Identity in Imperial Britain, 1890s–1990s', *Gender & History* vol. 15, no. 2 (August 2003): 319–41.

18. Shompa Lahiri, *Indians in Britain: Anglo-Indian Encounters, Race and Identity, 1880–1930* (London: Frank Cass, 2000), pp. 1–7.

19. Burton, *At the Heart of the Empire*, chapter 4.

20. Mulk Raj Anand, *Conversations in Bloomsbury* (Delhi: Oxford University Press, 1995).

21. 'Colonials at Home', *The New Idea* vol. 1 (Sept. 1, 1902), p. 95.

22. 'The Imperial and American Club', *The British-Australasian*, 9 July 1885, p. 646.

23. *The British Australian and New Zealander*, 17 June 1937, p. 8.

24. *The British-Australasian*, 3 November 1898, p. 1973; 22 January 1903, p. 104; 19 November 1903, pp. 1653–4.

25. 'The Overseas League: An Account of Its History, Aims and Progress', *The British-Australasian*, 25 May 1922, p. 15.

26. For more on the Royal Colonial Institute, see Woollacott, *To Try Her Fortune in London*, pp. 105–110.

27. *The British Australasian*, 15 February 1912, p. 18.

28. Mary Gaunt, *Alone in West Africa* (New York: Charles Scribner's Sons, 1912); Mary Gaunt, *The Uncounted Cost* (London: T. Werner Laurie, 1910). On the large number of reviews of her books, see Ian F. McLaren, *Mary Gaunt, A Cosmopolitan Australian: An Annotated Bibliography* (Parkville, Vic.: University of Melbourne Library, 1986).

29. Alice Grant Rosman, 'An Australian in West Africa: Mary Gaunt Talks to "Everylady's" ', *Everylady's Journal*, 6 June 1912, p. 330.

30. Mary Gaunt, 'The Sheltered-Life Girl: An Australian View of Her "Soft" Up-Bringing', *The Daily Chronicle*, 15 April 1912, p. 4.

31. Mary Gaunt, 'Woman in Australia', *The Empire Review* 1 (March 1901): 211–16.

32. Angela Woollacott, 'Creating the White Colonial Woman: Mary Gaunt's Imperial Adventuring and Australian Cultural History', in Hsu-Ming Teo and Richard White (eds), *Cultural History in Australia* (Sydney: University of New South Wales Press, 2003), pp. 186–200.

33. Katie Pickles, *Female Imperialism and National Identity*, and 'A Link in "The Great Chain of Empire Friendship": The Victoria League in

New Zealand', *The Journal of Imperial and Commonwealth History* vol. 33, no. 1 (January 2005): 29–50.

34. 'Women and the Empire', *United Empire* vol. 18 (January 1927): 47.

35. See Woollacott, *To Try Her Fortune in London*, pp. 124–37.

36. Caroline Chisholm, *The ABC of Colonisation* (London, 1850; reprinted in *Colonial Discourses* Series 1, Part 1, Reel 22 (Adam Matthews Publications)).

37. On the gendered meanings surrounding the emigration of 'distressed gentlewomen', see A. James Hammerton, *Emigrant Gentlewomen: Genteel Poverty and Female Emigration, 1830–1914* (London: Croom Helm, 1979).

38. Marilyn Barber, 'Sunny Ontario for British Girls, 1900–1930', in Jean Burnet (ed.), *Looking Into My Sister's Eyes: An Exploration in Women's History* (Toronto: The Multicultural History Society of Ontario, 1986), pp. 56–61.

39. Jean Jacques Van-Helten and Keith Williams, ' "The Crying Need of South Africa": The Emigration of Single British Women To the Transvaal, 1901–10', *Journal of Southern African Studies* vol. 10, no. 1 (October 1983): 17–38.

40. Lisa Chilton, 'A New Class of Women for the Colonies: *The Imperial Colonist* and the Construction of Empire', *Journal of Imperial and Commonwealth History* vol. 31, no. 2 (May 2003): 39.

41. Julia Bush, 'Emigration'. *Edwardian Ladies and Imperial Power* (London: Leicester University Press, 2000), chapter 9.

42. Jan Gothard, *Blue China: Single Female Migration to Colonial Australia* (Carlton South, Vic.: Melbourne University Press, 2001), p. ix.

43. YWCA Papers, MSS. 243/131/8/ii.i, Modern Records Centre, University of Warwick.

44. Quoted in *New Horizons: A Hundred Years of Women's Migration* (London: HMSO, 1963), pp. 96–7.

45. Hsu-Ming Teo, 'Romancing the Raj: Interracial Relations in Anglo-Indian Romance Novels', *History of Intellectual Culture* vol. 4, no. 1 (2004): 8.

46. Teo, 'Romancing the Raj', p. 14.

47. John M. MacKenzie, *Propaganda and Empire: The Manipulation of British Public Opinion 1880–1960* (Manchester: Manchester University Press, 1984), pp. 98–109.

48. Nupur Chaudhuri, 'Shawls, Jewelry, Curry, and Rice in Victorian Britain', in Nupur Chaudhuri and Margaret Strobel (eds), *Western Women and Imperialism: Complicity and Resistance* (Bloomington: Indiana University Press, 1992), pp. 231–46.

49. McClintock, *Imperial Leather*, pp. 210–19.

50. On late twentieth-century continuities of this aspect of imperial culture, see Jeffrey Auerbach, 'Art, Advertising, and the Legacy of Empire', *Journal of Popular Culture* vol. 35, no. 4 (Spring 2002): 1–23.

51. Frederick Cooper and Ann Laure Stoler, *Tensions of Empire: Colonial Cultures in a Bourgeois World* (Berkeley: University of California Press, 1997), pp. 9–10.

52. McClintock, *Imperial Leather*, pp. 104–18.

53. Nupur Chaudhuri, 'Memsahibs and their Servants in Nineteenth-century India', *Women's History Review* vol. 3, no. 4 (1994): 550.

54. Elizabeth Buettner, 'From Somebodies to Nobodies: Britons Returning Home from India', in Martin Daunton and Bernhard Rieger (eds), *Meanings of Modernity: Britain from the Late-Victorian Era to World War II* (Oxford: Berg, 2001), pp. 228–9.

55. Wendy Webster, *Imagining Home: Gender, 'Race' and National Identity, 1945–64* (London: UCL Press, 1998), pp. 36–9.

56. Buchi Emecheta, *Second-Class Citizen* (London: Allison & Busby, 1974), pp. 45–6.

57. Emecheta, *Second-Class Citizen*, p. 47.

58. Emecheta, *Second-Class Citizen*, p. 64.

59. David Lodge, *Nice Work* (London: Penguin Books, 1989), pp. 123–30.

Conclusion

A primary aim of this book has been to consider how feminist scholarship has recast historical understanding of the British Empire from the eighteenth to the twentieth centuries. The recent revolution in historical scholarship on imperialism and colonialism sprang from multiple sources at slightly different moments over the last ten to twenty years, yet diverse streams of revisionist thought have had convergent effects. If subaltern studies has sought to investigate the silenced position of the colonized in imperial regimes; critical race theory has explicated the complex workings of racial subordination; and feminist theory has insisted on the centrality of sexuality and hierarchies of gender to colonialism, the current field of postcolonial studies brings all three streams of historical analysis into play. 'The new imperial history' has revealed the highly political effects of imperial culture and colonial regimes, as well as insisting on the simultaneous constitution of metropolitan and colonial societies. Currently, when some strands of world history marginalize both gender as a category of analysis and the historical impact of feminist movements, postcolonial histories of the European empires show the imbrication of gender in political metaphor and discourses, the masculinism of colonial elites and governments, and the intersections of gender and race in quotidian life under colonial regimes. If some historians of the British Empire continue to worry that 'in trying to write in a role for women, there is a risk of exaggerating their importance',[1] this book has sought to demonstrate that women were everywhere, in the colonies and the metropole, and that the empire was sustained through their labour, both productive and reproductive. Ideologies of gender shaped the lives of women and men, colonized and colonizer, 'black' and 'white', and structured the empire itself throughout the modern period. Notions of gender were fully interwoven with those of race, both intersected with hierarchies of class, and sexuality was integral to everyday life in a circulating culture of empire.

This book has been both thematically and roughly chronologically arranged, moving from the period of slavery in the eighteenth century, to that of decolonization in the latter twentieth century. There were enormous historical changes during the period it covers. The British Empire itself now exists only vestigially with one or two tiny colonial outposts and through its descendant organization the British Commonwealth. Slavery was officially brought to an end in the British Empire (although forms of it still exist illegally in places), convict transportation ended and indentured labour has atrophied. Women have gained full political citizenship in most parts of the former empire, even if they remain underrepresented in government executives and legislative bodies, as well as poorer economically, and socially subordinated. The undemocratic, indeed violent and oppressive, nature of colonialism continues to shape multiple former British colonies, as various independent nation states struggle with autocratic leaders, corruption and internal racisms. Racial hierarchies continue to exist, along with those of gender. Tempting though the idea might be, it is simply not possible to outline a graphic or narrative historical profile of changes in gender practices or ideology over time. Gender as a complex interplay of cultural prescriptions, and hierarchies of economic, social and political power, is too plastic and pervasive an organic system to be reduced to a historical trajectory. Its workings continue and are ubiquitous, despite the fundamental changes in relations between women and men over the last two centuries. Despite economic and political gains particularly for some groups of women, the most repressive aspects of gender hierarchies, including sexual exploitation and physical violence, are still with us.

If we cannot easily depict historical trajectories within gender relations, we can identify historiographical shifts over the last twenty years and grapple with their significance. Along with other areas of women's history, in the early stages of the field as a disciplinary specialty, much of the history of women in the British Empire was individualist, recuperative and concerned with white women. We learned the stories of intrepid women travellers and explorers who contravened Victorian gender ideology and braved physical hardships and dangers. Studies showed that missionaries in diverse parts of the empire had been women, and that some had performed philanthropic and reform work to improve the lives (in European views) of colonized peoples. While much of the early work on women's history in the empire dealt with individual or small numbers of European women in the colonies, in the field of Caribbean history several scholars began to focus on the lives and historical experiences of enslaved women. Scholars like Hilary Beckles, Rhoda Reddock and Barbara Bush researched the daily lives, work, acts of resistance and reproductive practices of enslaved African-Caribbean women, influenced by the growth of the history of slavery and labour history.[2] One of the enduring challenges for the broader field of gender history of the British Empire has been the fragmented and geographically compartmentalized nature of scholarship on British colonies. Indeed, until recently, there was little conception of a broader field such as gender and the British Empire. Historians interested in the Caribbean were influenced by work on parts of the Caribbean beyond their own focus, histories of slavery in other locations and the history of the Americas as a wider canvas. At the same time, scholars interested in other parts of the empire did not always pay a great deal of attention to work on the Caribbean, and thus could overlook the mounting evidence of the centrality of sexual exploitation to plantation economies and racial and gendered hierarchies. It is only very recently, for example, that research by scholars such as Ian Duffield and Cassandra Pybus has sparked awareness of the connections between slave systems in the Caribbean, Mauritius and elsewhere, and convict transportation to Australia, in the embodied form of black convicts, both women and men.[3] The transcolonial workings of gender and race within systems of unfree labour continue to demand further research in order for us to fully apprehend their empire-wide interconnections.

Another geographical locus for relatively early work on nonwhite women in systems of slavery and racialized economic subordination was South Africa. If scholarship on sub-Saharan Africa has been strongly tied to Marxist analysis, it has influenced work on gender and colonialism elsewhere through its use of anthropology, and its explorations of the complex operations of hegemony and subordination under colonialism. From the work of historians such as Pamela Scully, on the integral role of gender in the postemancipation restructuring of South African class and racial hierarchies, to that of Timothy Burke on consumerism and cleanliness in the postcolonial negotiations within Zimbabwean society both before and after independence, and the intersections of gender with notions of bodily hygiene, scholarship on southern Africa has raised new questions that have drawn attention across geographical boundaries.[4] Some geographical origins of particular issues have been perhaps unsurprising – such as the work on Canadian and New Zealand frontier contact zones that has foregrounded the gendered dimensions of white-settler colonialism – yet even here the recent inclination and abilities of scholars from different global sites to engage in dialogue has enhanced the analysis of specific historical contexts and episodes. For example, the connections between the captivity narratives from North America, North Africa and early nineteenth-century Australia, and the narratives of sexual assault on white women perpetrated by indigenous men, as discussed in Chapter 2, has enriched our understanding of colonialism in each location as well as illustrating the circulation of imperial culture.

A major historiographical development for the field, of course, was that of the profound shift from the focus on women to that on gender as a structural and relational category. In the wake of 1980s feminist theory, particularly Joan Scott's exposition of gender as a category of historical analysis,[5] like the broader field of women's history, work on British colonialism embraced the study of masculinity as integral to the sex/gender system. Perhaps the most influential work has been Mrinalini Sinha's book *Colonial Masculinity*,[6] widely read and cited because of its detailed exposition of the interlinked historical construction of English manliness and imagined Bengali effeminacy in a series of political and legislative controversies in late nineteenth-century colonial India. Sinha's suggestion of the concept of an imperial social formation, with simultaneous and interconstitutive shifts in imperial culture in both metropole and colonies, has been provocative. Other works on the imperial construction of masculinity have included Graham Dawson's analysis of the figure of the 'soldier hero' such as Lawrence of Arabia as an iconic figure representing bravery and exoticized adventure.[7] More recently, through a cultural approach that looks at the racialized and gendered construction of ideas of the body, E.M. Collingham's work on the sahib in colonial India has explicated the connections between masculinity and imperial rule through the physical details of daily colonial life.[8] If more work is needed on the shifting understandings of masculinity on the part of colonized men, it is now widely understood that the field of gender in an imperial framework is no longer only the study of women and femininities.

Related to work on masculinity has been a recent flourishing of studies on homosexuality in imperial contexts. If this issue was first raised some time ago by Ronald Hyam in his explicitly anti-feminist study *Empire and Sexuality*,[9] it is only in recent years that more nuanced studies such as Robert Aldrich's *Colonialism and Homosexuality* have demonstrated the significance of European empires for male homosexual possibilities, and the extent of homosexual relations both across racial divides and among colonizing men.[10] Studies such as Christopher Lane's literary analysis have further pointed to the significance of representations of homosexual desire in imperial culture.[11] What is now most striking about this field on homosexuality and the British Empire is the glaring underrepresentation of studies on lesbianism. There are no comparable works demonstrating and analysing female homosexuality as integral to imperial history and culture. We do have some discussion of women's sexual relationships with other women in particular contexts, such as the women's factories in early colonial New South Wales and Van Diemen's Land,[12] and the significance of London as imperial metropolis in facilitating women's same-sex relationships and cohabitation.[13] Beyond those partial discussions, the subject of the interconnections between colonialism and lesbianism – whether cross-racial or among colonizing women – is a problematic lacuna.

An important development in the field, of course, has been interdisciplinarity, the borrowing of approaches and methods by historians from other fields such as anthropology, literary criticism, cultural studies, art history, international relations and elsewhere. Interdisplinary self-consciousness has enabled particular topics to be unpacked in fruitful ways. I have already referred to the impact in historical work of anthropological and literary approaches. Art history and the study of material culture have also been productive of a broader understanding of imperialism and its pervasive representations. Beth Fowkes Tobin's rich analysis of the manifold ways in which the empire appeared in eighteenth-century British painting shows contemporary fascination with cross-cultural mixing, with portraits and groups staged to tell stories with gender and racial dimensions.[14] More disturbingly, Lisa Z. Sigel's work on the connections between misogyny, racism and imperialism in nineteenth-century British pornography has illustrated very graphically just how central eroticized masculinist power was to imperial culture.[15] One of the most important effects of the range of anthologies on gender in the new imperial history that we have seen in recent years has been the juxtaposition of essays using different kinds of sources, as well as presenting episodes from the colonial pasts of many different parts of the globe. In Antoinette Burton's collection titled *Gender, Sexuality and Colonial Modernities*, for example, the essays jostling together cover places including Hong Kong, Niagara Falls, India and Australia, with analyses of sources from medical discourse on hygiene, travellers' narratives, postcards, a Home Science textbook and testimony presented to a royal commission.[16] This kind of suggestive juxtaposition, as well as the diversity of sources available to scholars, has been enabled too by the recent publication of collections of historical documents on empire, including recently the availability of a large online database on the British Empire since the late fifteenth century.[17]

Postcolonial approaches to the British Empire have insisted on seeing the British Isles as one imperial site, through which a constant traffic in goods, cultural representations and imperial subjects all flowed. It is impossible to understand imperial culture without recognizing the ways in which it circulated, both between metropole and colonies and among diverse colonial sites. Things did not happen first or originally in London or England; both colonialism and modernity sprang from scattered parts of the empire in complicated, interconstitutive ways. Racial and gender hierarchies were central to modernity, as were beliefs in material progress and technological miracles – influential examples of which were perceived as occurring in the colonies. Recent work has explicated the multiple ways in which the empire appeared in the metropole. Kathleen Wilson has explained the ways in which in the eighteenth century notions of masculinity, generated in imperial mercantilism, wars and expansion, became tied to notions of British national identity and the British empire, even as imperial associations with effeminacy had to be parried and resisted. British politics and national identity were both gendered and fundamentally shaped by the empire.[18] In contrast, one of the expanding number of studies on colonial subjects in the metropole is Cecilia Morgan's sensitive account of the English sojourns of two Canadian Mohawks, Pauline Johnson and John Ojijatekha Brant-Sero, at the turn of the twentieth century. Both Johnson and Brant-Sero played with gendered concepts of the primitive and savage North American Indian, in their entrepreneurial careers based on performing their indigenous culture, even though they themselves displayed a modern penchant for adopting and shedding ethnic personas.[19] Such work has demonstrated the utter permeability of the metropole to the empire, and the significance of its shaping by imperial culture, subjects, traffic and discourses. Despite the import of this work, we must be careful, as Durba Ghosh has urged, not to emphasize the metropole so much as to return to the very inadequate perspective of it as the determining centre. As Ghosh contends, 'it is important that we do not reproduce imbalances of power and authority in studying gender relations between colonizing and colonized societies.'[20]

An enormous amount of research demands to be done on aspects of the intersections of gender and colonialism that have barely been opened up to view. We know so little, still, of the perspectives of colonized peoples compared to the vast amount of work that has been written on the views, experiences and actions of the colonizers and imperial rulers. The history of the British Empire is still largely a story being told by the winners, or by their descendants. Racial privilege still skews much of the archives, research, interpretation and accounts presented by historians. For all of the two decades of work on gender and sexuality in the British Empire, the field is still dominantly understood as having men as its main protagonists. It is, of course, imperative to reject essentialist notions that only the colonized can write their own histories, only members of particular ethnic or sexual groups can undertake research into their specific histories. The past, as has so influentially been said, is another country – no matter what country, region, ethnic or sexual group, religion or sex one identifies with. Historical work can only be based on research, whether it is through oral histories, documentary sources, material culture or representations. There are many questions to be addressed, and many lines of enquiry to be traced. There is still much to understand about how colonial subjects moved from place to place, region to region, colony to colony, and what profound effects their migration or circulation had on colonial and imperial cultures. Evolving notions of race were suffused with gendered conceptions, and ideas of gender were shaped by imperial circumstances realized through forms associated with particular class rankings. This infinitely convoluted set of meanings shifted and circulated along shipping and trade routes, and through political and cultural circles, as well as in the proliferating media of Anglophone culture.

If much work remains to be done, the history of the British Empire has indeed been recast. No matter how vociferously some historians reject feminist and postcolonial interpretations, the field cannot return to its blinkered status of two decades ago. Even the more traditional organs of scholarship on the empire and colonialism have opened their pages to women's history, and to the histories of the colonized, albeit in a circumspect fashion. The more recalcitrant members of older historiographical schools have become belligerent in the face of what they see as attacks on their field and the incursions of those who do not belong or do not appreciate the nuances of established scholarship. For all of the best efforts of such scholars to defend the battlements, scholarship on gender and colonialism is growing at a rapid rate. The increased numbers of conference papers in this area has led Ghosh to hail 'the globalization (and feminization) of imperial history'.[21] The expanding number of monographs, journal articles, anthologies and conferences themselves in the field signals the same thing. Even the staid *Oxford History of the British Empire* series responded to criticisms of the absence of gender in its initial five volumes, and last year published a companion volume on the subject of gender.[22] It would be very difficult, in the early twenty-first century, to seek to synthesize the field of empire history without incorporating women as historical subjects, or the gendering of political discourses of nation and empire, or the foundational presence of sexuality as a daily shaping force under colonial regimes. Feminist scholars increasingly recognize the historical imbrication of racial categories with gender and sexuality. The 'new imperial history', postcolonial studies, and the broader history of the European empires must now fully account for the integral contribution of women as both colonizers and colonized, the racialized meanings of masculinity and sexuality, and the ideological work of gender in imperial culture.

Notes

1. Robert Johnson, *British Imperialism* (Houndmills, Basingstoke: Palgrave), p. 127.
2. For example, Hilary McD. Beckles, *Natural Rebels: A Social History of Enslaved Black Women in Barbados* (London: Zed Press, 1989); Rhoda Reddock, 'Women and Slavery in the Caribbean: A Feminist Perspective', *Latin American Perspectives* Issue 40 (1985); Barbara Bush, *Slave Women in Caribbean Society 1650–1838* (London: James Currey, 1990).
3. For example, Ian Duffield, 'Daylight on Convict Lived Experience: The History of a Pious Negro Servant', *Tasmanian Historical Studies* vol. 6, no.2 (1999): 29–62; Cassandra Pybus, 'The world is all of one piece: The African Diaspora and Transportation to Australia', in Ruth Hamilton (ed.), *Routes of Passage: Rethinking the African Diaspora* (Michigan State University Press, 2002).
4. Pamela Scully, *Liberating the Family? Gender and British Slave Emancipation in the Rural Western Cape, South Africa, 1823–1853* (Portsmouth, NH: Heinemann, 1997); Timothy Burke, *Lifebuoy Men, Lux*

Women: Commodification, Consumption, & Cleanliness in Modern Zimbabwe (London: Leicester University Press, 1996).

5. Joan Scott, *Gender and the Politics of History* (New York: Columbia University Press, 1988).

6. Mrinalini Sinha, *Colonial Masculinity: The 'Manly Englishman' and the 'Effeminate Bengali' in the Late Nineteenth Century* (Manchester: Manchester University Press, 1995).

7. Graham Dawson, *Soldier Heroes: British Adventure, Empire and the Imagining of Masculinities* (London: Routledge, 1994).

8. E.M. Collingham, *Imperial Bodies: The Physical Experience of the Raj, c.1800–1947* (Cambridge: Polity Press, 2001).

9. Ronald Hyam, *Empire and Sexuality: The British Experience* (Manchester: Manchester University Press, 1990).

10. Robert Aldrich, *Colonialism and Homosexuality* (London: Routledge, 2003).

11. Christopher Lane, *The Ruling Passion: British Colonial Allegory and the Paradox of Homosexual Desire* (Durham: Duke University Press, 1995).

12. Daniels, *Convict Women*, pp. 175–83; Damousi, *Depraved and Disorderly*, pp. 69–72.

13. Angela Woollacott, 'White colonialism and sexual modernity: Australian Women in the Early Twentieth Century Metropolis', in Antoinette Burton (ed.), *Gender, Sexuality and Colonial Modernities* (London: Routledge, 1999).

14. Beth Fowkes Tobin, *Picturing Imperial Power: Colonial Subjects in Eighteenth-Century British Painting* (Durham: Duke University Press, 1999).

15. Lisa Z. Sigel, *Governing Pleasures: Pornography and Social Change in England, 1815–1914* (New Brunswick, NJ: Rutgers University Press, 2002).

16. Antoinette Burton, *Gender, Sexuality and Colonial Modernities* (London: Routledge, 1999).

17. The *Empire On-Line* database published by Adam Matthews incorporates scholarly essays with hypertext links to thousands of primary source documents from across the British Empire.

18. Kathleen Wilson, 'Empire, Gender, and Modernity in the Eighteenth Century', in Philippa Levine (ed.), *Gender and Empire* Companion Volume in the *Oxford History of the British Empire* series (Oxford: Oxford University Press, 2004), pp. 14–45.

19. Cecilia Morgan, ' "A Wigwam to Westminster": Performing Mohawk Identity in Imperial Britain, 1890s–1990s', *Gender & History* vol. 15, no. 2 (August 2003).

20. Durba Ghosh, 'Gender and Colonialism: Expansion or Marginalization?', *The Historical Journal* vol. 47, no. 3 (2004): 755.

21. Ghosh, 'Gender and Colonialism', p. 738.

22. Levine (ed.), *Gender and Empire*.

Select Bibliography

Aldrich, Robert, *Colonialism and Homosexuality* (London: Routledge, 2003).

Ballantyne, R.M., *The Young Fur-Traders* (London: Thomas Nelson and Sons, n.d. (1856)).

Beckles, Hilary McD., *Afro-Caribbean Women & Resistance to Slavery in Barbados* (London: Karnak House, 1988).

Beckles, Hilary McD., *Centering Woman: Gender Discourses in Caribbean Slave Society* (Kingston: Ian Randle Publishers, 1999).

Bristow, Joseph, *Empire Boys: Adventures in a Man's World* (London: HarperCollins Academic, 1991).

British Parliamentary Papers, *Colonies. West Indies, Vol. 4. Jamaica Royal Commission 1866. Papers Laid Before the Commission by Governor Eyre.*

British Parliamentary Papers, *Colonies. West Indies, Vol. 5. Minutes of Evidence and Appendix to the Report of the Jamaica Royal Commission 1866.*

Burton, Antoinette, *At the Heart of the Empire: Indians and the Colonial Encounter in Late-Victorian Britain* (Berkeley: University of California Press, 1998).

Burton, Antoinette, *Burdens of History: British Feminists, Indian Women, and Imperial Culture 1865–1915* (Chapel Hill: University of North Carolina Press, 1994).

Bush, Barbara, *Slave Women in Caribbean Society 1650–1838* (London: James Currey, 1990).

Bush, Julia, *Edwardian Ladies and Imperial Power* (London: Leicester University Press, 2000).

Carr, Julie E., *The Captive White Woman of Gipps Land: In Pursuit of the Legend* (Carlton South, Vic.: Melbourne University Press, 2001).

Cary, Joyce, *Mister Johnson* (originally published 1939; New York: New Directions Books, 1989).

Chaudhuri, Nupur and Margaret Strobel (eds), *Western Women and Imperialism: Complicity and Resistance* (Bloomington: Indiana University Press, 1992).

Clancy-Smith, Julia and Frances Gouda (eds), *Domesticating the Empire: Race, Gender, and Family Life in French and Dutch Colonialism* (Charlottesville, VA: University of Virginia Press, 1998).

Coates, Colin and Cecilia Morgan, *Heroines and History: Madeleine de Verchères and Laura Secord* (Toronto: University of Toronto Press, 2002).

Collingham, E.M., *Imperial Bodies: The Physical Experience of the Raj, c. 1800–1947* (Cambridge: Polity Press, 2001).

Cooper, Frederick and Ann Laura Stoler (eds), *Tensions of Empire: Colonial Cultures in a Bourgeois World* (Berkeley: University of California Press, 1997).

Crotty, Martin, *Making the Australian Male: Middle-Class Masculinity 1870–1920* (Melbourne: Melbourne University Press, 2001).

Damousi, Joy, *Depraved and Disorderly: Female Convicts, Sexuality and Gender in Colonial Australia* (Cambridge: Cambridge University Press, 1997).

Daniels, Kay, *Convict Women* (St. Leonards, NSW: Allen & Unwin, 1998).

Driver, Felix, *Geography Militant: Cultures of Exploration and Empire* (Oxford: Blackwell Publishers, 2001).

Duffield, Ian and James Bradley (eds), *Representing Convicts: New Perspectives on Convict Forced Labour Migration* (London: Leicester University Press, 1997).

Emecheta, Buchi, *Second-Class Citizen* (London: Allison & Busby, 1974).

Evans, Julie, 'Re-Reading Edward Eyre: Race, Resistance and Repression in Australia and the Caribbean', *Australian Historical Studies* Vol. 33, No. 118 (2002): 175–98.

Ferguson, Moira (ed.), *The History of Mary Prince, A West Indian Slave, Related by Herself* (Ann Arbor: University of Michigan Press, 1993).

Fleischmann, Ellen L., *The Nation and Its 'New Women': The Palestinian Women's Movement, 1920–1948* (Berkeley: University of California Press, 2003).

Hall, Catherine, *Civilising Subjects: Metropole and Colony in the English Colonial Imagination 1830–1867* (Chicago, IL: University of Chicago Press, 2002).

Hall, Catherine, *White, Male and Middle Class: Explorations in Feminism and History* (New York: Routledge, 1992).

Hall, Douglas, *In Miserable Slavery: Thomas Thistlewood in Jamaica, 1750–86* (Basingstoke: Macmillan, 1989).

Henty, G.A., *Jack Archer: A Tale of the Crimea* (first pub. 1884; New York: W.L. Allison Co., ca. 1900).

Henty, G.A., *The Dash for Khartoum: A Tale of the Nile Expedition* (London: Blackie and Son, n.d. (1890s)).

Hunt, Tamara L., 'Wild Irish Women: Gender, Politics, and Colonialism in the Nineteenth Century', in Hunt and Micheline R. Lessard (eds), *Women and the Colonial Gaze* (New York: New York University Press, 2002).

Inglis, Amirah, *'Not a White Woman Safe': Sexual Anxiety and Politics in Port Moresby 1920–1934* (Canberra: Australian National University Press, 1974).

James, C.L.R., *Beyond a Boundary* (London: Hutchinson & Co. Ltd., 1963).

Jayawardena, Kumari, *Feminism and Nationalism in the Third World* (London: Zed Books, 1986).

Kipling, Rudyard, 'The Bridge-Builders', in his *The Day's Work* (Garden City, NY: Doubleday, Page & Co., 1919).

Kumar, Radha, *The History of Doing: An Illustrated Account of Movements for Women's Rights and Feminism in India, 1800–1990* (London: Verso, 1993).

Lal, Vinay, 'The Incident of the "Crawling Lane": Women in the Punjab Disturbances of 1919', *Genders* No. 16 (Spring 1993).

Lane, Christopher, *The Ruling Passion: British Colonial Allegory and the Paradox of Homosexual Desire* (Durham: Duke University Press, 1995).

Levine, Philippa (ed.), *Gender and Empire*, Volume in *The Oxford History of the British Empire* series edited by Wm. Roger Louis (Oxford: Oxford University Press, 2004).

Levine, Philippa, *Prostitution, Race & Politics: Policing Venereal Disease in the British Empire* (New York: Routledge, 2003).

Mani, Lata, *Contentious Traditions: The Debate on* Sati *in Colonial India* (Berkeley: University of California Press, 1998).

Maugham, W. Somerset, *The Explorer: A Melodrama in Four Acts* (London: William Heinemann, 1912).

McClintock, Anne, *Imperial Leather: Race, Gender and Sexuality in the Colonial Contest* (London: Routledge, 1995).

McCulloch, Jock, *Black Peril, White Virtue: Sexual Crime in Southern Rhodesia, 1902–1935* (Bloomington: Indiana University Press, 2000).

Midgley, Clare (ed.), *Gender and Imperialism* (Manchester: Manchester University Press, 1998).

Midgley, Clare, *Women Against Slavery: The British Campaigns, 1780–1870* (London: Routledge, 1992).

Orwell, George, *Burmese Days* (San Diego: Harvest Books, 1934).

Otieno, Wambui Waiyaki, *Mau Mau's Daughter: A Life History*, edited by Cora Ann Presley (Boulder, CO: Lynne Rienner Publishers, 1998).

Paxton, Nancy L., *Writing under the Raj: Gender, Race, and Rape in the British Colonial Imagination, 1830–1947* (New Brunswick, NJ: Rutgers University Press, 1999).

Pedersen, Susan, 'National Bodies, Unspeakable Acts: The Sexual Politics of Colonial Policy-Making', *Journal of Modern History* Vol. 63, No. 4 (Dec. 1991): 647–680.

Perry, Adele, *On the Edge of Empire: Gender, Race, and the Making of British Columbia, 1849–1871* (Toronto: University of Toronto Press, 2001).

Pickles, Katie, *Female Imperialism and National Identity: Imperial Order Daughters of the Empire* (Manchester: Manchester University Press, 2002).

Pratt, Mary Louise, *Imperial Eyes: Travel Writing and Transculturation* (London: Routledge, 1992).

Presley, Cora Ann, *Kikuyu Women, the Mau Mau Rebellion, and Social Change in Kenya* (Boulder, CO: Westview Press, 1992).

Procida, Mary A., *Married to the Empire: Gender, Politics and Imperialism in India, 1883–1947* (Manchester: Manchester University Press, 2002).

Reddock, Rhoda, 'Indian Women and Indentureship in Trinidad and Tobago 1845–1917: Freedom Denied', in Hilary Beckles and Verene Shepherd (eds), *Caribbean Freedom: Economy and Society from Emancipation to the Present* (Princeton, NJ: Markus Wiener Publishers, 1996).

Russell, Lynette (ed.), *Colonial Frontiers: Indigenous-European Encounters in Settler Societies* (Manchester: Manchester University Press, 2001).

Sarkar, Tanika, *Hindu Wife, Hindu Nation: Community, Religion, and Cultural Nationalism* (Bloomington: Indiana University Press, 2001).

Sattin, Anthony (ed.), *An Englishwoman in India: The Memoirs of Harriet Tytler 1828–1858* (Oxford: Oxford University Press, 1986).

Schaffer, Kay, *In the Wake of First Contact: The Eliza Fraser Stories* (Cambridge: Cambridge University Press, 1995).

Schaffer, Kay and D'Arcy Randall, 'Transglobal Translations: The Eliza Fraser and Rachel Plummer Captivity Narratives', in Graeme Harper (ed.),

Colonial and Postcolonial Incarceration (London: Continuum, 2001), pp. 105–23.

Scully, Pamela, *Liberating the Family? Gender and British Slave Emancipation in the Rural Western Cape, South Africa, 1823–1853* (Portsmouth, NH: Heinemann, 1997).

Sharpe, Jenny, *Allegories of Empire: The Figure of Woman in the Colonial Text* (Minneapolis: University of Minnesota Press, 1993).

Shepherd, Verene, Bridget Brereton, and Barbara Bailey (eds), *Engendering History: Caribbean Women in Historical Perspective* (Kingston: Ian Randle Publishers, 1995).

Sigel, Lisa Z., *Governing Pleasures: Pornography and Social Change in England, 1815–1914* (New Brunswick, NJ: Rutgers University Press, 2002).

Sinha, Mrinalini, *Colonial Masculinity: The 'Manly Englishman' and the 'Effeminate Bengali' in the Late Nineteenth Century* (Manchester: Manchester University Press, 1995).

Stoler, Ann Laura, *Race and the Education of Desire: Foucault's History of Sexuality and the Colonial Order of Things* (Durham: Duke University Press, 1995).

Streets, Heather, *Born Warriors? The Military, Martial Races, and Masculinity in British Imperial Culture, 1857–1914* (Manchester: Manchester University Press, 2004).

Strobel, Margaret, *European Women and the Second British Empire* (Bloomington: Indiana University Press, 1991).

Sussman, Charlotte, *Consuming Anxieties: Consumer Protest, Gender, and British Slavery, 1713–1833* (Stanford, CA: Stanford University Press, 2000).

The Amritsar Massacre, 1919: General Dyer in the Punjab (1920; London: The Stationery Office, 2000).

Vance, Jonathan F., *Death So Noble: Memory, Meaning, and the First World War* (Vancouver: University of British Columbia Press, 1997).

Vibert, Elizabeth, 'Real men hunt buffalo: Masculinity, race and class in British fur traders' narratives', in Catherine Hall (ed.), *Cultures of Empire: Colonizers in Britain and the Empire in the Nineteenth and Twentieth Centuries: A Reader* (New York: Routledge, 2000).

Webster, Wendy, *Imagining Home: Gender, 'Race' and National Identity, 1945–64* (London: UCL Press, 1998).

White, Luise, *The Comforts of Home: Prostitution in Colonial Nairobi* (Chicago, IL: University of Chicago Press, 1990).

Wilson, Kathleen, *The Island Race: Englishness, Empire and Gender in the Eighteenth Century* (London: Routledge, 2003).

Woollacott, Angela, *To Try Her Fortune in London: Australian Women, Colonialism, and Modernity* (New York: Oxford University Press, 2001).

Index

Printed in the United States
154270LV00003B/33/P

9 780333 926451